Rebecca's Children

REBECCA'S CHILDREN

Judaism and Christianity in the Roman World

ALAN F. SEGAL

HARVARD UNIVERSITY PRESS
*Cambridge, Massachusetts
and London, England
1986*

Library of Congress Cataloging-in-Publication Data

Segal, Alan F., 1945–
Rebecca's children.

Bibliography: p.
Includes index.
1. Christianity and other religions—Judaism.
2. Judaism—Relations—Christianity.
3. Rome—Religion.
4. Rome—Social conditions.   I. Title.
BM535.S329   1986   296.8'1   85-17656
ISBN 0-674-75075-6 (alk. paper)

To my parents and my children

Acknowledgments

The controversial ideas in this book have been a long time coming. They have stimulated debate in my seminars and classrooms at Yale, Princeton, the University of Toronto, the Aspen Institute, and Barnard College at Columbia University. The controversy helped me refine the ideas.

It is impossible to thank every student whose hunches, questions, or suggestions added to the book, though I try to remember them all. Two in particular offered outstanding help in preparing the manuscript: Leonard Gordon and the late Frances M. Schwartz. Their and many other students' enthusiasm for seeing Judaism and Christianity from the perspective of social science, sympathetically, unifies this effort.

Other people consented out of collegiality to read the manuscript. Let me thank especially Bernard Barber, Thomas Boslooper, Leon Festinger, Holland Hendrix, John Gager, Claude Gerstle, Wayne Meeks, Elaine Pagels, Gilles Quispel, Willard Oxtoby, James Schwartz, and Morton Smith, all of whom made important contributions to the book by sharing their insights with me.

I would like to thank Robert Juckiewicz, Mark Lerner, and Francine Ovios of Columbia University's Computer Center for their patient help in gaining access to Columbia's computers. I am indebted to the National Endowment for the Humanities and to Barnard College for giving me time free from classes to finish the manuscript and for underwriting other costs in preparing it. For drawing up the indexes, I am grateful to Avent

Beck and Thomas Boslooper. Special thanks are due to Aida Donald and Elizabeth Suttell of Harvard University Press, who liked the manuscript even in its primitive state, and to Virginia LaPlante, who prodded it into literary form.

My thanks, as ever, to my wife, Meryl.

Contents

	Introduction. Myth in Israelite Society	1
I.	Israel Between Empires	13
II.	Society in the Time of Jesus	38
III.	Jesus, the Jewish Revolutionary	68
IV.	Paul, the Convert and Apostle	96
V.	Origins of the Rabbinic Movement	117
VI.	Communities in Conflict	142
VII.	The Ways Divide	163
	Notes	183
	Scriptural Index	197
	General Index	199

Rebecca's Children

Two nations are in thy womb;
And two peoples shall be separated from thy bowels;
And one people shall be stronger than the other people
And the elder shall serve the younger.

Genesis 25:23

INTRODUCTION

Myth in Israelite Society

The time of Jesus marks the beginning of not one but two great religions of the West, Judaism and Christianity. According to conventional wisdom, the first century witnessed the beginning of only one religion, Christianity. Judaism is generally thought to have begun in the more distant past, at the time of Abraham, Moses, or even Ezra, who rebuilt the Temple destroyed by the Babylonians. Judaism underwent radical religious changes in response to important historical crises. But the greatest transformation, contemporary with Christianity, was rabbinic Judaism, which generally became the basis of the future Jewish religion.

So great is the contrast between previous Jewish religious systems and rabbinism that Judaism and Christianity can essentially claim a twin birth. It is a startling truth that the religions we know today as Judaism and Christianity were born at the same time and nurtured in the same environment. Like Jacob and Esau, the twin sons of Isaac and Rebecca, the two religions fought in the womb. Throughout their youth they followed very different paths, quarreling frequently about their father's blessing. As was the case with Rebecca's children, the conflict between Judaism and Christianity molded their characters and determined their destinies.

When Jesus was born, the Jewish religion was beginning a new transformation, the rabbinic movement, which would permit the Jewish people to survive the next two millennia. The complex of historical and social forces that molded rabbinic Judaism also affected the teachings of Jesus, helping to form Christianity into a new and separate religion. Dislocation, war, and foreign rule forced every variety of Jewish community to rebuild its ancient national culture into something almost unprecedented, a religion of personal and communal piety. Many avenues were available to Jews for achieving this new sense of personal piety, one of which was Jesus' movement. Although the way ultimately taken by the majority of Jews differed from the way offered by Christianity, at the time of their inception rabbinic Judaism and Christianity were twin alternatives for achieving similar goals.

The period of the birth of rabbinic Judaism and Christianity, from roughly 200 before the common era (B.C.E.) to 200 of the common era (C.E.), was like modern times in important ways.[1] It was characterized by a degree of cosmopolitanism, individualism, and technology that the West would not experience again until the Renaissance. Like the present, the Roman world knew war, imperial domination, and human tragedy on such a mammoth scale as to challenge the validity of inherited beliefs. Then, as now, the events of history and the increased ease of communications between cultures fostered a quest for new ways to understand the meaning of life.

The understanding of Judaism and Christianity as twin religions reared in the same environment comes from examination of the historical reports about Judaism and Christianity in the first centuries. Though incomplete, biased, and often puzzling, these accounts continue to be of importance to modern life. They are here scrutinized with the same methods that are used to deal with bias, incomplete data, and puzzlement in the contemporary disciplines of philology, literary criticism, history, political science, economics, psychology, sociology, and anthropology—in short, all relevant humanities and social sciences. As a result, these two great religions are analyzed within their social, economic, and political context. Just as the early theologies of Judaism and Christianity were embodied within their particular communities, so a comparison of these religions must attend to the real social matrix in which the religious thought existed. Insights gained from studies of religion in the modern as well as the ancient period help to frame the history of early Judaism and Christianity, where the social setting might otherwise be obscured by the profound and timeless values in the texts.

A clear definition of religion is hard to achieve, because religion takes such different forms in different societies. The religion of any society embodies its ultimate assumptions, but not every society expresses its religious beliefs in the same sentiments, customs, or ceremonies. The problem of definition becomes manageable, however, when religion is broken down into smaller parts. When the ultimate assumptions of a society are articulated in allusive or analogical language, they are designated by a variety of nearly synonymous technical terms—root metaphor, conceptual archetype, or more simply, myth.[2] Though comparing single beliefs instead of a whole religion can be misleading, in this case the Israelite root metaphors were inherited equally by both Judaism and Christianity. The root metaphors shared by both communities serve to highlight divisions and contrasts between Judaism and Christianity.

Use of the term *myth* for a religious story does not suggest that the story is false. Rather, it means that the story is considered true by someone in a literal or metaphoric sense. The tenets of modern American democracy, especially as interpreted by the popular media, can be described as myths, since they are treated as self-evident truths. In this technical usage, a "foolish myth" is a contradiction in terms, at best referring to a myth that has ceased functioning in a mythological way. But because myth continues in ordinary parlance to have the unwanted implication of a false or foolish story, neologisms like "root metaphor" or "conceptual archetype" are used here when dealing with biblical religion and other religious writings to which we still give credence.

A root metaphor or myth usually takes the form of a story about the cosmos.[3] Although the story may be amusing or enjoyable, it also has four serious functions: to order experience by explaining the beginning of time and of history; to inform people about themselves by revealing the continuity between key events in the history of the society and the life of the individual; to illustrate a saving power in human life by demonstrating how to overcome a flaw in society or personal experience; and to provide a moral pattern for individual and community action by both negative and positive example. Around the world, root metaphors or myths are often connected with ritual actions, such as dancing, reciting, singing, eating, and bathing. The ritual, whether a complete dramatization of the story or just a casual reference to it, is an expression and embodiment of the root metaphor within the society.

The root metaphor underlying Hebrew society is expressed in the word *covenant* (Hebrew: *brith*). Covenant is a theological term that means much the same thing as *contract* does today. According to the ancient Israelites of the Hebrew Bible, the relationship between themselves and their God—a supernatural person called the LORD or, as His name is conventionally figured in Hebrew, Yahweh—was governed by the rules of a contract, which specified the divine nature of their societal laws.[4] The root metaphor itself came from formal agreements in ordinary human relationships, such as treaties and commercial or marital contracts. One central concept uniting these areas of human endeavor was the use of an oath to guarantee the contract between the two parties. In the case of the Hebrew covenant, the two parties were Israel and its God. All those who were party to the covenant became known as the people of Israel, whether they lived in the southern kingdom of Judah or the northern kingdom, also called Israel.

The Hebrew claim of the divine origin of law was in no way unusual. All the great ancient Near Eastern cultures at the time of the Hebrews, as well as for centuries before them, thought of themselves as subject to laws given to them by their gods. For example, the Babylonian king Hammurabi was said to have received his law code from the god of wisdom, Shamash. Furthermore, gods were almost always called upon to witness and protect the integrity of oaths. Every treaty between nations in the ancient Near East contained a list of gods who had witnessed and were responsible for protecting the sanctity of the oaths sworn by the two parties.

But the Hebrew concept of covenant was unique in crucial respects. It conceived of the entire universe as under the sway of one deity. The law was not simply revealed; it was based upon an actual agreement and guaranteed by an actual oath sworn between the people and that God. Furthermore, the Hebrew God was not only single and unique but also reliable and just in His responses to His people. Hence, His ordinances of law were for the common human good. Nowhere else in the ancient Near East was there so systematic an appropriation of the concept of lawful, contractual obligation to express the relationship between a whole people and their god and consequently to define morality within society. These concepts, derived from the root metaphor of covenant and later expressed by terms like *monotheism* and *ethics*, evolved through many stages in Hebrew thought as the social institutions and historical situation of Israel changed.[5]

The Hebrew concept of the covenant was not merely a theological idea but also model of social practice. The Hebrews' legendary ancestors—Abraham, Isaac, Jacob, and Moses— were pictured as having made archetypal covenants with God. These legendary accounts paralleled the historical covenant-making of such figures as David, Solomon, Josiah, and Ezra.

The interspersing of covenantal, legal material with historical narrative, epic, and saga in the Bible is a unique aspect of Hebrew covenant literature. Depending on the time and place in which the account was written and the purposes for which it was written, the covenant, like a contract, could be described differently. Biblical stories of the covenant express the perspectives and politics of the narrators. Even in the accounts of the patriarchal covenants, which were supposed to have taken place in the most distant past, the assumptions of the narrators are apparent, as in Genesis 15:

> After these things the word of the LORD came to Abram in a vision, "Fear not, Abram, I am your shield; your reward shall be very great. But Abram said, "O LORD, what wilt thou give me, for I continue childless, and the heir of my house is Eliezer of Damascus?" And Abram said, "Behold, thou hast given me no offspring; and a slave born in my house will be my heir." And he

brought him outside and said, "Look toward heaven, and number the stars, if you are able to number them." Then he said to him, "So shall your descendants be." And he believed the LORD and he reckoned it to him as righteousness.

And he said to him, "I am the LORD who brought you from Ur of the Chaldeans, to give you this land to possess." But he said, "O LORD God, how am I to know that I shall possess it?" He said to him, "Bring me a heifer three years old, a she-goat three years old, a ram three years old, a turtledove and a young pigeon." And he brought him all these, cut them in two and laid each half over against the other; but he did not cut the birds in two. And when birds of prey came down upon the carcasses, Abram drove them away.

As the sun was going down, a deep sleep fell on Abram; and lo, a dread and great darkness fell upon him. Then the LORD said to Abram, "Know of a surety that your descendants will be sojourners in a land that is not theirs, and will be slaves there, and they will be oppressed for four hundred years; but I will bring judgment on the nation which they serve, and afterward they shall come out with great possessions. As for yourself, you shall go to your fathers in peace; you shall be buried in a good old age. And they shall come back here in the fourth generation; for the iniquity of the Amorites is not yet complete."

When the sun had gone down and it was dark, behold a smoking fire pot and a flaming torch passed between these pieces. On that day the LORD made a covenant with Abram, saying, "To your descendants I give this land, from the river of Egypt to the great river, the river Euphrates, the land of the Kenites, the Kenizzites, the Kadmonites, the Hittites, the Perizzites, the Rephaim, the Amorites, the Canaanites, the Girgashites and the Jebusites."[6]

Yahweh appears here to Abraham during a vision, which for the narrator expressed the transcendance of the encounter and the awesomeness of the divinity. Yet the model for this covenant is a human legal transaction, treaty-making. The flaming torch, connoting the presence of Yahweh, passes between the pieces of the animals to signify that Yahweh has sworn Himself with an oath. This strange ceremony has analogies with the treaty ceremonies of ancient Near Eastern emperors, but it may also reflect less stylized agreements used by tribal chieftains.

Apparently, the purpose of cutting up the animals is to invoke a curse upon any person who violates the oath. This story depicts a late Bronze Age practice of covenanting. The central feature of the ceremony was a solemn oath, to which the Bible makes Yahweh a partner. The metaphor of a covenantal treaty with Yahweh gives reality to the concept that God will continue to oversee the destiny of the people descended from Abraham. In this epic layer of the biblical tradition, the true and enduring aspect of God's providence is expressed as a treaty between two great though dissimilar chiefs—Abraham, the ancestor of all the people of Israel, and Yahweh, the God who promised to be faithful to his descendants, provided they behaved in a way befitting Yahweh's people.

Many other aspects of Hebrew society are reflected in the story. Offspring and homeland have paramount importance. These benefits will accrue to the descendants of Abraham as long as they keep faith with Yahweh's bond. Abraham himself, on account of his deep faith, is rewarded by being allowed to live to an old age and to be buried with his ancestors.

The story omits any doctrine of reward after death. This society understands ultimate rewards concretely: an easy death after a long and comfortable life, with many descendants to carry on afterward. There is no interest in the final disposition of souls after death. Rather, the story describes the benefits of the covenant to the living people, Israel. After the time of David and Solomon, when Israel had separated into two Kingdoms, the stories of Abraham and Jacob functioned to unify all those who claimed common descent from these patriarchs. The root metaphor of family relation to Jacob—the person whose alternate name, Israel, became the name of the entire people—originated with the ten Hebrew tribes in the northern kingdom of Israel, while the root metaphor of family relation to Abraham, who lived south of Jerusalem, solidified the remaining two Hebrew tribes in the southern kingdom of Judah. All the stories were adopted by the whole people when Israel was unified. The root metaphor of family descent set the Israelites apart from the Canaanites, earlier inhabitants of the land of Israel, whom the Israelites partially defeated but whose religion they were tempted to emulate. Yahweh, the Israelite God, was not neutral toward the Israelites' accommodation to Canaanite ways after their settlement in the promised land. He found the Canaanite religion abhorrent because of its practices of ritual prostitution and child sacrifice. He wanted the Israelites to separate from the Canaanites, forbad them to sacrifice their children, gave them Canaan as punishment for the Canaanites' sins, and promised the Israelites progeny and long life if they obeyed His covenant. This moral is apparent in the epic, the law, and the prophecy contained in biblical writings. For instance, the story of the forestalled sacrifice of Isaac emphasizes the opposition of Yahweh to the religion of the Canaanites, while praising Abraham's obedience.

The Ten Commandments in Exodus 20:2–17 are a concrete example of the covenant with Israel, specifying the terms for the people to follow as well as the promises of the divinity. Again the biblical narrative describes a covenant ceremony, this time complete with a communal oath-taking. The whole people, not just the eponymous ancestor, swear to obey all the ordinances laid down by Yahweh. According to the narrative, the stipulations of the covenant, which follow immediately after the oath-taking, begin with the Ten Commandments.

The story of the giving of the commandments shows evidence of many different kinds of narrator. Priestly aspects of the covenant ceremony are stressed in some places, details of treaty-making in others. These differences suggest that the scribal and priestly voices in the society all made contributions to the text. The Sinai event was told and retold by each generation in ancient times, and several originally differing concepts of covenanting were combined into a single biblical narrative. Yet the unity of the narrative is what chiefly impresses today's reader, because all the voices have been harmonized into a narrative whole. The biblical description stresses all the grandeur and wonder imaginable in that day. Yahweh's divinity is expressed by supernatural fire, while His presence is so exalted that it cannot be seen with the naked eye. With all the redaction and editing, the covenant metaphor nevertheless remains clear.[7]

Even more interesting, this story parallels the actual covenant-making described in the historical books of the Bible. The resemblance reflects the relationship between root metaphors and cultic or ritual enactments which is apparent in any society. The ancient stories legitimate the practice, while the rituals reenact and reiterate the root metaphors.

Since so many different biblical writers use the explicit metaphor of a treaty to express the relationship between themselves and their God, a treaty was presumably the highest form of contractual arrangement to most of the narrators. This suggests that most of the biblical writers were educated people—courtiers, royal scribes, and administrators who were charged with writing treaties in their professional lives. In the Sinai story they transform the earlier prose epic from their special perspectives, clarifying that the contract between Israel and its God is the basis of a social contract as well. The Ten Commandments emphasize human social responsibilities, as does the Book of the Covenant, the extended law code that immediately follows the commandments. In like fashion the priestly narrators, who tended to the liturgical aspects of the covenant ceremony, portray Moses as an intermediary between God and the people.

The writings of the prophets communicate the concept of covenant not in the narrow technical language of treaties but in the broader language of root metaphor. Many prophets speak directly of covenant but do not envision it as a treaty. When the prophet Amos delivers the words of Yahweh, "You only have I known of all the families on earth. Therefore I will punish you for all your iniquities," he is not speaking the words of a divine despot. Rather, he is speaking the words of Yahweh, who is publicly claiming a grievance. Amos is reminding his hearers that Israel entered into a contract with Yahweh, sealed by an oath, on which the people have defaulted. Yahweh must therefore seek redress by lawful means. Amos assumes the original agreement and concentrates on describing a divine lawsuit against Israel. Even the words *love* and *lover, know* and *knower, master* and *servant* have covenantal implications in the mouths of the prophets. They are technical terms referring to covenantal partnerships in ancient Near Eastern texts, and their legal implications are exploited by the prophets. The

Bible suggests the variety of ways in which the covenant metaphor could be expressed at different stages in Israelite history.

The legal implications of the covenant metaphor allow the
prophets to range widely in their search for language adequate
to their task. The prophet Hosea pictures the covenant relationship between Yahweh and Israel as a marriage, though a
bad one that has to be repaired or ended. A marriage, too, is a
contractual arrangement which, unless the father or husband is
a king, cannot fairly be reduced to a treaty form. Like treaties,
however, marriage contracts are covenants, enforced by
oaths.[8]

Only one type of biblical marriage alludes directly to treaty
forms, the marriage between kings which cements national alli-
ances between nations. Given the Israelite predilection for
endogamy, the diplomatic necessity for Solomon and his successors to acquire foreign wives becomes a biblical target for
moral criticism on the grounds that it violates the basic covenantal arrangement between Israel and their God. The historical books of the Bible are critical of these diplomatic marriages,
but the prophets scarcely mention them. Instead, the prophet
Hosea relies on marriage imagery to express the covenantal relationship between God and Israel. The accusations of seduc-
tion and adultery in Hosea 2:16–20 gain their power by
conceiving of the covenant between Israel and Yahweh as a
marriage, with Yahweh describing how He plans to win back
His misled wife and to forgive her even for adultery with the
Canaanite fertility gods:

> Therefore, behold I will allure her, and bring her into the wil-
> derness, and speak tenderly to her. And there I will give her her
> vineyards, and make the Valley of Achor a door of hope. And
> there she shall answer as in the days of her youth, as at the time
> when she came out of the land of Egypt. And in that day, says
> the LORD, you will call me, "My husband," and no longer will
> you call me, "My ba'al." For I will remove the names of the
> ba'als from her mouth, and they shall be mentioned by name no
> more . . . And I will betroth you to me forever; I will betroth you
> to me in righteousness and in justice, in steadfast love and in
> mercy. I will betroth you to me in faithfulness; and you shall
> know the LORD.

If the people give up their sinful relationship with the Canaanites' goddesses and gods, including their sexual rituals of fertility and abhorred child sacrifice, Yahweh will renew His covenant with them. The force of this prophetic writing depends on the prophet's effective use of the metaphors of love and betrothal for covenantal obligation. Since the name of the Canaanite god, Baal, also means "husband," it too has become part of the extended metaphor of the adulterous corespondent.

Israelite culture was nonmythological in the sense that it demythologized nature, replacing the nature gods of the ancient Near East with the bare objects of the physical universe. The heavens of Israelite culture were merely heavens, the earth merely earth; they were not gods. Throughout the Bible, the Israelites maintain that there is only one God, who controls the forces of nature. More important, this God causes historical events. The very name of Yahweh is grammatically related to the causative form of the verb *to be* in Hebrew. Its original meaning may have been "He who causes to be." This helps explain what Yahweh tells Moses at the burning bush. When asked for His name, Yahweh replies, "I am who I am," which may mean, "I am the one who causes things to happen." If so, embedded in this etymology are far-reaching intuitions about the uniqueness of events. God causes history, not just the endless seasonal repetition that characterizes the concept of time in fertility cults. This Hebrew insight about Yahweh gives to each member of Israel and of humanity a special individuality, besides suggesting that the goals of human destiny are bound up with the various covenants that Yahweh has revealed to Israel and to mankind.

Yet the Israelites did not lack a mythology, a situation that would have been unique among human cultures, for covenant is itself a root metaphor or myth. The Israelite myth of covenant simply has unique characteristics that allow it to address history along with cosmology. The events of Israelite history itself were interpreted in terms of the root metaphor of the covenant relationship, since the people of Israel considered all historical events to result from the direct intervention of God in continual and unique response to their communal behavior.

The various Israelite groups and classes from the period of the Babylonian exile to the time of Jesus interpreted the events of their history in terms of the covenantal root metaphor. The fact that different groups found very different and, in some cases, opposing meanings in these historical events points up the differences between Judaism and Christianity.

Israelite history is mythical in the further sense that it sees the past as a paradigm for the present. Past events are consciously used as liturgical models for the covenantal meaning of human destiny. For instance, the entire people, whether they actually came from Egypt or only knew of the story, took the event of the Exodus to be a metaphor of going from slavery to becoming a people with a destiny and a purpose. The Passover liturgy today contains the ancient lines, "Every Jew should look upon himself as though he too came forth out of Egypt." As the service continues, each Jew is instructed to hope for the future redemption of Israel and humanity. Thus, identification with the history of the covenantal community helps define an individual Jew's religious purpose.[9] Fidelity to the covenant makes deliverance possible. Past historical events, remembered either directly or within a liturgical context, express evolving notions of the covenant and the salvation it offers.

With the rebuilding of the Israelite state after the Babylonian captivity, Jewish groups and sects proliferated, each based on its own definition of covenant. The period between the destruction of the first Temple by the Babylonians in 586 B.C.E. and the destruction of the second Temple by the Romans in 70 C.E. produced an enormous variety of Jewish communities, adapted to the plethora of new and different social, political, and economic environments brought about by the dispersion of Jews throughout the ancient world. In each place where Jews sought to dwell, the meaning of the covenant seemed different. This spectrum of opinion, influenced by the historical and social circumstances of Jewish life, is a key to new insights about the differences between Judaism and Christianity. Like Rebecca's children, Judaism and Christianity had a history of conflict. But like them, they may reach a reconciliation based upon mutual understanding and respect.

❧ I ❧

Israel Between Empires

By the waters of Babylon, there we sat down and wept,
  when we remembered Zion.
On the willows there we hung up our lyres.
For there our captors required of us songs,
and our tormentors, mirth saying, "Sing us one of the
  songs of Zion."

How shall we sing the LORD's song in a foreign land?
If I forget you, O Jerusalem, let my right hand wither!
Let my tongue cleave to the roof of my mouth, if I do not
  remember you,
if I do not set Jerusalem above my highest joy!

Psalm 137:1–6

Despite the warnings of the prophets, the nation of Israel drifted toward ruin. The literary prophets recorded the destruction of the northern and southern kingdoms. Some of the prophets had been against the political establishment; others favored it. But their successful predictions of national destruction convinced later Israelite society that they all spoke the word of Yahweh.

The razing of the Temple of Solomon in Jerusalem in the sixth century B.C.E. by Nebuchadnezzar, the sovereign of a newly constituted Babylonian Empire, was the beginning of several tragic crises of national existence that the people of Israel faced. The theology, beliefs, and hopes of modern Judaism were greatly influenced by these historical catastrophes. The crisis of confidence brought on by the destruction of the Temple stemmed not from the fact that Yahweh was viewed as a regional God only, because He was viewed as the Lord of all creation, but from the fact that He had been worshiped in a single, principal location for so long. The Temple, the central place where the unity of Judean society had been expressed, was now destroyed. Did that mean that Yahweh had finally abandoned His people? The crisis was summed up by the author of Lamentations 5:19–22:

> Why dost thou forget us for ever, why dost thou so long forsake us?
> Restore us to thyself, O LORD, that we may be restored! Renew our days as of old!
> Or hast thou utterly rejected us? Art thou exceedingly angry with us?

Together with the Israelites' fervent desire for restoration to wholeness and national independence went their need for a sign that God had not permanently rejected them. This, the prophets supplied, giving comfort and signaling the continuation of national purpose by refusing to abandon the metaphor of covenant. As if in answer to the question of the psalmist, the prophet Ezekiel articulated the bizarre vision of a heavenly chariot driven by the glory of God. The specially magnificent vehicle is an appropriate conveyance for the God of Israel. According to this account, Ezekiel saw Yahweh's heavenly chariot and the radiance of His presence approach Babylonia in a storm cloud, just as in Psalm 29. The throne chariot was borne by four fantastic creatures—cherubim, who are not the fat little cupids of greeting cards but fantastic beasts, like the sphinx or the winged lions of Babylonian art. Next to them were the four wheels of Yahweh's chariot, wheels within wheels, as in the black American spiritual based on this passage. Above the creatures was a crystal platform, as in Exodus 24:10. Higher still was a sapphire throne and above that a human figure, later identified as "the appearance of the likeness of the glory" of Yahweh. The prophet wanted to distinguish the essential personhood of God from the human figure, the form in which He manifested himself. It was God's glory, not He himself, who has a human form. Ezekiel and his generation were already sensitive to the issue of anthropomorphic descriptions of God. Whether the figure is an angel or a divine hypostasis becomes an important issue in the Hellenistic period. Once it is clear that God's sacred presence itself cannot be clearly seen, the human value of the vision becomes evident. God's presence moves like an earthly caravan, albeit a splendid one. Having abandoned the Temple just before its destruction, God's entourage travels the caravan routes, avoiding the deserts and thus arriving from the North instead of flying directly from the West.

Yahweh literally removed His presence with the Israelites when they went into exile. The answer to the psalmist's lamentation is that one can continue to worship Yahweh, because He came into exile with the people. This is a dramatic, concrete, mythological portrayal of God's continued interest in His people, Israel.

The Persians as National Saviors

Thus, when Cyrus the Persian conquered Babylon in 539 B.C.E., he was seen by the Israelites living there as part of God's plan.[1] Although the Persian Empire was to effect drastic changes in the ancient Near East, Cyrus did not describe himself as the bringer of a new order to the world. He styled himself as the restorer of the ancient regimes destroyed by the Babylonians, hence the champion of all the old gods. He allowed the traditional priesthood of Marduk to practice their own religion. And he allowed the Jews to go back, as many as wanted, to the land of Israel to set up their Temple. When Ezra later described the Persian permission to set up a new Temple to Yahweh, he made Cyrus sound like a worshiper of Yahweh:

> In the first year of Cyrus, king of Persia, that the word of the LORD by the mouth of Jeremiah might be accomplished, the LORD stirred up the spirit of Cyrus, king of Persia so that he made a proclamation throughout all his kingdom and also put in writing: "Thus says Cyrus king of Persia: 'The LORD, the God of heaven, has given me all the kingdoms of the earth, and he has charged me to build him a house at Jerusalem, which is in Judah. Whoever is among you of all his people, may his God be with him, and let him go up to Jerusalem, which is in Judah, and rebuild the house of the LORD, the God of Israel—he is the God who is in Jerusalem.' " (1:1–2)

By now, the Israelites had vivid proof that Yahweh directed all of world history, not just the destiny of Judah. It was not true, of course, that Cyrus was an exclusive worshiper of

Yahweh. But the announcement of return was not out of keeping with Cyrus's policy of patronizing the priesthoods and
cults of the old order.[2] Isaiah was so impressed with God's
presence in the events surrounding Cyrus's rise to power that
he called Cyrus "the Messiah," anointed by God to fulfill a
certain destiny. What he means by "messiah" is that Cyrus is
Yahweh's chosen instrument.

Not all the Jews wanted to return to the land of Israel. It
took some persuading to bring the prospering artisan and aristocratic class back from Babylonia, the land where for a half-
century of exile they had sought and sometimes found their
fortunes. Many resisted any persuasion and stayed. The Babylonian Jewish community, so influential in the writing of the
Talmud in the second through seventh centuries C.E., was
founded at this time.

So too was historical Zionism, founded by the post-exilic
Isaiah. By means of prophetic rhetoric Isaiah attempts to bring
the people home. He maintains that God is on the verge of re-
peating all His past deliverances. The new Persian policy signals the end of the period of tribulation in Isaiah 40: 1–2:

> Comfort, comfort my people, says your God.
> Speak tenderly to Jerusalem, and cry to her
> that her warfare is ended, that her iniquity is pardoned,
> that she has received from the LORD's hand double for all her sins.

The exiles are to be drawn from the far corners of the earth.
The new ingathering will be like a new Exodus, bringing the
people of Israel across water and fire. Isaiah (43:15–19) says
that, just as at the Red Sea (Exodus 15:3), Yahweh will appear
as a man of war doing battle:

> "I am the LORD, your Holy One, the creator of Israel, your king."
> Thus says the Lord, who makes a way in the sea, a path in the
>   mighty waters,
> who brings forth chariot and horse, army and warrior;
> they lie down, they cannot rise, they are extinguished, quenched
>   like a wick:
> "Remember not the former things, nor consider the things of old.
> Behold, I am doing a new thing; now it springs forth, do you not
>   perceive it?
> I will make a way in the wilderness and rivers in the desert."

New heavens and a new earth will be created because the old ones were witnesses to the breaking of the covenant by the people in the first Temple period. This new Israelite commonwealth will be a fresh start, even a new creation, according to Isaiah (60:1–3):

> Arise, shine; for your light has come and the glory of the LORD has risen upon you.
> For behold, darkness shall cover the earth, and thick darkness the peoples;
> but the LORD will arise upon you, and his glory will be seen upon you.
> And nations shall come to your light, and kings to the brightness of your rising.

These prophecies culminate in the arrival at Jerusalem of the Lord at the head of His returning exiles. Isaiah is not saying simply that the history of Israel will repeat itself. In a new mythological breakthrough, Isaiah declares that the events of the past are paradigms for the present and future. His message is that after the punishment Yahweh intends a restoration that will be no more nor less miraculous than Yahweh's previous creation of the world and election of Israel.

Isaiah's words are among the most stirring biblical passages. Unfortunately, the condition of the returning exiles was still poor. The almost total lack of archaeological remains from this period suggests that the buildings were small and quickly decayed. In fact, the beginnings of the second commonwealth were so meager that it is hard to reconstruct the actual events.

The fate of the succession of Judean kings is not known for certain. The Davidic king, son of Yehoiachin, who adopted the Babylonian name Sin-Ab-Usuru, or Sheshbezzar in Hebrew, arrived in Jerusalem during the reign of Cyrus. Thereafter the descendants of David were called *nasi* (prince) rather than *melekh* (king), perhaps in deference to the Persian Empire that ruled over the country from the East. Zerubbabel, another descendant of David's line, apparently arrived in the land of Israel during the reign of Darius I. The second Temple was then completed in 515 B.C.E. After that, there is complete silence about Zerubbabel or the fate of the kingship.[3] The mysterious end of Israelite kingship stimulated legends about a future messianic king.

Ezra and Nehemiah, who established firm government in Israel, came there as court officials of the Persian Empire. The date or order of their administration is not certain, but the government that they set out was explicitly based upon the covenantal formula used in the first Temple period. In describing the "constitutional assembly" convened by Ezra, for instance, the book of Nehemiah turns the Sukkoth ("Tabernacles") holiday into a covenant renewal ceremony, though the crops are now promised to Persian overlords:[4]

> Behold, we are slaves this day; in the land that thou gavest to our fathers to enjoy its fruit and its good gifts, behold, we are slaves. And its rich yield goes to the kings whom thou hast set over us because of our sins; they have power also over our bodies and over our cattle at their pleasure, and we are in great distress.
>
> [Even with] . . . all this, we make a firm covenant and write it, and our princes, our Levites, and our priests set their seal to it.   (Nehemiah 8:13–9:38; 10:1 in Hebrew)

Covenant was still possible, even in the occupied state, though a covenant renewal ceremony such as that organized by Ezra could not inaugurate independence from Persia. Instead, it served as the establishment of a new regime and continued as a national day for the new, satellite state. The place to which the Judeans returned was now called *Yahud*, the Aramaic term for the tribal territory of Judah. From this word came the Greek, Latin, and English words for the area, Judea. An inhabitant of this region was known as *Yehudi*, a Judean. This is the word that would later take on the implication of the English word "Jew." During this period and throughout the entire New Testament period, *Yehudi* could mean simply Judean. The term gained its modern sense of a member of the Jewish religion during the first and second centuries, which added a unique ambiguity to the term just when the New Testament was being written.

Endogamy, or marriage only within the group, is the most common marriage system in human society. But in the Hebrew case it is also part of a larger symbolic system in which the holiness of the people is protected by concentric circles of exclusion, ending in the purity of the High Priest as he enters the inner sanctum of the Temple on Yom Kippur. Avoiding foreign women was part of the system of moral prohibitions within the dominant strand of pre-exilic traditions, since Canaanite religion, as practiced by Canaanite wives, accepted child sacrifice (a practice that continued even into Roman times). Worship of Yahweh necessarily entailed the command to marry within Abraham's family, thus guaranteeing a national life through the gift of progeny, the very opposite of Canaanite child sacrifice.

Intermarriage was known in pre-exilic times. Moses, for one, took his wife, Zipporah, from among the Midianites. Many of the kings of Israel and Judah married foreigners. The Judeans were forced to make marriages of state to enforce oaths of allegiance between themselves and their suzerain allies. The judgment of the biblical narrative is always negative in these cases. Deuteronomy's law on female war captives implies that foreign women could be brought into Israelite society, presumably if they were properly socialized, and the Book of Ruth records some ancient practices about how such "conversions" took place. But in the post-exilic idealistic restoration of government, the countervailing tendency to oppose contact with foreign women needed emphasis because of the extent of intermarriage during the exile.

Although the actual practice of endogamy varied considerably and was not always or in all places part of Israelite law, the explicit biblical discussions of marriage always favor strict endogamy. The second Temple period, however, was ushered in with more than the ordinary warnings against intermarriage because of an unprecedented new crisis, brought about by a half-century of national disruption: considerable intermarriage had taken place in the years of exile. Intermarriage was no longer functional for king or commoner. There was now no need to be deferential to marriages of state because the land of Israel no longer had an independent king. Rather it was part of a larger bureaucratic empire, and imperial status no longer necessitated royal marriages. Instead, the old ideal of national family unity could be promulgated without opposition from above, though it was challenged in a new way, by the sheer number of intermarriages that had taken place among the ordinary people. Since the second commonwealth was a deliberate attempt to repattern the original kingdom without the sinful practices that had led to destruction, the new social experiment was planned to allow only pure Israelite marriages. The result was an idealized conception of the people, resting on the most widely understood basis of national definition, family structure.

Conversion into Judaism was the countervailing policy that allowed the program to work. The biblical Book of Ruth, named for the Moabite woman who was the ancestress of King David, was edited as a polemical tract dramatizing a new change of status that would later be called conversion. According to this romance, the covenant metaphor defined ideological as well as genealogical peoplehood. The implicit metaphor of the Book of Ruth is marriage into the family, the opposing counterpart to intermarriage, which is marriage out of the family. That David's ancestors could themselves have entered the family from without legitimizes the practice for later generations.

Practical means of entering the community are mentioned in the covenant swearing ceremony. The *nilvim* joined by agreeing to abide by the Torah and so were "attached to the Lord."[5] Henceforth, the family metaphor contained "adoption" possibilities. The myth of a common national parentage could thus be maintained, but the parentage was in important ways superseded by ideological siblinghood: all Israelites were like brothers and sisters either by marriage or by some other generalized form of adoption. Eventually the practices would evolve into a formal conversion ceremony. The Hebrews were from their beginning ethnically and culturally mixed, yet national mythology required use of a family metaphor.

Another anomaly that was as puzzling as intermarriage to the newly reconstructed second commonwealth had to do with the Judeans' political fortune. As Ezra said, they were not the masters of their own land. The Davidic king had in effect disappeared. This led to an enormous amount of speculation about the meaning of the Second Book of Samuel, which promised that the Davidic kingship would continue forever. Thus the idea was born that a king of David's line would return and bring with him a perfect order.

Since the legitimate king had disappeared, most of the affairs of state came under the purview of the priests. The term *theocracy* has been used inexactly to refer to this system of government, for God did not rule directly; rather, the rule was given to priests who claimed to be undertaking God's purposes. One result of this form of theocratic rule was to transform some of the priests into political bureaucrats with priestly ordination.

The most notable achievement of this period was the editing or redaction by the priestly aristocracy of the books now known as the Five Books of Moses. Most of the traditions contained therein were already part of an informal state constitution, with the possible exception of the first chapter of Genesis, the grand seven-day creation story, which has every mark of being written by a priestly hand, a fitting beginning to the whole story. Better known in the first Temple period was the Adam and Eve story, which appears to have functioned independently until this point. The seven-day creation has affinities with the Babylonian creation story and was adapted to Israelite purposes during this time of increased cultural interchange.

Biblical traditions had never before been put together in a single book. During this period the document came to be known as the Torah, a word originally signifying a priestly ordinance and reflecting the priestly editorial activity. But the priestly redactors did not basically alter the original epic stories in the document. Often they combined conflicting accounts of the same events and made a seeming whole out of the "traditions" in front of them. Gathering past traditions for posterity was characteristic of many countries in the Persian Empire and was, as in Israel, an attempt to preserve the traditions destroyed by the Assyrians and Babylonians. The Torah became the foundation document of the nation in the second commonwealth period in somewhat the same way that the collected body of British law serves as their constitution. However, the Hebrew constitution came complete with cosmogonic myth, epic, and narrative history, because of the conventions in which covenants were written. We today rely more on other documents to express our root metaphors and myths.

The Greek Conquest and Accelerated Hellenization

In 333 B.C.E. the greatest empire in the world, Persia and its possessions, fell into the hands of a young conqueror, Alexander the Macedonian. Like Cyrus before him, Alexander had little ambition to change the order of the empire he had conquered. Yet his military achievements transformed the world. When Alexander the Great defeated the Persian Empire, he was so impressed with the variety and civility of oriental culture that he married a princess of the realm and compelled most of his army to marry Persian women. This public marriage, symbolizing an attempt to meld cultures, contrasts sharply with the group divorce of Ezra and Nehemiah's time. The two ceremonies, so opposite, anticipate the conflict that eventually arose between Judaism and Hellenism. The surprise is that the conflict took so many centuries to evolve and that, in the meantime, many different ways of accommodation between Judaism and Hellenism were successfully discovered. Only in the later Roman period in the second, third, and fourth centuries C.E. did Jews begin to believe that they could no longer co-exist within the Roman Empire, and it was a Roman Empire heavily influenced by Christianity that brought them to this conclusion.

Hellenization began on a much more promising note, with the adoption of the Greek language by many of the indigenous populations of the eastern Mediterranean basin. The word *Hellenizō* in Greek, cognate with the English word *Hellenization*, means literally "to speak Greek"—aptly so, for the Hellenistic age, as opposed to the Hellenic age of the city-states in classical Greece, was characterized by the learning of Greek by non-Greek peoples all over the Mediterranean. Greek remained the major language of trade in the eastern Mediterranean, even after the Romans arrived. Yet the common culture that evolved out of Greek communication had little to do with the values of ancient Greece. The cultural process that gave the Hellenistic age its characteristic stamp was largely oriental and actually began before Alexander's conquests.

In the larger economic, social, and political sense, the changes that were brought about by the Hellenistic age were already under way before Alexander. The empires of the ancient Near East had always been centered in the river valleys. The Persians were the first to form a huge, road-connected, political entity, which ruled from the Danube to the upper Indus rivers.[6] The center of the Persian Empire was on the high plateau of modern Iran, overlooking the ancient Near Eastern capitals in the Tigris and Euphrates river valleys of Iraq. Ruling at such a distance from the ancient river trade was made possible by the development and effective protection of overland trade routes. Along with road building and military control, trade was facilitated by the spread of gold coinage, which had been invented in Lydia.

All of these developments tended to decrease the traditional importance of the agricultural interests in every ancient Near Eastern state. With the diminution of agriculture came a loss of prestige for the traditional, national, agricultural divinities and their priesthoods. The increased communication between states also brought a loss in the prestige of each nation's traditional mythology. The effect of greater world organization and communication was to call into question by conquest and rational comparison the traditional basis of all the ancient civilizations, including the cult of Yahweh.

The characteristic sociology of the Hellenistic age was also initiated by the Persians. From the Persian conquest in the sixth century B.C.E. through the next millennium, until the Arab conquest in the seventh century C.E., the ruling class of the Near East spoke an Indo-European language and oversaw an indigenous population which spoke a Semitic language. While the new Greek conquerors took on the cultural habits of their conquered lands, they did not much desire to blend in with the indigenous population. Furthermore, language differences made any significant communication between the two populations difficult.

Even though the land of Israel had been rebuilt under the Persians, the economic burdens that the Israelites were forced to bear were extensive. They therefore welcomed Alexander as a national liberator. To this day Jews continue to name their children Alexander or Alexandra, or Sandor in Yiddish, to commemorate the liberation from the Persians.

This positive attitude toward Greece and Hellenistic institutions continued largely unabated from the fourth century for the next century and a half, while Judea was ruled by the Ptolemies living in Egypt. During this period, Hellenization continued apace in the land of Israel. Not only Greek names but Greek styles of architecture and dress were adopted—in short, all the things that normally go along with learning the Greek language.

The culmination of the first stage of contact was the translation of the Bible into Greek. According to legend, this volume was the product of seventy scholars who, working independently, by a miracle produced the exact same translation for King Ptolemy in Egypt. The edition is thus called the Septuagint (abbreviated LXX because *Septuaginta* means "seventy" in Greek). Though the story is only a fable, it illustrates both the respect in which the Septuagint was held and the novelty of translating the constitution of the Hebrew state into a foreign language, where it became an object of literature and meditation more than a political document. The translation of the document was largely for use by the large and influential Alexandrian Jewish community, most of whose members had lost the ability to read Hebrew. Philo, one of the foremost members of the community during the time of Jesus and Paul, seems to have known a few Hebrew etymologies and some Hebrew exegesis, but he was well versed in the Greek Septuagint. The Septuagint was clearly accepted as a legitimate version of the Bible. The situation was similar to that of the contemporary American Jewish community which, in spite of its commitment to Judaism, has not kept close touch with either Hebrew or Yiddish.

Although Hellenization affected all parts of Jewish society, both in the diaspora and within the land of Israel, it did not infuse all parts of Jewish society equally. The community still living in the land of Israel may have kept more of its native ways, but Hellenization was pronounced even there. First of all, the very small district of Judea was not even as big as the modern state of Israel. It was closer to the limits of modern metropolitan Jerusalem. Surrounded by cities founded or settled on Greek models, it could hardly ignore Hellenistic culture. Second, there was a good deal of Hellenistic influence within the confines of Jerusalem itself, a city where Hellenization took on unique forms but flourished nevertheless, as evidenced by the amphitheater and gymnasium constructed there in the second century B.C.E.

The process of Hellenization was similar to two contemporary types of cultural contact: modernization, a phenomenon in the third world, or secularization, a phenomenon of religious transformation in Western societies. These transformations are stimulated by the society's need to acculturate a new world-system. They also involve a breakdown of the power, wholeness, and appeal of the traditional religion. In modernization, the stimulus comes from Western industrial or colonial rule. In secularization, the stimulus comes from the intellectual structures of a philosophy that challenges traditional religion. In both cases, the traditional unity of the culture is broken down. Often this outcome is accompanied by an ideology of pluralism and free competition between varieties of religious expression. The key commonality in the two developments is that the religious establishments can no longer take for granted the allegiance of their populations. As a result, the religious tradition, which was an almost unconscious, self-evident assumption about the world, becomes a set of beliefs that has to be marketed.[7]

The situation in second commonwealth Israel was similar in that Greek culture and the spread of trade made an entirely new world perception necessary and eroded the automatic assent of Judeans to the religion of their forefathers. The religion had to explain itself in new ways and had to evolve new ways of understanding itself in a Greek environment. Furthermore, the process of Hellenization progressed at different rates in different classes, making more distinct separations between the social classes of Judea and exacerbating class conflicts. Basically, those people who were interested in a life of leadership within the community and could afford the education sought out Greek educational institutions. They consisted mostly of the traditional rural aristocrats and the priests entrusted with running the country. A developing trades class also learned rudimentary Greek for use in international exchange. These Jews felt that Greek philosophy and culture did not interfere with their Jewishness.

For their own part, the Greeks were equally impressed with Jewish traditions. Hecataeus, for instance, lionizes Moses as one "who did not make any kind of picture of Gods, as he did not believe that God was in human form; rather the heaven which surrounds the earth was alone God and Lord of all." Although Hecataeus did not get the details right, the tone of admiration is perceptible. Theophrastus calls the Jews a "race of philosophers" because they "discourse on the divine . . . observe the stars at night . . . and call to them in their prayers" (Fr. 13). Since many of the schools of Greek philosophy had evolved monistic or monotheistic premises, explaining the ancient myths and stories of the *Iliad* and *Odyssey* as allegories representing moral virtues, it is not difficult to see why Hebrew monotheism was so impressive to them. In talking about "Jewish philosophy," the Greek philosophers were undoubtedly describing ordinary Judaism, even though they were also dressing it up to suit their own romantic notions of the philosophical peoples of the East.[8]

Not all pagan responses to Judaism were as positive. Anti-Semitism was known during the Hellenistic period. But it was not especially prevalent. More often than not the anti-Jewish writings of Greeks and Romans turn out to express a general dislike of all foreigners rather than a specific anti-Semitism.

In the case of Apion in the first century C.E. however, xenophobia crossed the line into anti-Semitism. According to Josephus, "Within this sanctuary, Apion has the effrontery to assert that the Jews kept an ass's head, worshiping that animal and deeming it worthy of the deepest reverence; the fact was disclosed, he maintains, on the occasion of the spoliation of the temple by Antiochus Epiphanes, when the head, made of gold and worth a high price, was discovered" (*Against Apion*, 2.79–80).

Apion spread the incredible story that the Jews practiced human sacrifice and that they were incarcerating a young man in the Temple for such a purpose when Antiochus luckily intervened. Josephus reports that Apion had learned of this from the writings of Posidonius and Apollonius Molon, respectable intellectuals of the first century. Yet Apion's overt anti-Semitism was an exception. He was known by Roman aristocrats to be a self-promoter and bounder in the society of Alexandria and Rome. His anti-Semitism was part of his program to recommend himself as one of the guardians of classical culture against foreign dilution, and he failed to gain the acceptance he wanted.

Hellenistic thought was accepting of foreign religions. The rule seems to have been toleration of Jewish presence combined with a genteel discrimination against nonclassical cultures. Given even that degree of Roman and Greek prejudice, Jews had sufficient reasons not to seek out Hellenistic culture. But discrimination certainly did not deter Jews from seeking their success in various Hellenistic occupations.

The principal factor in determining whether a Jew would Hellenize was neither prejudice nor religion. Rather, Hellenistic sociology and economics affected the decision significantly. Rural people, who had no need of developing international trade or formal education, continued within their native Hebrew and Aramaic languages and distrusted the new cultural forms. The city populations, containing aristocrats, venture capitalists, merchants, and skilled tradesmen, were necessarily more affected. In Judea, as in the rest of the Hellenistic world, Hellenization was largely an urban phenomenon and also a necessary fashion for the wealthier classes.

Prominent among the literary production of the first period of Jewish Hellenization was wisdom literature, an ancient Semitic genre of proverbs and inquiry into the ethical underpinnings of the universe. Probably the entire Book of Ecclesiastes, with its stoic acceptance of what is, was written under Hellenistic influence, although it was later attributed to Solomon and canonized. Proverbs had praised Wisdom as a handmaiden of God to the extent of personifying her. In the Hellenistic age she easily became Sophia, a personification of the Greek virtue of wisdom. Hellenistic Jewish culture could easily emphasize the virtues of studying wisdom, continuing to equate it with the correct service of the Lord. *The Wisdom of Jesus ben Sira*, which is a native book of Hebrew wisdom written during this period, shows the growing popularity of wisdom literature. Once it was translated into Greek, *The Wisdom of Jesus Ben Sira* was widely disseminated, even after the original Hebrew was lost, showing that the genre of wisdom literature could continue independently in its new Greek environment.

The Maccabean Revolt

According to legend, Alexander the Great willed his empire not to a specific person but "to the strongest." His generals and their successors each took whatever piece of the empire they could control, while their descendants spent centuries trying to prove that they were the sole heir stipulated by Alexander's legendary will. The wars that resulted between the two Greek dynasties, the Ptolemies of Egypt and the Seleucids of Syria, unalterably changed the history of the land of Israel.

During the first century of Hellenization, Judea fell peaceably into the domains of the Ptolemies. In 223 B.C.E. Antiochus III the Great came to the Seleucid throne in Antioch. After more than two decades of war against the Ptolemaic rulers of Egypt, he won a decisive victory over Ptolemy V at Panias, the source of the Jordan River in northeast Galilee. As a result of his victory, the land of Israel passed from the control of the Ptolemies into the empire of the Seleucids.

Antiochus III's son, Antiochus IV Epiphanes ("The God manifest"), is the Seleucid king whose villainy is recounted in the story of Hanukkah. The traditional version, which treats Antiochus as an insane and irrational tyrant, has little credibility. What Antiochus did was more rational and more cynically political: he installed his own candidate, Jason, for the Jewish High Priesthood, over his rival and relative, Meneleus, and then changed his mind when Meneleus offered him more money. Apparently, Antiochus issued a decree offering the status of Antiochene citizenship to the cities of his empire who were ready to take on Hellenistic civic forms. A priest named Jason (Hebrew: Joshua), the brother of the reigning High Priest Onias, represented those Jews who thought this to be a good idea. Jason appeared before Antiochus, promising a large sum of money for the privilege of establishing a community of Antiochenes in Jerusalem. Antiochus promptly accepted the offer and appointed Jason to replace Onias. Antiochus may have been economically and politically expedient in changing his mind. But his demotion of the High Priest was a violation of the native Torah constitution, because the High Priesthood was an inherited office, hitherto independently chosen by Israelites and governed by Israelite rules of succession. In the past, the imperial rulers had been a little more discreet and circumspect in their use of power.

Jason returned home to draw up a list of citizens and to establish the institutions typical of a Greek polis. Within three years, however, Antiochus had changed his mind in at least one significant way. Meneleus offered Antiochus a greater bribe and succeeded in winning the High Priesthood for himself. In order to meet the terms of the agreement, Meneleus plundered the temple vessels. Onias, who publicly criticized Meneleus, was murdered by a retainer of Antiochus.

When Antiochus mounted an expedition against Egypt, Jason took advantage of his absence to attack Meneleus in Jerusalem. The result was urban rioting, with the supporters of Meneleus and of Jason battling each other. The ordinary Jews of Jerusalem objected to both candidates, presumably not wishing to give up an hereditary, God-ordained Torah constitution for Hellenistic civic forms. Antiochus returned from Egypt, stormed the city, plundered the Temple, slaughtered the population, and sold some into slavery. He also placed Meneleus back in the seat of the High Priesthood. Another horrible slaughter ensued two years later when Antiochus's officer Apollonius attacked the citizenry on the Sabbath. Antiochus was in danger of losing his hold on the city of Jerusalem by his unskillful and greedy meddling. More drastic action was definitely necessary to secure the area.

What followed is open to many interpretations. From the perspective of the Jewish writers, Antiochus began a persecution of Jews, who were causing the rioting against his appointees for the priesthood. This was followed by the transformation of the Temple into a cult place of Zeus, the supreme god of the Hellenized world and for centuries identified with Yahweh of the Hebrews. From Antiochus's perspective, however, the action may have been much more political, to declare martial law in Jerusalem and its environs by moving troops into the Temple area and hence to suspend the local Torah constitution. The effect was far greater than he expected: a general revolt broke out in the country, led by a group of resistance fighters called the Maccabees. The rebels ultimately regained independence for Judea and set themselves up as client kings called the Hasmoneans. Antiochus appears to have misunderstood the nature, the depth, and the extent of the religious sentiments of the Judeans, rather than to have desired specifically to persecute the religion. In any case, the result was the loss of his Judean province.

The primary source for these events is the highly tendentious First Book of Maccabees, which is an official history of the Maccabean dynasty. Compared to the story that most Jews know in the "Megilat Antiochus," however, 1 Maccabees is a model of restraint. The Maccabean Revolt was not just a response to a foreign invasion, as is ordinarily supposed. It also involved the active participation of a group of "reformers" within Israelite society.[9] But it is hard to know whether Antiochus and the reform group's interests were "religious" or merely "political." Furthermore, it is difficult to understand the motives of Antiochus and the reform group in persecuting and proscribing Judaism, as the tradition maintains, when such an act was so out of keeping with Hellenistic morals and the tolerant policies of the time.

One way of reconstructing these events is to compare the events of Hellenistic times with cultural conflicts in the modern period. Complex problems of assimilation or acculturation in the modern period can serve as paradigms for the Maccabean Revolt. One of the most obvious differences between acculturation and assimilation is that assimilation always assumes that the purpose of the reform is the total loss of previous identity.[10] Commentaries about Jewish assimilationism always assume that the purpose of assimilation is the complete loss of Jewish identity. Acculturation, sometimes called modernization or secularization, assumes many possible outcomes of the conflict between two different cultures, including the eventual rejection of the new culture by the native group.

The Maccabean Revolt was partly a civil war, caused by a difference in the acculturation of different classes in Judea to Hellenistic culture, and aggravated by external interference that went beyond most of the parties' wishes. The differences between the Hellenizers and the Maccabees was not wholly religious but also political and economic.[11] The most Hellenized faction is characterized in 1 Maccabees as guilty of apostasy against the covenant, the Torah of Moses, and the holiness of the people. But this account also hints that the reformers' motives were just more political than the Maccabees' and that the charge of heresy was an exaggeration.

The motives of the reformers are related to the fact that their revolt was a civil war, caused partially by a difference in acculturation of certain classes in Judea to Hellenistic society and partially by external interference. In acculturation, as opposed to assimilation, the differences between "religious" and "social" motives in situations such as this are not absolute; rather, they depend on the perspective of actors in the drama. The perspective of those people who had been more Hellenized, acculturated, or modernized in the life of the Hellenistic empire was more political. The natural perspective of the least acculturated party was religious. Both of these terms are relative, not absolute.

The First Book of Maccabees levies the tendentious charge of apostasy against the reformers and characterizes them as assimilationists, denying God, contradicting the divine Torah in both its civil and religious dimensions, and replacing it with an adventitious diplomatic covenant:

> At that time there appeared in Israel a group of renegade Jews, who incited the people. "Let us enter into a covenant with the Gentiles round about," they said, "because disaster upon disaster has overtaken us since we segregated ourselves from them." The people thought this a good argument, and some of them in their enthusiasm went to the king and received authority to introduce non-Jewish laws and customs. They built a sports stadium in the Gentile style in Jerusalem. They removed their marks of circumcision and repudiated the holy covenant. They intermarried with Gentiles, and abandoned themselves to evil ways.   (1:11–15)

The account imputes to these "radical Hellenizers" an intent to repudiate the covenant with Yahweh in several ways. To build a sports stadium is to introduce non-Jewish customs into Jerusalem. This is followed by the removal of the marks of circumcision, denoting the covenant itself, by means of a dangerous surgical procedure. The further sin of intermarriage makes evident the whole evil intent of the plan.

Merely building in the Greek style and setting up a gymnasium would not in itself have been a violation of the constitution, were the ancient Hellenistic gymnasium like a modern one. But the ancient institution was a major socializing school for Hellenistic culture, involving debates and other educational and civic affairs, and pre-eminently displaying naked males in athletic competition. The games always began with a public ceremony of worship to a foreign god. All this was offensive to many Jews for long-standing reasons.

Furthermore, those desirous of adopting this way of life needed surgery, since the mark of circumcision would have been evident in a naked competition. However, this was more than an operation to improve one's social acceptability.[12] Circumcision was the emblem of God's covenant, the basic sign of membership in the covenant community. Hellenized Jews would not often have considered such an extreme remedy. It is an exaggeration of the reformers' position from a traditionalist perspective, condemning all for the extremism of some.

The First Book of Maccabees provides an unambiguous example of how root metaphors and paradigms produce sociodrama within societies. The metaphor of covenant, which was used to organize reality within the society, impresses a particular pattern on the way in which social conflict is expressed.[13] It is theoretically possible that the removal of all peculiarly "Jewish" aspects of Jerusalem's government was in the minds of all the Hellenists, as 1 Maccabees explicitly states, but this would have been a radical solution for the time. The other side of the argument is equally possible, as shown by another case of Jewish acculturation in the modern period, to the dominant European culture. Modern Reform Judaism believes that it is preserving the essential qualities of Judaism and removing only unessential customs and ceremonies when it reforms worship and practice. Orthodox and Conservative Judaism see the matter as a mistaken violation of Judaism and even as a way to assuage consciences in the process of assimilating to European or American life. The positions on both sides are sincere. So even though there is no direct opposing testimony from the reformers themselves in the Maccabean period, the situation was probably more a matter of perspective than 1 Maccabees suggests.

Archaeological and inscriptional evidence from the Hellenistic world suggests that most Jews took a much more moderate position toward Hellenization. It shows that Hellenistic and Jewish civilizations were able to live symbiotically to an astonishing extent. The roots of the conflict between the two cultures were due not to any essential differences between them but to unbridgeable and uncompromisable positions brought on by the civil disorder in Jerusalem. In other environments the outcome of the mix of Judaism and Hellenism was different. Philo, a "Torah-true" Jew living in Alexandria, admired and justified Hellenistic institutions such as the gymnasium in *The Special Laws*. He saw Greek citizenship as a positive value, not conflicting with Jewish rites but benefiting them. It is plausible to assume that in Jerusalem 150 years earlier there were those who felt similarly. But as the political situation was then different, the moderate perspectives have been lost to historical record.

The situation in Judea, then, was like a drama—two groups of people interpreting the same action differently, each group from its own point of view. Most reformers probably thought they were advancing the political reputation of Jerusalem, whereas from the perspective of the Maccabees they were affecting the religious underpinnings of all organized life in Judea. To make matters worse, the reformers were priests of a high order changing the worship of the service in Jerusalem and bringing a foreign institution, the gymnasium, onto sacred ground. Changing these few customs, no matter how justified from the reformers' perspective, was perceived in the less Hellenized rural areas as a violation of the entire Torah constitution. If any of the Torah were to be replaced by Hellenistic law, the entire constitution would be endangered. There was at the time no radical separation of "church" and "state," but from the perspective of the outlying areas this was a far more serious religious issue than the reformers had intended, especially when Antiochus attempted to quell the conflict by moving Greek soldiers into the Temple compound and defiling the altar. This action went beyond any by the most extreme expectations. It was followed by a more general suppression of Jewish customs in the countryside, wherever the troops maneuvered.

In the traditional story told at Hanukkah, Antiochus is perceived as a persecutor of Judaism pure and simple. He forbad Jewish families to practice the law, even to circumcise their children. He polluted the Temple with pigs and bones. And he compelled Jews to eat pork publicly, as a test of obedience to his evil edicts. Avoiding pork (among other unclean animals) as well as practicing circumcision (which does not in itself confer membership in the community upon a believer) emerged at this point as symbolic boundary-marking actions far in excess of their original meanings within biblical lore. Because of the Maccabean Revolt, circumcision and abstention from pork became emblems of Jewish identity par excellence in ways that would have been inappropriate to earlier periods of Jewish history

With such general disapproval, Antiochus lost his hold upon the government of Israel. First, public opinion went against him. The excesses of his troops offended Hellenized and non-Hellenized alike. When the rural Jews revolted under the leadership of the Maccabee family, a clan of rural priests located in Modiin, the countryside went to their aid. Some Jews wanted an end to the political oppression; others saw in the persecution of Judaism a beginning of the end of time. Some Jews even refused to fight on the Sabbath and so risked martyrdom for their religious beliefs. The combination of all these forces in the Jewish society gave the Maccabees their chance for success.

The Maccabees were victorious and became the country's new rulers, calling themselves kings. But the rededication of the Temple was all that united the populace. The subsequent Maccabean military successes expanded the Jewish state to its pre-exilic boundaries. The Maccabees instituted a native dynasty, the Hasmonean house, which was to rule in shaky and feverish independence for more than a century, from 165 B.C.E. until Pompey's entrance into Jerusalem in 63 B.C.E. brought the land of Israel under Roman occupation. But the Hasmoneans were not anti-Hellenistic. Rather, they readily adopted Hellenistic culture, so Hellenism itself was not the perceived problem at the time.

There is no mention in the early sources of the cruze of oil that the rabbis say burned for eight days and caused the holiday of Hanukkah (Rededication) to be observed for that length of time annually. Nor is there any mention of the nine-branched Hanukkah menorah characteristic of the holiday today. Instead, the holiday of Hanukkah was instituted by the Maccabees as their independence day, the founding day of their dynasty. The First Book of Maccabees merely says that the holiday of rededicating the altar was celebrated for eight days. Probably, this was in deliberate imitation of the dedication of the first Temple under Solomon, which was held on the Sukkoth holiday. The dedication of the second Temple, under

Ezra and Nehemiah, emulated the dedication ceremonies of the first Temple (Ezra 6:16–18).

The Second Book of Maccabees begins with a letter addressed to the Jews of Alexandria, trying to convince them to celebrate a Judean national holiday that has no basis in the history of the Alexandrian community and, in fact, might be distasteful to them. The letter to the Egyptian Jews first calls the holiday "the Camping-Out Festival of Kislev"—in other words, the Sukkoth holiday celebrated in winter instead of fall when it normally falls. The letter goes on to say that a miracle happened when the Temple was rededicated, which the Jewish community in Jerusalem views as evidence that the Alexandrian Jews ought to celebrate it. Unfortunately, the miracle has nothing to do with Judas Maccabeus's time or the cruze of oil. Rather the miracle takes place in the time of Ezra when the sacrificial fire of the first Temple, hidden before its destruction, is miraculously rekindled by means of naphtha.

Josephus, in his *Antiquities of the Jews*, written at the beginning of the second century, acknowledges that the holiday is called a "Festival of Lights" but is not sure of the reason. He supposes that the lights have something to do with the regaining of freedom. Or the use of lights in celebration of this holiday may merely have come from its chance synchronization with the winter solstice, when many peoples perform rituals to mark the northward turning of the sun and the lengthening of daylight. In any event, Josephus, who is not reticent about talking of miracles, does not know of the one miracle crucial to Jewish folklore of Hanukkah—the minute amount of sacred oil which burned for eight days, giving the priesthood enough time to replenish the Temple's supply.

Consequently, the best explanation for the story of the miracle of the oil is that it was a folk tale, picked up by the later rabbinic community, which helped convince the Jewish community to continue celebrating Hanukkah as a religious holiday, even after the Hasmonean house ceased to be the official government of the country and the holiday was no longer an independence day of a particular regime.

The populace would have needed persuading to continue to

celebrate the holiday under any circumstances. Shortly after the time of Judas and his brothers, the Hasmonean house suffered a loss of esteem. Having started as rural priests, the Hasmoneans took the title of king as well as High Priest, which was a violation of the separation of powers in the Israelite constitution. Ironically, it was because Antiochus had attempted to place his own candidate into the High Priesthood that the revolt broke out. The Maccabees' successors took the title for themselves, though they were not of the high priestly family. Even more amazing, although they started as an anti-Seleucid party, the pressures of ruling the area soon made it necessary for the Hasmoneans to acquire as much Hellenistic education and Greek culture as their opponents in the Maccabean war. Opposition to Hellenistic culture itself was not the original issue, although in later times the holiday became a symbol of Jewish opposition to foreign influences. Rather, the issue was the use to which Hellenization was put. From one perspective, Hanukkah could later be seen as a holiday celebrating religious freedom. Yet in its own time, the original issue could not have been solely a problem of Hellenization. One needed to Hellenize in order to rule properly, for all international communication was carried out in Greek. Conflict broke out when Greek customs openly violated Israelite constitutional procedure.

The Maccabean Revolt was a watershed in the Hellenization process. Once Hellenization came into conflict with the traditional constitution, the Torah of Israel, it could no longer be tolerated. But the corollary was also true. A Greek custom, no matter how foreign, could be appropriated if a conflict with Torah could be avoided. Living in a foreign empire was acceptable provided it allowed for the Israelite constitution. Jews could not allow their national identity to be subsumed by a larger, secular code when the Laws of Moses were known to be divine in origin and convenantally guaranteed to them. Thus a second, more subtle period of Hellenization began, when Hellenistic ideas were adopted into Israelite culture after having been refashioned into uniquely Judean institutions.

❦ II ❦
Society in the Time of Jesus

The Maccabean Revolt ensured that the machinery of the Judean state under Hasmonean and Roman administration would be based on the covenant idea. More than that, it ensured that all Judean political institutions of the Hellenistic period had to be legitimated and rationalized by means of the constitution of the country—the Torah. As the root metaphor of Israelite society, the Torah functioned as the foundation of all the institutions and political parties, even though some of them originally had Hellenistic roots. In addition, the Torah formed an unwritten script for any drama of conflict within the society. The interpretation of specific biblical verses by means of exegetical principles was as important as the institutions and parties themselves, for these exegetical methods became the focal points of conflict about the legitimacy of various positions and institutions within Judea. To understand the conflict, one must analyse the scriptural supports for the major institutions—the Temple, the synagogue, and the Sanhedrin—as well as the Scripture supporting the major parties—the Pharisees, the Sadducees, the Essenes, the Samaritans, and the Hellenized Jews.

The Temple
The Temple had been a part of Israel's government since the days of Solomon. The desert tabernacle was the Temple's forerunner and, according to priestly traditions, its explicit model. Although during David's time the building of a temple for

Yahweh was a controversial idea, the Temple eventually became an integral part of the government and religious life of the Judeans. Thus, the Temple and the priesthood were the easiest institutions to justify.

From the sixth century through the end of the first century B.C.E., the Temple was even more central to the government, since the priesthood became the highest and most stable political power. Jews living in exile, as well as those living in the land of Israel, waited to hear the Temple messengers proclaim the holidays, feasts, and festivals. All who lived close enough and could afford the journey made the trip to the Temple on the great pilgrimage holidays. Furthermore, the second Temple, as the administrative center of native Judean government, had functions that went far beyond those of the first Temple. Much administration was handled from the courtyards surrounding the Temple, which had evolved by the first century B.C.E. into an institution in their own right. Some of the courtyards were secular enough to be visited by Gentiles or unclean Israelites. To be sure, neither the Persian governors nor the procurators of Rome could legally enter very far into the Temple precincts for, being Gentiles, they were too impure. So the purity of the Temple also acted as a barrier, ensuring the independent deliberations of the priesthood. At the same time, during Roman times ultimate power was clearly vested in the Roman procurators, not in the priesthood.

Whereas the institution of the Temple could be justified on the basis of the historical prophets and Torah, critical voices were often raised against the contemporary Temple administration. Many Israelites felt that the new Temple, modeled on Hellenistic conventions, did not live up to the ideals of the ancient institution. As had become clear during the Maccabean Revolt, the High Priest was not an independent ruler but was subject to confirmation or manipulation by the ruling authority—be it Persian, Ptolemaic, Seleucid, Roman, or native Hasmonean. The Hasmonean successors of the original Maccabees, in fact, were severely criticized by many sects—including the Essenes, the Pharisees, and later the rabbis and Christians—for having subverted the institution. The claim of the Maccabees to the offices of both king and High Priest, which could be viewed as a constitutional violation, may have been responsible for some of their unpopularity. Although Herod, who followed the Hasmoneans, was roundly hated by almost everyone, his extensive renovations and beautification of the Temple enhanced Jewish pride all over the Roman Empire. The High Priest or the priesthood was accused or criticized far more often than the building itself. Because the Temple symbolized government, people who were unhappy with the administration of the state could frame that disquiet as opposition to the Temple cult.

Holiness surrounded the Temple in concentric circles of increasing purity. At the very center of holiness was the dark chamber of the Holy of Holies, meant to be entered only by the High Priest and only once a year on Yom Kippur. When Pompey brought Judea under Roman rule in 63 B.C.E., he broke this rule by entering the Holy of Holies. According to rabbinic legend, Pompey subsequently suffered the apt retribution of God, who caused an insect to crawl into Pompey's ear and kill him—violating his own inner sanctum, as it were, and showing Pompey's true size in the eyes of God.

The basic duties of the Temple were performed by Levites, who were professional assistants trained in specific services. Serving the Jerusalem priesthood was a much larger cadre of amateur priestly volunteers. Most of these priests served on a regular schedule, taking leave from their ordinary occupations to come to Jerusalem for their prestigious service.

As enlarged and rebuilt by Herod on the earlier Persian structure, the Temple in Jerusalem was widely admired by Jews and Gentiles alike as a grand edifice in the Hellenistic style. Gentiles could donate some sacrifices and many did so as an act of piety toward the Jewish state and people. At holiday times Jews and Gentiles from all over the world converged on Jerusalem for pilgrimage. After special occasions like childbirth, Jews also made the journey. Whether or not they traveled to Jerusalem, all Jews were expected to contribute to the upkeep of the institution. Most honored that obligation, wherever they lived.

The Synagogue

The other major Jewish institutions of Hellenistic times—the synagogue and Sanhedrin—were defined by tradition rather than biblical statute, although a pretext had to be found in the Torah to justify the tradition after the fact. Like American political parties or the President's cabinet, many institutions were firmly rooted in tradition but were not mentioned explicitly in the constitution. The synagogue, for instance, was unmentioned by the Torah. No one knows how it came into being or what its original function was. Synagogues are known to have existed in the Holy Land in the first century only because they were described in Josephus and the New Testament. There is no unambiguous archaeological evidence for synagogues in Judea until the second century C.E.[1]

According to Philo, synagogues were plentiful in the Diaspora even before the destruction of the Temple. Galilean synagogues were famous, on account not only of the New Testament references to them but also for their well-preserved artwork and mosaic floors from the third and later centuries. Evidently, Judea had a lesser need for synagogues because of the multiple functions that the Temple provided. Alternatively, it is possible that in the land of Israel, wealthy patrons' houses served as synagogues. Synagogues apparently became independent public edifices earlier in the Diaspora than in the holy land. Rabbinic tradition maintains that there was a synagogue within the precincts of the Temple, but this may be an anachronism.

The synagogue, whatever and whenever its origin, was legitimated by its function. It was a place where the Torah was read, studied, and interpreted. This is clarified by the New Testament, as well as by Philo and Josephus, in describing synagogues in various places outside Judea.

Various scriptural pretexts were used to claim antiquity for the synagogue. The rabbis cited Ezekiel (11:16) to prove that the Israelites founded the synagogue in Babylonian exile. But according to both Josephus and Philo, Sabbath scriptural reading was prescribed by Moses. If the synagogue was also a place where prayers were offered, it was because the community was already there to hear Scripture read. After the Temple was destroyed, the synagogue took on many new holy functions, as did the home in general and the dinner table in particular.[2]

Archaeological data for first century C.E. Judean synagogues may be lacking because synagogues had not yet evolved a characteristic architecture. Large private homes served as places of worship for Jewish congregations elsewhere in the Hellenistic world, and they are not distinguishable from ordinary homes in the archaeological remains. At Gamle in the lower Golan heights, archaeologists have uncovered a synagogue oriented toward Jerusalem that may date from the first century. Benches line all four sides of the building, and no remains suggest separate seating for men and women. In the center of this building may have been a *bema*, or podium.

Third-century Galilean synagogues are more numerous and more uniform architecturally, reflecting the shift of Jewish population into Galilee after the destruction of the Judean state by the Romans. The great synagogue at Meiron incorporates the typical basilica architecture, with a triple-doored front entrance, a rectangular plan inside, and two rows of supporting columns running down the center of the building. As at Gamle, there is no evidence for an ark on the wall. Rather, it appears that the ark of Hellenistic times was sometimes portable, probably a four-wheeled cart resembling the *naiskos*, or model temple, used in pagan processionals, which was wheeled into place for Torah reading. Other archaeological sites in Galilee, including Baram, Capernaum, Khirbet Shema, and Beth Alpha, reveal the extent to which Hellenistic art and culture had influenced Jewish sensibilities.[3]

The most famous synagogue excavation is outside Israel in Syria, at a place the ancients called Dura Europos. This third century synagogue is extremely well preserved, because it was deliberately filled with sand in order to strengthen the city's fortifications in time of siege. It has an elaborate Torah shrine, the niche for displaying the Torah, which corresponds to the ark in modern synagogues. Colorful wall paintings of great beauty depict scenes from the Torah in Hellenistic style.[4]

Evidence about the governance of synagogues has come down from ancient writing and archaeological remains. The synagogue leaders were called *archontes*, as was standard in many Greek organizations. A prominent congregant might refer to himself or herself as a mother (*mater*) or father (*pater*) of the synagogue on a burial inscription. The president of the synagogue could be called the *archisynagogos*. Laypersons led prayers and Torah readings. There was nothing that corresponded to the modern practice of hiring a rabbi to supervise the religious life of the congregation, both because the rabbinic movement was in its infancy and because the whole idea of a specific ministry to a community had not yet evolved.[5] Philo remarks that each trade—glassblowing, goldsmithing, silversmithing—had its own synagogue in Alexandria, where a principal synagogue also served the whole community. The synagogue was the focus of Jewish activity in the Diaspora, but the life that centered there was quite different from the one that the rabbis were later to ordain.

Besides Jews, a group of Gentiles called "God-fearers" (*Sebomenoi* or *Phoboumenoi*) is mentioned in the New Testament and synagogue inscriptions. They were evidently an unorganized group of fellow travelers, who attended services in the synagogue or contributed to its upkeep. Some of them wanted to convert; others, favorably impressed with Judaism, wanted only to bestow some civic honor upon the local synagogue. In an inscription from Aphrodisias, a list of synagogue patrons is followed by a list of the God-fearers, who have Greek names and occupations. The contention that early Christian support in synagogues came from these God-fearers, based on the report in Acts, can no longer be dismissed as the imagination of Luke.

The Sanhedrin

The Sanhedrin (Greek: *Synhedrion*) was an innovation to the Jewish scene. In municipal and provincial administrations during the Hellenistic period, a council called by the king or notable for the purposes of advising or confirming his decisions was called a *synhedrion*. There was no native Torah justification for the institution until the rabbinic period when the rabbis used the term to describe their own court, also called Beth Din ("Courthouse"). Probably, the term *sanhedrin* attached itself to a body of civil leaders identifiable in Maccabean times as "the council" (*boulé*), but possibly going back to a council of elders in earlier biblical times.

The Sanhedrin is a controversial body not just because of its role as the Jewish court in the trials of Jesus and Paul but because of irreconcilable differences in Greek and Hebrew descriptions of the institution. Presumably the reason for their conflicting eveidence is that the Sanhedrin changed character after 70 C.E. when the rabbis took it over. Before the war against Rome in 66 C.E., the institution was not solely in the hands of the Pharisees. The New Testament reports that the Pharisees and Sadducees shared power in the Sanhedrin, and Josephus observes that the two parties had periods of ascendancy and decline, at least in the time of the Hasmoneans. Josephus says, however, the Pharisees were the party whose opinions the people respected, and they were in the majority at the end of the first century. Yet for most of that century, the Sanhedrin was presided over by the High Priest.[6]

After the Sanhedrin became a rabbinic institution and started to serve as the central government body of the postwar administration in Galilee, the rabbis entered into elaborate exegeses to justify and legitimate the institution, based on the description of the seventy elders who had accompanied Moses into the cloud to receive God's revelation (Sanhedrin 1:1). The tractate of the Mishnah devoted to the organization of courts and punishment is called *Sanhedrin* in Hebrew. But the term used inside the tractate is always *Beth Din*. The officers of the Sanhedrin are described as rabbinic officials, the "Prince" and the "Father of the Court" (*Ab Beth Din*), not as the High Priest. It seems likely, then, that the Sanhedrin evolved into a rabbinic institution only after the rabbis had taken it over in the second century. The institution itself acquired its standard definition in the rabbinic period.[7]

Just as the major institutions of the period were legitimated through the Torah constitution (even when the legitimation appears forced), so too the major parties and sects of that day grounded their social charter in the Torah constitution.[8] The beliefs of each of the many parties and groups had to be based on Scripture. There were two reasons for the proliferation of competing sects and interpretations of Scripture. First, the text itself is refractory. What the Torah means to say is not always clear. Second and more important, Hellenization of the country made a greater variety of responses to the ancient document both possible and necessary, in order to comprehend the wider diversity of opinion and the individualism encouraged by Hellenistic society.

Though each sect felt that its distinct perspective was determined by the meaning of Scripture, each sect was also heavily affected by sociological forces. The sects at the time of Jesus read the Bible in the light of their own experience and situation. Since they felt sure that their own beliefs, in which they had been reared or to which they had been converted, were uniquely confirmed by Scripture, they quite naturally read the Torah as if it uniquely prophesied their position.

The Sadducees

The Sadducees have been universally maligned not only because they did not believe in resurrection but also because they were an aristocratic, heavily Hellenized class, closely connected with the management of the Temple. Although no one line of identifiably Sadducean text has survived, the reports in Josephus make it possible to reconstruct the likely Sadducean perspective:

> The Sadducees . . . do away with Fate altogether, and remove God beyond, not merely the commission, but the very sight of evil. They maintain that man has the free choice of good or evil and that it rests with each man's will whether he follows the one or the other. As for the persistence of the soul after death, penalties in the underworld, and rewards, they will have none of them. (*War* 2.164–166)[9]

> The Sadducees hold that the soul perishes along with the body. They own no observance of any sort apart from the laws;

in fact, they reckon it a virtue to dispute with the teachers of the path of wisdom that they pursue. There are but few men to whom this doctrine has been made known, but these are men of the highest standing. They accomplish practically nothing however. For whenever they assume some office, though they submit unwillingly and perforce, yet submit they do the formulas of the Pharisees, since otherwise the masses would not tolerate them. (*Antiquities* 18.16–17)

The claims of the Saducean party are the easist to support in Scripture. At no place in the Torah is general resurrection promised. Only in a late book, Daniel, is resurrection discussed at all. There, it is promised to those who help out in the final battle at the end of time. The period when the Book of Daniel came to be regarded as canonical is not known, though the Sadducees would have been suspicious of its claims. Since the Sadducees were the priestly aristocrats, they would have Hellenized faster than the surrounding community. They would have needed a Greek education to carry on the role of statecraft for the restored community of Israel.

No specifically Sadducean sectarian documents need have been written to justify Sadducean inherited rights, for it would have been easy to legitimate the traditional role of the priests. That role was explicitly outlined in the Torah constitution. The difficulty that the Sadducees faced was to legitimate their Greek philosophy and way of life. They could have accomplished this task through a variety of arguments that Homer and Socrates were actually students of Moses, an apologetic tradition of several Hellenistic Jewish writers. Furthermore, the mixture of stoicism and platonism that was most favored among the educated classes of the Hellenistic world had considerable philosophical affinities with the wisdom literature of the Hebrew Bible. Though there is no identifiably Sadducean literature, passages from the *Wisdom of Ben Sira* (also known as *Sirach*), for instance, express ideas that were also central to Sadduceeism (14:16–19):

Give, and take, and beguile yourself, because in Hades one cannot look for luxury.
All living beings become old like a garment, for the decree from of old is: "You must surely die!"

Like flourishing leaves on a spreading tree, which sheds some and puts forth others,

So are the generations of flesh and blood: one dies and another is born.

Every product decays and ceases to exist, and the man who made it will pass away with it.

The Samaritans

Samaria, capital of the northern kingdom of Israel, was destroyed by Assyria in 722 B.C.E., and its tribes deported or diluted by idolatrous population settled there by the Assyrians. Thus, the Samaritans are considered in the Bible to be religiously suspect, having given up pure Yahweh worship. Yet the Samaritans regarded themselves as the true remnants of the tribes of Ephraim and Manasseh. By the time of Jesus, however, the Samaritans had emerged as an identifiable sect with a characteristic set of beliefs. There are hints that religious schisms like gnosticism affected the Samaritan community in the second century C.E. and thereafter.[10]

The Samaritans, like their forebears, rejected the canonicity of the prophets and writings, together with the primacy of Jerusalem or the Davidic king. Instead, they shaped their own traditions from the much more limited text of the Pentateuch, developing an expectation for the return of a prophet like Moses. Beneath the doctrinal differences smoldered the original geographical and regional differences traceable to the time of Solomon and before, namely the rivalry between the northern and southern districts over the proper way to worship Yahweh. In the first commonwealth the northern tribes, who had more arable land and were more affluent than the southern Judeans, refused to accept the dynastic principle of the southern Davidic monarchy and seceded from the federation to form a separate northern kingdom. The southerners viewed the northerners as rebels who had always flirted with heresy and had on several occasions warred with the Judean kingdom. During the Persian period, the inhabitants of Samaria opposed the building of the second Temple. Later John Hyrcanus, a Maccabean king, destroyed their temple at Samaria. So there were ample historical reasons for Judeans and Samaritans to dislike each other, which were paralleled by the theological disputes. In general, the Samaritans are pictured as strict fundamentalists by the rabbis, who disapproved of their practices but gave grudging admiration to their zeal.

Though Samaritans were in many ways considered coreligionists by the Judeans, other issues separated the two communities. The story of the good Samaritan in the New Testament assumes a considerable level of animosity between the two groups by the first century C.E. This animosity suggests a relationship between Jesus' movement in Galilee and the neighboring Samaritans. In John the Samaritans are portrayed as especially friendly to the Christian community. Samaria and Galilee were alike in that they had always cherished certain customs and feelings of independence from Jerusalem. Throughout the Roman period, these two areas fomented rebellion quite often, though in the end the crowds that gathered for pilgrimages in Jerusalem proved as incendiary as the rural revolutionaries.

The Essenes

Philo, a Jewish philosopher and resident of first century C.E. Alexandria, mentions a select group among Alexandrian Jews who had tried to put all of Moses' ordinances into action. Called the Therapeutae or "Healers," they lived a monastic life. Though the group is not known from any other literature, they appear to be related to the Essenes described by both Philo and Josephus. Because of the sensuality that prevailed among the uneducated pagan classes, a life of chastity and abstinence was viewed by educated Jew and Gentile alike as the sign of a morally serious religion.

In Palestine these sects had an added political dimension. The Dead Sea Scrolls found at Qumran were the product of a cloistered group that closely resembled the Essenes of Josephus's description:

> The doctrine of the Essenes is wont to leave everything in the hands of God. They regard the soul as immortal and believe that they ought to strive especially to draw near to righteousness.

They send votive offerings to the temple but perform their sacrifices with a different ritual of purification. For this reason they are barred from those precincts of the temple that are frequented by all the people and perform their rites by themselves. Otherwise they are of the highest character, devoting themselves solely to agricultural labor . . . Moreover, they hold their possessions in common, and the wealthy man receives no more enjoyment from his property than the man who possesses nothing. The men who practice this way of life number more than four thousand. They neither bring wives into the community nor do they own slaves, since they believe that the latter practice contributes to injustice and that the former opens the way to a source of dissension. Instead they live by themselves and perform menial tasks for one another. They elect by show of hands good men to receive their revenues and the produce of earth and priests to prepare bread and other food. (*Antiquities* 18.18–22) [11]

Apparently, the Essenes formed a separate group when a High Priest not to their liking was appointed in Jerusalem. They had supported an alternate candidate who taught righteously and was therefore called the Teacher of Righteousness. With him they retired to the desert to establish their own center of priestly purity. Though they did not set up a temple in the desert, they interpreted their communal body as the temple of the Lord, an idea that was to be paralleled in Christianity. The Essenes were distinguishable from other protest groups of their day by their priestly character.

The communuty believed that the Torah indicated the imminent approach of the apocalyptic end. In order to demonstrate the Torah's meaning, the Essenes devised a special kind of exegesis, similar to that developed by other apocalyptic groups and early Christians. The term *pesher*, a modern coinage meaning "solution" or "interpretation," is used to describe this exegesis. The word points up the methodological similarity in the scriptural commentaries found in the Dead Sea Scrolls:

A star shall come out of Jacob, and a sceptre shall rise out of Israel. He shall smite the temples of Moab and destroy all the children of Seth. He shall rule out of Jacob and shall cause the survivors of the city to perish. The enemy shall be his possession and Israel shall accomplish mighty deeds. (Numbers 24:17–19)

> By the hand of your anointed ones, the seers of your testimonies, you have related to us the [times] of the wars of Your hands to conquer our enemies that You may be glorified by levelling the battalions of Belial, the seven nations of vanity, by the hand of Your poor whom You have redeemed [by might] and by the fullness of Your marvelous power. (You have opened) the door of hope to the melting heart. You will do to them (as you did) to Pharaoh, and to the captains of his chariots in the Red Sea. You will kindle the downcast spirits as a flaming torch in the straw to consume evil and never to cease until iniquity is no more. (*The War of the Children of Light against the Children of Darkness* (1 QM) 11.6–10)

The passage in Numbers describes a war against Moab in the time of Moses. The interpretation by the Essenes looks at this description not just as history but as a prophecy for the future. Moreover, the Essenes regard the passage as referring to their own group explicitly, written in a kind of code that needs a divinely revealed solution. As far as the Qumranites are concerned, the Moabites are in reality the followers of Satan, or Gentiles and Jews with un-Qumranite views. The Dead Sea text uses the past typologically to explain the present and prophesies what is about to come true historically.

The Essenes were not the only group to interpret this passage in Numbers as a prophecy describing a messianic war. "The Star Emerging from Jacob" was the title given to the man called Bar Kokhba (literally "Son of the Star") who in the second century C.E. led the second great Jewish revolt against Rome and died attempting to overthrow Roman rule. Prophetic interpretations of the Numbers passage doubtless added to the wide support that Bar Kokhba enjoyed, much to the chagrin of most of the rabbinic leadership.

The Essenes cherished a militant body of tradition. They thought of themselves as the children of Israel who, after spending a second forty years in the desert, would reconquer the Promised Land. The Qumran sect regarded the Hellenized Jews and Gentiles as the new Canaanites, the iniquitous nations who needed to be wiped out before a new community of redeemed Israelites could be formed. Their especially prominent observance of priestly purity laws allowed them to associate with the angels, who were going to help them fight the battle against the children of darkness at the end of time. So they read the past described in the Torah as if it were the prophecy and true model of their future. In other words, their way of life and their understanding of Scripture were perfectly parallel. They lived like the children of Israel under Moses, still in the desert but poised in highest purity for retaking by miraculous means the land of Israel from the sinners, as Joshua was supposed to have done.

In order for this monastic community to remain in perfect symmetry with the biblical record, some parts of Scripture had to be interpreted in a very loose way. For instance, in *The Manual of Discipline* (1 QS 9:10–11), a prophet, a royal messiah, and a priestly messiah are mentioned alongside one another. These three figures are the future leaders of the community to be restored at the end of time, according to the plan for a new government read into Deuteronomy 18:18 and 33:8–11, as well as Numbers 24:15–17. Therefore, the Dead Sea community appointed three office holders: an interpreter of Torah, a head priest, and a lay leader. The Essenes apparently believed in two messiahs, a messiah of Aaron and a messiah of Israel. Since they were a profoundly priestly community, the messiah of Aaron had the highest rank and the most important responsibilities. The royal messiah was much less important to the Essenes because they opposed the royal pretensions of the Maccabees. The Essenes' priestly beginnings preceded their exegesis, naturally determining the way in which the role of the eschatological priest would be interpreted from Scripture.[12] Their method of exegesis, like Philo's, the Christians', and the rabbis', was perfectly suited to demonstrating their views.

The Revolutionaries

At the far ends of the political spectrum were groups who refused to live under Roman authority under any circumstances. Most of the information about these groups comes from Josephus, who imposes his own perspective on the events and describes as bandits people who appear to have had truly political motives. Foremost among these groups was an extended family in Galilee, which constantly fomented trouble against Herod and the Roman rulers. Ezekias, Judas of Galilee, James and Simon, Menahem, and Eleazer—all members of this family— are mentioned by Josephus in ways that suggest they were revolutionaries.[13]

The most famous of the revolutionary groups, called either the Fourth Philosophy or the Zealots, coalesced to make war against Rome in 66 C.E.[14] John of Gischala was an important figure in this movement, from the beginning of the revolt in Galilee until the final destruction of Jerusalem, when he was captured. Simon bar Giora, another zealot, was the rebel leader who oversaw the Jewish defense of Masada, and in Josephus's narrative he was given the stirring words recommending death over slavery that preceded their mass suicide.

The Pharisees

The Pharisees are vilified in the New Testament, as the result of both sectarian rivalry and the Pharisaic interest in ritual purity. But the Pharisees were both the most popular sect and the ancestors of the rabbinic movement. Josephus speaks of them with real respect:

> The Pharisees, who are considered the most accurate interpreters of the laws and hold the position of the leading sect, attribute everything to Fate and to God; they hold that to act rightly or otherwise rests, indeed, for the most part with men, but that in each action Fate cooperates. Every soul, they maintain, is imperishable, but the soul of the good alone passes into another body, while the souls of the wicked suffer eternal punishment. (*War* 2.162–163)

> The Pharisees had passed on to the people certain regulations handed down by former generations and not recorded in the laws of Moses, for which reason they are rejected by the Sadducean group, who hold that only those regulations should be considered valid which were written down, and that those which

had been handed down by former generations need not be observed. And concerning these matters the two parties came to have controversies and serious differences, the Sadducees having the confidence of the wealthy alone but no following among the populace, while the Pharisees have the support of the masses. (*Antiquities* 13.297–298)

The Pharisees were disposed to interpret the scriptural text broadly. Unlike the allegorizers and the apocalyptic *pesher* writers, however, the Pharisees tried to lay down rules and procedures of exegesis by which the Scripture could be understood. They were the counterparts of the Sadducees in this respect. To use an analogy from American jurisprudence, the Pharisees were "loose constructionists" of the Torah, whereas the Sadducees were "strict constructionists." Since there is no Pharisaic document accurately datable to the first century, little can be said with certainty of their doctrine at that time. But there are rabbinic writings from the second century and also the reports of Josephus and Paul, who claim to have been Pharisees at different periods in their lives.

Rabbinic thought from a more mature time, around 200 C.E., illustrates the principles that were being formulated in the first century and represents the views of the Pharisees on the topic of resurrection:

All Israelites have a share in the world to come, for it is written (Isaiah 60:21): "Your people shall all be righteous, they shall possess the land forever; the branch of my planting, the work of my hands, that I may be glorified."
Mishnah 1: Moses received the Torah on Sinai and handed it down to Joshua, and Joshua to the elders, and the elders to the prophets, and the prophets handed it down to the men of the great assembly. They said three things: be deliberate in judgment, raise up many disciples, and make a fence around the Torah. (*Mishnah Pirke Aboth* 1:1)

The rabbinic traditions transmitted from the first century are not actual quotations or the *ipsissima verba* of the Pharisees but are rather rabbinic *dicta* coded for easy memorization and retelling.[15] This particular fragment of rabbinic lore can serve as representative of the beliefs of the Pharisees, only because it coincides with the descriptions of the Pharisees given by Josephus around 70 C.E.

The passage from Isaiah is interpreted in a way that never would have occurred to the prophet. He is talking about living in the land at the end of time. The Pharisees use the remark to prove resurrection. Next they maintain that a chain of transmission links them with the actual words which Moses received on Sinai. They can thus claim that their traditions were the actual divine revelation from Sinai. Building on this idea, the rabbis would later maintain the explicit doctrine of an "oral Torah" as well as a "written Torah," by which they could prove that their own scriptural interpretations were just as divine as the doctrines written explicitly in the Torah constitution. The Pharisees, far from agreeing that the Sadducean priests are the traditional rulers of the country, relegated the priesthood to purely cultic functionaries.

The social position of the Pharisees was not so high as that of the Sadducees. The Sadducees represented the upper reaches of society, whereas the Pharisees represented the middle classes. Some Pharisees were landowners. Others were skilled workers. Scribal occupations, which many of them followed, were middle-class skilled professions. Pharisees also followed occupations like tent-making, carpentry, or glass-blowing. Their later legal interpretations favor some kinds of commerce. Yet since they constantly ascended in power in this society, their class interests were not static.

After the destruction of the second Temple in 70 C.E., the Pharisees migrated to the smaller towns of Galilee, just as some Christians did. In fact, the Mishnah gives evidence that, in order to remain in the holy land after the war, the Pharisees had to get used to a small-town existence.

Philo, the Diaspora Jew

Philo was an Alexandrian Jewish philosopher and a great intellectual of his day. Though he was hardly representative of ordinary persons, his opinions give hints about a large group of Hellenized Jews, including the Sadducees of Judea, whose be-

liefs would otherwise be mostly unknown. Philo's more sophisticated arguments are often found in less sophisticated
form in the Jewish Diaspora, the community of Jews living
outside of the land of Israel. Philo demonstrates that in the
Diaspora, too, Jews interpreted the Torah as part of their fundamental rule of life. But the most characteristic aspect of
Diaspora thinking was its attempt to show that Scripture and
Greek philosophy were in complete harmony over the essential
issues, and that Jewish ethics and morality were superior.

A resident of first century Alexandria, roughly contemporary with Jesus and Paul, Philo held many views similar to
those of the Sadducees. His literary purpose was to show how
the Bible agrees with Greek philosophy. Since this agreement
is not evident from a literal reading of Scripture, he had to
adopt a systematic method of interpretation, allegory, which
had been developed by the Greeks in order to understand the
Homeric epics and hymns. By allegory, Philo means the use of
a story to symbolize the development of the soul's moral virtues. The Garden of Eden and the other creation stories, for
example, are allegorically but not literally true. Although they
show how God created the world of ideas before He created
the material world and other parts of the cosmos, the stories
did not actually happen. In this respect, Philo's system of exegesis is quite modern. His insistence that all the laws in the
Bible are to be carried out as they were written is one connection between Philo and the Sadducees.

Another important connection between Philo and the Sadducees is that, like them, he came from an aristocratic environment and tried to justify the importation of Greek culture into
Hebrew thought. Philo was evidently one of the leaders of the
Alexandrian Jewish community, since he was a relative of the
alabarch, the leader of the Jewish community in Alexandria,
and was also a relative of one of the Roman procurators of
Judea. Toward the end of Philo's life he was called upon to
head a delegation to Gaius Caligula to explain the Jewish side
of the urban rioting in Alexandria.

In good Greek manner, Philo refuses to predicate evil of
God. Any evil that humanity perceives, Philo holds, is a prod-

uct of material processes or merely a misunderstanding. This view harmonizes with the beliefs of the Sadducees. Philo also believes that good moral men of any type—by which he means not only converts to Judaism but also moral pagans who profess a monotheistic system and eschew idolatry and sexual immorality—will win deliverance. He does not speak of conversion *per se* but rather says that "other people, particularly those who take more account of virtue, have so far grown in holiness as to value and honor our laws" (*Life of Moses* 2.17). This was presumably a common apologetic belief of Hellenized Jews, who saw both the valuable and the immoral aspects of Hellenistic life and could on occasion appraise it favorably. This kind of culturally plural toleration of Greek philosophical ideals was characteristic of upper-class and Hellenized Jews and was distinctly different from the extremist sectarian condemnation of pagan and most Jewish behavior as sinful.

In other ways Philo is like the Pharisees. He believes in the immortality of the soul, which is not a Saducean idea. However, Hellenistic philosophy contained the same differences of opinion on the immortality of the soul. Philo knows the oral traditions for interpreting the Bible, having learned them from his elders. But he is much more interested in justifying the stories and principles of the Hebrew Bible to a Greek-speaking audience than in explicating the exact meaning of the laws.

Philo wants to say that God is immutable and immaterial. He therefore calls Him the Existent One, or Being itself. All the anthropormorphic descriptions of God in Scripture, together with the descriptions of angels, Philo ascribes to a mediational creature called the *logos*, meaning the "blueprint" or "pattern," often mistranslated the "Word." This ascription allows Philo to maintain, in spite of biblical evidence, that God lives only in the realm of pure spirit or ideals, while His appearances on earth are due to the *logos*, one of His emanations, a figure shaped like a man only in order that humanity can understand and relate to Him. In so doing, Philo proposes a radical change in Greek philosophy, because the *logos* had never before been personified. Thus Philo provides a necessary step in the development of Christian theology in the first chapter of the Gospel of John where the *logos* is mentioned. Philo's purpose, however, differs from that of John, since he would not have agreed that the personified *logos* can be made flesh.[16]

In his own Alexandrian context, Philo sets a middle course between the literalism of groups like the Sadducees, on the one hand, and the reform position of those he calls "extreme allegorizers," on the other. Apparently Philo knew and disapproved of a group of Jews who took allegory so far as to maintain that it was no longer necessary to observe Judaism; it was necessary only to understand the moral virtues that were represented and advocated by the biblical allegory:

> There are some who, regarding laws in their literal sense in the light of symbols of matters belonging to the intellect, are overpunctilious about the latter, while treating the former with easy-going neglect. Such men I for my part should blame for handling the matter in too easy and off-hand a manner: they ought to have given careful attention to both aims, to a more full and exact investigation of what is not seen and in what is seen to be stewards without reproach. As it is, as though they were living alone by themselves in a wilderness, or as though they had become disembodied souls, and knew neither city nor village nor household nor any company of human beings at all, overlooking all that the mass of men regard, they explore reality in its naked absoluteness. These men are taught by the sacred word to have thought for good repute, and to let go nothing that is part of the customs fixed by divinely empowered men greater than those of our time. (*On the Migration of Abraham* 89)[17]

Once Philo has stated that the law is a symbol whose purpose is most evident when it is practiced, he can understand any anthropomorphic or anthropopathic description of God in the Bible as necessary for mankind's instruction. The philosophical God is the Existent One beyond all comprehension. Philo uses the biblical covenant as a useful instrument for human moral education:

> Why then did it seem well to the prophet and revealer to represent God as binding himself by an oath? It was to convince created man of his weakness and to accompany conviction

with help and comfort. We are not able to cherish continually in
our souls the thought which sums so worthily the nature of the
cause, that "God is not like a man" (Num. 23:19), and thus rise
superior to all the human conceptions of Him. In us the mortal is
the chief ingredient. We cannot get outside ourselves in forming
our ideas; we cannot escape our inborn infirmities. We creep
within our covering of mortality, like snails into their shells, or
like the hedgehog we roll ourselves into a ball, and we think of
the blessed and the immortal in terms of our own natures. We
shun indeed in words the monstrosity of saying that God is of
human form, but in actual fact we accept the impious thought
that He is of human passions. And therefore we invent for him
hands and feet, incomings and outgoing, enmities, aversions, es-
trangements, anger, in fact such parts and passions as can never
belong to the Cause. And of such is the oath—a mere crutch for
our weakness.   (*On the Sacrifices of Cain and Abel* 94–97)

Even where there are few political implications of the term
covenant, Jews continued to find the root metaphor useful to
explain their religious life.

The Function of Sectarian Strife

The sects represented rough sociological groupings within Israelite society. The Sadducees were an upper-class political
and occupational group intimately connected to Temple life.[18]
The Pharisees behaved more like a sect, instituting rules of purity and tithing that distinguished members in good standing
from the general populace. They lived near their fellowship
brothers within the general population and were highly respected. The Essene groupings were even more sectarian in
nature, having retreated to monastic communities.

The Sadducees' center of power was the Temple. They
were in charge of its proper running. The Pharisees were more
at home around the synagogues of Judea. The Essenes were
found mostly in monastic retreats like the one excavated at
Qumran, but they reportedly lived in cities as well. The Pharisees and Sadducees shared power in the Sanhedrin in the first
century, but after the war the Sanhedrin became more and
more a Pharisaic institution until it evolved into a rabbinic in-

stitution. This system of shared power, without any single predominant sect, was the norm in the first century.

Indeed, in a society as dedicated to individualism and cosmopolitanism as was the Hellenistic world, sectarian life was functional because the culture encouraged different and opposing concepts of truth. For Judaism to ignore the variety of Hellenistic life in favor of a single orthodox interpretation would have been futile. Sectarianism was a more practical method for gaining stability. It organized and handled conflict in a regular way, just as modern American political life organizes and channels social conflict. Neither the Republican nor the Democratic party defines the American political philosophy of the whole twentieth century, but certainly the two-party system is the norm of American political life. In first century Israel, the sharing of power between Pharisees and Sadducees served a similar purpose.

As long as the sectarian groups agreed on the basic meaning of the root metaphor of covenant, their conflict helped Jewish society express the same sort of individualism and cosmopolitanism that was evident in the larger Hellenistic society. This kind of conflict resolution has been described by Lewis Coser.

> Conflict may serve to remove dissociating elements in a relationship and to re-establish unity. Insofar as conflict is the resolution of tension between antagonists, it has stabilizing functions and becomes an integrating component of the relationship. However, not all conflicts are positively functional for the relationship, but only those which concern goals, values or interest that do not contradict the basic assumptions upon which the relation is founded. Loosely structured groups and open societies, by allowing conflicts, institute safeguards against the type of conflict which would endanger basic consensus and thereby minimize the danger of divergence touching core values. The interdependence of antagonistic groups and the criss-crossing within such societies of conflicts, which serve to "sew the social system together" by cancelling each other out, thus prevent disintegration along one primary line of cleavage.[19]

As long as the sectarian groups tacitly agreed to the root metaphor of covenant, their conflict helped the Judean society express the same sort of individualism and cosmopolitanism that was evident in the larger Hellenistic society. The drama of opposing forces created by the differing views of the meaning of covenant was functional in Judean society because it allowed the various views of Hellenistic values to be expressed and handled within the society. The balance created by this system was slowly tilting in the direction of the Pharisees when it was destroyed by two overwhelming new forces, the birth of Christianity and the war against Rome.

Resurrection

There was no strict distinction between body and soul in ancient Hebrew thought, so the idea that something of importance could survive death was not prominent. The Hebrew word *nefesh*, which is often translated as "soul," did not pertain to something that could be separated from the body. The word might be better translated as "person," because while Adam is called a living soul, a corpse is described as a dead soul, as in Leviticus 21:11 or Numbers 6:6.

The life-sustaining essence of creatures was normally understood to be their blood, as the dietary laws demonstrate. But the disappearance of breath was also observed as a characteristic of dying, abetting the idea of the spirit ("wind" or "breath") of the dead. No sense of reward or desirability was attached to the idea of becoming a spirit.

While the Hebrews may have formulated ideas about what happens to a person after death, nothing in Hebrew thought anticipated the postbiblical ideas of paradise or resurrection as a reward for a righteous life. The original solution to the problem of where personality goes after death was Sheol, a place like the Greek Hades, where the person resides in greatly attenuated form. Sheol certainly is not equivalent to heaven or hell. It is a pit, a place of weakness and estrangement from God, from which the spirits of the dead issue on the rare occasions when they can be seen on the earth.[20]

On the whole, ancient Hebrew society was hardly preoccupied with the question of whether there is life after death.

Whenever the question is raised as a direct issue, the answer seems to be No. Consider Ecclesiastes 3:19: "For the fate of the son of man and the fate of the beasts is the same; as one dies, so dies the other. They all have the same breath, and man has no advantage over the beasts; for all is vanity." This passage says only that all men die, but it implies more than that. The Book of Job (14:14) asks directly whether men live again after they die: "If a man die, shall he live again?" Job's answer (14:20–22) appears to be that men grow old and die, and there is nothing else:

> Thou prevailest forever against him, and he passes; thou changest his countenannce, and sendest him away.
> His sons come to honor, and he does not know it; they are brought low, and he perceives it not.
> He feels only the pain of his own body, and he mourns only for himself.

In another passage that has suffered in transmission, Job's death is not clearly stated, though his death and resurrection have often been understood (19:25–27):

> For I know that my redeemer (or vindicator) lives, and at last he will stand upon the earth;
> and after my skin has been thus destroyed, then from my flesh I shall see God, whom I shall see on my side, and my eyes shall behold, and not another.

Although this passage is often read as a prediction of Job's resurrection, it appears only to affirm that Job wants to be vindicated while still alive in a heavenly court by a heavenly vindicator or lawyer, as the logical outcome of his challenge to the justice of God. The original context for these statements must be extrapolated from ancient Near Eastern mythology, where the high god was pictured as a judge or king in a heavenly courtroom. The passage does not suggest there is life after death; rather, it portrays a man seeking redress from God in His own heavenly court. The Book of Job almost seems to argue explicity against any simple pietistic belief in immortality, in direct contradiction to the way the book is usually understood today.

As time went on, subtler ideas of immortality developed

within Judaism. In the later prophetic books especially, the Canaanite mythological battle between Death and Ba'al is reused as a metaphor for the power of Yahweh. Isaiah 25:8 says, "God will swallow up death forever." Isaiah 26 and Ezekiel 37 speak of the restoration of the people as a resurrection of buried bones. But nothing in these verses implies the expectation of a literal resurrection. The metaphor of resurrection is explicitly interpreted as a description of the people when they begin to live again under prophetic influence. Even the stirring phrases in Isaiah 26:19, which have contributed to the sophisticated doctrine of resurrection in later Judaism, appear to mean more than they do in fact:

> Thy dead shall live, their bodies shall rise. O dwellers in the dust, awake and sing for joy!
> For thy dew is a dew of light, and on the land of the shades thou wilt let it fall.

This has been taken as a literal statement of resurrection. But like the vision of the dry bones in Ezekiel, Isaiah is speaking of the end of spiritual death and actual poverty that the nation was experiencing. The revived bones are part of Isaiah's metaphor for national deliverance (26:15–16):

> But thou has increased the nation, O LORD, thou hast increased the nation; thou are glorified; thou hast enlarged all the borders of the land.

In other words, the dwellers in the dust are the symbolically dead in the nation, whom God will cause to revive by prophecy. All of these references were to be creatively reunderstood when the note of resurrection was clearly sounded within the society, in the first and second century C.E.

The first indubitable reference to resurrection in biblical literature comes from the visions of the Book of Daniel, which date to the years of oppression in the Maccabean Revolt, not to the earlier Persian and Babylonian period, as the book purports. Daniel 12:2 states: "And many of those who sleep in the dust of the earth shall awake, some to everlasting life, and some to shame and everlasting contempt. And those who are wise shall shine like the brightness of the firmament; and those who turn many to righteousness, like the stars for ever and ever."

No general theory of immortality is articulated here, only the resurrection of the many, which satisfies the Hebrew concept of justice. Those who suffered and died in remaining true to God's Torah will be vindicated. The reference to the saved as "sleepers in the dust" may be a reinterpretation of Isaiah 26:19. Those who persecuted the righteous of Yahweh will also be resurrected so that they can be punished. Judaism evidently developed the doctrine of resurrection in response to the problem of righteous suffering and martyrdom. The doctrine of resurrection is this-worldly in orientation, imagining the next life to take place in roughly the same place and circumstances as the present one but with the injustices removed. Not all Hebrew conceptions of the afterlife evince this kind of directness, but in general Hebrew concepts of resurrection tend toward this model.[21]

Another aspect of the tradition of resurrection is the theme of ascension to the eternally constant, deathless heaven where the most deserving and righteous go. The story of the seven martyred sons in 2 Maccabees 7 clarifies the importance of this idea. Several of the sons, who are tortured because they will not eat pork, report that they expect to be transported to heaven as an eternal reward after a short period of pain and suffering on earth. Immortality becomes a special reward for martyrs in Judaism, just as it was in Greek mythology for the heroes like Hercules and Perseus who accomplished superhuman tasks.

In none of these stories is the journey to heaven itself an important motif. But the heavenly journey motif is important in 1 Enoch and other apocalyptic and pseudepigraphical literature. In most cases, a journey to heaven is assumed to take place at death, for paradise and hell are both thought to be located in one of the several heavens. Great personages or mystics could undertake heavenly ascent during life by means of ecstatic trance or other extracorporeal experiences. Mystical techniques appear in some Jewish apocalypticism, and the resulting heavenly journey functions as verification for the eschatological beliefs of the community. Once a credible prophet actually is said to have visited heaven and seen the ultimate rewards there, the notions of eternal life and compensation after death are demonstrated vividly to the community.

The expectation that Jesus might survive death on the cross is understandable in the context of his death as a martyr. As the Book of Daniel shows, whoever else may have deserved immortality, martyrs pre-eminently were granted the privilege of immortality, because they had died sanctifying God's name. In the time of Jesus and Paul the concept of resurrection was nevertheless debated. The Sadducees rejected it entirely, as did the Book of Job and the Wisdom of Ben Sira.[22] Pharisaism accepted the idea, as did Christianity. The idea of resurrection was still one of the more extreme views of the culture. Not until Christianity and rabbinic Judaism began to dominate the Jewish scene did resurrection become a general belief.

The Messiah

Although the messianic hope is thought to be the main element of continuity between the Old and New Testaments, the concept of the messiah, as it exists in Christianity, scarcely appears in the Hebrew Bible at all and only vaguely appears in the other sectarian literature of the day. *Messiah* is an anglicized form of the Hebrew word for "an anointed one," *mashiah.* Anointing was a characteristic Hebrew ritual for inaugurating a personage into a divinely sanctioned official position. In Hebrew society, kings mostly but also prophets and sometimes priests were appointed to office by pouring oil over their heads. When the word *mashiah* was translated into Greek, it became *christos,* which had few associations of consequence to a Greek. Winners of races and kings were crowned with the branches of various shrubs and bushes in Greek tradition, not anointed. So there was no royal association for the term *christos* in Greek. One Greek connotation of *christos* was with athletes who oiled their bodies before competing. This association is rare in the New Testament. Another association, which was also largely ignored except at Jesus' burial, was with luxuriant grooming. Thus, before a Christian could convert a Greek to the religion of the "crucified messiah," he had to explain to the Greek what a "messiah" was. In doing so, he imposed a Christian connotation on the term.

The Christian concept of the messiah, as it appears in the New Testament, would not have been self-evident or even comprehensible to a Hebrew living in the first Temple period. The noun *mashiah* appears only thirty-nine times in the Hebrew Bible. Mostly it appears in the same context with the king, referring to his installation to office. Sometimes it appears in reference to priests, and twice in reference to the patriarchs. Saul's shield is once described as "anointed," showing that the process of ordaining something for special service is more basic than the royal meaning of the word. And once it refers to Cyrus the Persian. Obviously the word does not designate a person so much as a divinely sanctioned function of appointment.

The Hebrew Bible expresses the expectation in several places, especially in the books of the prophets, that God will raise up a king who will rule with justice and righteousness. Experience with less than perfect kings, as well as with foreign domination of the country, probably stimulated the belief in an ideal kingship. The idea was greatly augmented when the last heir to the Davidic throne disappeared without historical trace during the Persian period. Since 2 Samuel 7 promised that Israel shall never fail to have a king of the seed of David, the Jews naturally began to expect that the messianic king would reappear.

Yet the term *messiah* is not used in the Hebrew Bible to describe an idealized future king. The expected king is sometimes called the son of David (Isaiah 11; Ezekiel 34; Micah 5); or he is called the "branch," ostensibly a "new shoot of the Davidic family tree" (Jeremiah 23). The explicit concept of a messianic hope does not develop until much later.

One thing is very sure: the messiah is never viewed as weak or suffering. As the Lord's anointed, he is, according to Isaiah 11:3–4 the strong vindicator who will carry out God's vengeance against the unjust enemies of Israel:

He shall not judge by what his eyes see, or decide by what his ears hear;
but with righteousness he shall judge the poor, and decide with equity for the meek of the earth;
and he shall smite the earth with the rod of his mouth, and with the breath of his lips he shall slay the wicked.

Ideas of a future king also appear in apocalyptic and pseudepigraphical writings, a few of which may be earlier than Christianity. In the pseudepigraphical Psalms of Solomon, dated variously to the first century B.C.E. or C.E., the theme of the victorious battles of the messiah is extended to all those Gentile nations who have harmed Jerusalem, and the messiah himself is seen as a blameless ruler (17:36–37a, 17:39–40):

And he himself [will be] pure from sin,
So that he may rule a great people.
He will rebuke rulers,
And remove sinners by the might of his word . . .

His hope will be in the Lord;
Who then can prevail against him?
(He will be) mighty in his works,
And strong in the fear of God,
(He will be) shepherding the flock of the Lord . . .
Faithfully and righteously.

Essentially the messiah is the ideal future king who contrasts with the iniquitous Roman rulers and will lead Israel to victory against them. Yet there are many descriptions of the end of time that do not include a messiah. For instance, Daniel does not describe a messiah accompanying the coming of God's kingdom (7:9; 12). Rather he talks about the coming of the "son of man" figure, which appears to be angelic. The important characters in God's redemption tend to be either the leaders of the people or the angels, though the leaders may become angels in the end. In other words, even in apocalyptic literature, the presence of the messiah is not a *sine qua non* for the redemption.

At one place in apocalyptic literature the death of a future messiah is mentioned (2 Esdras, or 4 Ezra, 7:28–30): "For my son the messiah shall be revealed with those who are with him, and those who remain shall rejoice four hundred years. And after these years, my son the messiah shall die, and all those who draw human breath. And the world shall be turned back to primeval silence for seven days, as it was at the first beginnings; so that no one shall be left." The scene is the establishment of God's kingdom, under His messiah who, along with those who helped establish the kingdom, will live four hundred years. At the end of an extended but natural period, they will all die. Then the world will return to chaos, followed by the general resurrection of the righteous.

In Qumran, the concept of the messiah was tailored to fit the Essene community of the last days. The generic term *messiah* was used to describe both the priestly and the royally anointed leaders of the people. Furthermore, the priestly messiah was by far the most important.

Philo also refers in a veiled way to the messiah. He thinks of an actual future of victory over evil and unjust rulers (*On Rewards* 115–119). Tactfully, he does not make explicit his criticism of the present political order or his hope for the pre-eminent role of the Jewish people in the coming revolution.[23]

Nowhere before the start of Christianity is there any evidence that the messiah will suffer. In fact, no matter who among the righteous is pictured as suffering, the important aspect of the pre-Christian concept of the messiah is that he is the one person who is finally going to bring God's justice to the world. Thus, nowhere before the start of Christianity is there any evidence that the messiah was expected to die for humanity's sins.

❦ III ❦

Jesus, the Jewish Revolutionary

Although Christianity's destiny brought it to Rome and world prominence, its beginnings were in sectarian Judaism. Like the other sects, Christianity was based on an interpretation of the Torah constitution, as is evident in the term *new testament,* from the Latin term meaning "new covenant" which in turn came from the Greek, itself an interpretation of Jeremiah 31. Jeremiah's consoling prophecy that God would renew the destroyed country of Israel with a new covenant was reunderstood as a prophecy of Jesus' incarnation. This reinterpretation was advanced by the church, not by Jesus himself. Jesus' own message is often more difficult to isolate. But it is certain that Jesus headed an apocalyptic movement, not just a movement of educational social reform.[1]

In his own day many of Jesus' hearers understood his meaning to be apocalyptic. This does not mean that all of Jesus' teaching was apocalyptic. He was also a pre-eminent teacher of wisdom. But the part of his teaching that can be identified as uniquely his own and that most affected his contemporaries was apocalyptic. Since the later church would not eliminate authentic Jesus traditions yet at the same time did not favor apocalypticism, the presence of apocalyptic in early Christianity must be attributed to Jesus himself.

Tracing the apocalyptic traditions in Christianity reveals an irony in New Testament methodology: the historicity of teachings ascribed to Jesus can confidently be asserted only when they conflict with the teachings of the church that followed him. In Norman Perrin's phrase, every statement about Jesus must pass a "criterion of dissimilarity" before it can be accepted as historical.[2] Clearly, this test of evidence can call into question many authentic traditions about Jesus. It is nevertheless necessary, because Christian tradition was transmitted by well-meaning followers who found it inconceivable that Jesus had not spoken directly about every one of the church's fundamental beliefs. If any non-Christian or anti-Christian reports of the mission of Jesus had survived, the criterion of dissimilarity might have been unnecessary. But the only extant historical reports about Jesus come from his followers, all of whom had accepted similar ideas about the meaning of his mission before they wrote.

Apocalypticism

Until recently, apocalypticism was defined solely by the literary apocalypses, especially the Book of Daniel in the Hebrew Bible and the Revelation of Saint John in the New Testament. Apocalypticism, coming from the Greek verb meaning to "disclose," "uncover," or "bring to light," has always implied the revelation of the secret of the coming end of time, apocalyptic books have in common the violent end of the world and the establishment of God's kingdom. They are replete with arcane symbolism and puzzling visions, the meaning of which is hardly clear from a first reading. And they are often pseudepigraphical, fictitiously ascribed to an earlier hero or patriarch.

Discovery and renewed study of many noncanonical apocryphal and pseudepigraphical books of the Old and New Testament has changed the definition of apocalypticism by providing insight into the conditions that produced the literary genre.[3] The Dead Sea Scrolls give a totally unexpected glimpse of Jewish sectarian life, for they are concerned with the nature of the actual community as well as its expectations about the end of time. Since the Dead Sea Scrolls reflect an Essene group, they make it possible for the first time to view the workings of an actual ancient apocalyptic community, comparing their social organization with their apocalyptic writings.

Although the sociological picture of ancient apocalypticism is incomplete, apocalyptic movements in the modern period, particularly those in Melanesian and North American Indian religions, evidence clear sociological commonalities. The modern data also have limitations, but because they are complete by comparison to data in the ancient period, they serve as a practical guide. The Melanesian and native American Indian societies during the last century, though far removed from the world of first century Judaism in history, geography, and material culture, exhibited some of the same social forces. They, too, had to deal with problems of acculturation and disorganization brought on by European domination, in ways similar to those used by ancient Jewish society in dealing with the problem of Greek culture and Roman domination.

The most important similarity between ancient and modern apocalypticism is that both movements characterize time as a linear process which leads to the future destruction of the evil world order. For both modern and ancient apocalypticists there will be an "end of days," a decisive consummation of history. As opposed to holding an optimistic view of progress, which moves toward the final goal by slow approximations, apocalypticists are totally impatient with the corrupt present, seeing it as a series of unprecedented calamities. Usually, the "end of days" is viewed as a sudden, revolutionary leap into an idealized future state, when the believers will finally be rewarded for their years of suffering, while their oppressors and the other evil infidels will be justly punished.

There are important analogies between apocalyptic movements and political revolutions. Though the apocalyptic view of the ideal future is not always revolutionary in a political sense, it necessarily entails the destruction of the present evil political order. The new order is always an idealization, often of a recaptured past state of perfection, as the term *paradise* implies in the West.[4]

Though ancient apocalypticism and modern millennial cults have perceptible similarities, the relevance of the modern data becomes clear only when seeking the causes and motivations of apocalypticism from the refractory and incomplete ancient record. Among the underlying commonalities in apocalyptic and millennial cults is the role of the leader. His individual skills and talents, as well as his ideals, necessarily have a strong effect on the movement. The leader must be revered by the community, not necessarily as a strong political leader but as a person whose example dramatizes the movement for the believer.[5] The leader should be the best moral example of the values that the movement endorses. Normally, the leader fulfills the function of modeling the ideals of the group.

Common motivations also underly any millennial movement. People who join apocalyptic groups feel deprived of something meaningful or valuable to the society but unavailable to all people equally. Marxism stresses the appeal of apocalypticism to colonized peoples who have no access to the rewards of their labor, since it has been disassociated from the rewards of production. There are more varieties of deprivation than the economic. Epidemics, famine, war, or other disasters may stimulate millenarian movements, for the disaster can be seen as the penultimate stage before the victory of the good. Relative deprivation can also lead to the formation of apocalyptic movements.[6] The group does not have to be deprived in absolute terms—by famine, war, or poverty—for apocalypticism is occasionally popular among affluent classes. There only has to be a lack of social or religious attainment commensurate with the economic level, or rising expectations without any real possibility for improvement in status.

Other motivations are involved as well. Deprivation, whether absolute or relative, is not enough to ensure the rise of an apocalyptic movement. Some of these movements arise out of ambiguities in the way a religion is interpreted by different classes. Though all people require norms for orienting their lives, religious systems at times provide better norms for some parts of a society than for others. When groups see themselves as cut off from the goals of the society, in terms of power, ethics, or status, and from the feelings of self-worth that arise from achieving these goals, they may coalesce into antisocial movements of *communitas*, or communitarian idealism. Such movements, which stress an alternative social structure to that of the dominant majority, can appeal widely to one whose status is ambiguously defined by a society. Status ambiguities were common in Roman society because class was defined by law, not by occupation and buying power. Therefore, people who succeeded in a trade often achieved a status above their legal station in life. Reform of the basic social categories appeals to such people. While deprivation of both material needs or spiritual status is necessary for the development of apocalypticism, it, too, is not sufficient to produce an apocalyptic movement. To develop an apocalyptic cult, in contrast to a purely political movement, people must have a propensity to impose religious meanings upon events and must be searching for a more satisfactory system of religious values. The factors of need, deprivation, anxiety, leadership, and the propensity to interpret events in a religious framework all came together in first century Judea. The result over the next two centuries was the rise of a variety of apocalyptic cults.[7]

Apocalyptic groups have the propensity to mix political and religious motives to such an extent that the actors in the drama have difficulty distinguishing between them. As a general rule, members of apocalyptic movements hold a variety of positions about political change. At times an apocalyptic movement has a retarding effect on simple political revolution because the explicitly religious symbolism of its leaders tends to make the group more interested in theological goals than in political ones. At other times, even in the same movement, earnest political revolutionaries may be present among the apocalyptic cult members. These cults engage in a wide spectrum of political action, ranging from passive to active, and depending on the faction in the group that dominates at any one moment, their participation may change in character. But regardless of the disposition of a group toward political action, either active or passive, the distinction is lost on the ruling powers. The opposition of rulers to the group is constant, no matter what the group itself may think of armed intervention. The various actors within a society may interpret the movement differently, but the rulers almost always interpret the threat as a political one and deal with it accordingly. Moreover, since the political or nonpolitical aims of the movement start out fairly confused, often some historical development in the conflict between the apocalyptic group and the power structure confirms, disconfirms, or reaffirms the political intentions of the group.[8] Many of the apocalyptic groups of Hellenistic Judea, including Christianity, underwent such a moment of political decision.

The Book of Daniel

The Book of Daniel purports to be the writings of a prophet who lived during the reigns of Nebuchadnezzar, Cyrus, and Xerxes, but the visions at the end of the book, in chapters 7–12, are from a much later time, during the Maccabean Revolt. This dating is established by the prophecies in Daniel 7:8 and 8:9, where "the little horn speaking great things" is Antiochus Epiphanes.[9] In a perplexing vision a divine figure called "the Ancient of Days" (7:9) presides over the heavenly council at the last judgment and sentences the fourth kingdom, the one ruled by Antiochus, to destruction. Then there appears in the clouds of heaven "one like a son of man" (7:13), an expression that in Aramaic means only "a human figure." His human appearance contrasts with the monstrous animal figures that have preceded him in the vision and is clearly designed to signify the good forces. An angel interprets the figure as symbolizing "the holy community, the saints of the most high" (7:27). Probably, the "son of man" or manlike figure is simply an angel, since angels are human figures in heaven. It is even possible that the figure is one of the archangels, perhaps Michael or Gabriel, who are mentioned in other visions. In any case, the angelic status of the "son of man" seems sure. Instead of a transient kingdom, he establishes an everlasting and universal dominion, which will begin after "a time, two times and a half a time of the little horn," which is a cryptic reference to the three and one-half years when Antiochus persecuted the Jews, 168–165 B.C.E. The mention of the abomination of desolation is probably a reference to the stationing of Syrian troops in the Temple and the desecration of the Temple purity (11:31, 12:11).

The fact that the author of the Book of Daniel was not making a prediction about the Babylonian Exile rather looking back at the Maccabean Revolt as if that event of his recent experience had been predicted by Daniel, a legendary hero of the Babylonian captivity, has religious connotations. The writer is saying that the days of Antiochus are numbered, because he has insulted God by desecrating the altar. The clock is beginning to strike midnight, when God will intervene and set everything to rights. In fact, the author's skill in describing the events of the Maccabean Revolt reveals when the book was written. The only prediction that did not come true, besides the final consummation, is the prophecy concerning the death of Antiochus on his return to Jerusalem after his war with Egypt (11:40–45). Antiochus in fact died in Persia in 163 B.C.E. Daniel is concerned not only with the fate of the world empires but with the aftermath of the judgment and the setting up of an ideal community on earth. In this earthly kingdom, the righteous and the illustrious dead will partake in everlasting harmony (12:2).[10]

According to modern observations of millenarianism, books like Daniel are normally written by an apocalyptic sect. The identity of this particular sect cannot be fixed with accuracy, but some hints of its existence can be coaxed from the ancient documents. Although in Daniel the angelic princes of the evil nations fight against Michael, "Prince of Israel," the protagonists are not the entire community of the Jews. Both the text of Daniel and the events of the Maccabean war suggest that a smaller group than the whole Jewish nation was intended.[11] When the book was being written, the Jewish state was in the midst of a civil war, with Antiochus intervening on the side of the most Hellenizing party. The party of faithful Jews are identified in Daniel as *maskilim*, the "wise" or "enlighteners" (11:2, 34). The visionary identifies with this group of Jews. They are the ones who will be rewarded by shining as the stars in heaven (11:2). Their job is to impart to the many the apocalyptic teachings about the end of time and so save people from the coming annihilation. The "people of the saints of the most high" are likely to be the same group, who will share in the final victory, live in the re-established state of Judah, and become what they are not when the book was written, the sole inhabitants of the land of Judah. The entire plan is predestined and has nothing to do with the ability of the group to fight in battle.

Although this apocalyptic group is opposed to Antiochus, it does not share the position of the Maccabees, for the religious goals of Daniel contrast with the political position taken by the Maccabees in their official history of the Maccabean Revolt. In the First Book of Maccabees, an active militarist and political view is taken of the events that founded the Hasmonean house. There are few references to God's miraculous intervention in history. But there is indirect evidence for a second, more passive group of revolutionary allies to the Maccabees. Judas was joined by "a company of Hasideans [Hasidim in Hebrew, though not related to the modern Hasidim], mighty warriors of Israel, everyone who offered himself willingly for the law" (1 Maccabees 2). Shortly thereafter part of the force of Judas was caught in a cave and martyred, because they refused to fight. On account of the close juxtaposition of the two events, the martyrs of the cave are thought to have belonged to the Hasidim. As opposed to Judas, the Hasidim seem to have been more passive in their resistance and interested in restoring acceptable religious conditions, purifying the altar, and reinstating the legitimate priesthood. Although the Hasidim fought together with the Maccabees, they also disputed with them. They gave up resisting once the Temple was restored, whereas the Maccabees continued much longer to fight for land and position.

The Hasidim broke decisively with the Maccabees in 142 B.C.E. when Simon Maccabee was proclaimed "high priest forever, until a faithful prophet should arise" (1 Maccabees 14:41). The issue that set the Maccabees and Hasidim unalterably against each other was the founding of a new Maccabean High Priesthood for their own political ends. According to Frank Cross, this incident led to the founding of the Dead Sea Scroll Essene community.[12] The Essene community at Qumran was thus an apocalyptic community historically related to the sentiments expressed in Daniel, founded after it became clear that the Maccabees would not bring about the religious reforms for which the authors of Daniel hoped. Indeed, the Maccabees were as cynical in the election of the High Priesthood as Antiochus had been before them. But the Hasidim and subsequently the Essenes harbored eschatological expectations for the divine restoration of correct worship in Jerusalem.

Just as in the modern period, so too in the ancient world there were differences between active and passive revolutionaries. The Book of Daniel gives evidence of a more religious wing of the opposition to Antiochus, while 1 Maccabees suggest an overly political group of militants. The subsequent efforts of the Maccabees to take over the High Priesthood as well as the kingship led to the final break between the apocalypticists who wrote Daniel and the ruling Maccabean party. Historical events helped to differentiate the political and nonpolitical aims, but even before the events, the distinction was already moot.

The Book of Daniel is the first book in the Bible to stress the concept of resurrection, together with the idea that the *maskilim* will ascend to heaven for astral immortality. Through these ideas the apocalypticists both explained the years of persecution and kept true to their faith that God would intervene to re-establish justice. The form of immortality that was envisioned may well have been angelic. The angels had been identified with the stars as early as the first Temple period. Several strands of late Hellenistic spirituality apparently involved the way in which astral immortality was gained. For instance, the Books of Enoch are obsessed with the notion of astral journey, as are the Hekhaloth texts of Jewish mysticism, which were traditionally thought to date from Islamic times but are now thought to have been written in the Hellenistic period. Aramaic fragments of 1 Enoch have now been found at Qumran, giving witness to the earliest, Aramaic version and showing that the Enoch literature was known to the Dead Sea Scroll sectarians.[13] The so-called Mithras liturgy, found in the third century C.E. Paris Magical Papyrus, describes one such heavenly journey in an Egyptian magical context, culminating in a personal encounter with a heavenly god, Helios Mithras, and resulting in the "immortalization" (*apanathanatismos*) of the adept. Astral mysticism permeated Judaism as well.

Talmudic texts hint that the earliest rabbis occasionally practiced mystical ascension techniques, but there is even clearer evidence of apocalyptic Judaism's use of ascension techniques and traditions.[14] For instance, Josephus reports that the Essenes "immortalize" (*athanatizousin*) souls, almost the same term that appears in the Mithras liturgy (*Antiquities* 18.18). In another phrase that suggests the theme of the rivalry between angels and men over the approach of a mystic making a heavenly ascent, Josephus says that they "think the approach of the righteous to be much fought over." The Dead Sea Scrolls also report that the members of the Qumran group are "together with the angels of the Most High and there is no need for an interpreter."[15] The location for this meeting must be either heaven or the recreated ideal earth. The Qumran community probably believed its forebears to have ascended to heaven as angels after their deaths, as Daniel 12 implies.

The Qumran community held that the angels were their close companions. The scroll entitled "The War of the Children of Light upon the Children of Darkness" describes a military plan in which the angels of God descend to lead the numerically insignificant Qumran community to victory. Its priestly preoccupation with ritual cleanliness is functional for a group that desired angelic company. Angels would not consent to enter an Essene camp unless the Qumranites were in a sufficient state of ritual purity, the same state recognized by the rabbis as a necessary precondition for ascent to the heavenly Temple.

The Qumranites also cherished traditions about the angelic captain of the forces of light, who is named Melchizedek. Although the identification of this angelic intermediary with Melchizedek is an unusual aspect of the Dead Sea Scroll tradition, many other apocalyptic writings emphasize helping human or angelic figures in heaven. For instance, in Daniel 7:13 the figure of the "son of man" appears to take over the role of punishing the evil. These mystical traditions in apocalyptic

Judaism are of fundamental importance for the rise of Christianity.

Even the Greek Bible connected Adam's prelapsarian divine image—the image of God in which Adam was made and which, according to some legends, he lost after he sinned—with the image of God's glory seen in Ezekiel's chariot vision. Probably this manlike manifestation of divinity was associated with the angelic "son of man" figure of Daniel as well. The association of the discussion of the heavenly man in Ezekiel with the description of God in Moses' vision on Sinai in Exodus 19–34 and even with the description of Adam before the fall in Genesis is an antique one. The First Book of Enoch, now known to be mostly pre-Christian, and the vision of Moses in the remaining fragments of the work of Ezekiel the Tragedian, a pre-Christian writer, evince well-developed enthronement traditions.[16] The Qumranites probably felt that they could ascend to the heavenly Temple before death and that they would one day be translated into angels who would help destroy the children of darkness on earth.

Christianity as Apocalyptic Judaism

Jesus also spoke of himself as a "son of man." The early church associated these statements with Daniel 7:13, prophesying the coming of an angelic son of man. Yet what Jesus meant about himself is not at all clear. The most apocalyptic statements about "the son of man" satisfy the criterion of dissimilarity, for the later church knew that Jesus' return was not imminent. The only reason to preserve the apocalyptic "son of man" statements in church tradition was that they were already believed to be authentic, even when they appeared not to have come true as predicted. Some statements of the apocalyptic "son of man" apparently came from the earliest, apocalyptic church tradition:

> For whoever is ashamed of me and of my words in this adulterous and sinful generation, of him will the son of man also be ashamed when he comes in the glory of his father with the holy angels.   (Mark 8:38)

And I tell you, every one who acknowledges me before men, the son of man will acknowledge before the angels of God; but he who denies me before men will be denied before the angels of God. (Luke 12:8–9)

For truly I tell you, you will not have gone through the cities of Israel before the son of man comes. (Matthew 10:23)

Truly, I tell you that there are some of those standing here who will not taste death until they see the son of man coming in his kingdom. (Matthew 16:28)

Truly, I tell you that in the generation when the son of man shall sit on the throne of his glory, you also who have followed me shall sit on twelve thrones judging the twelve tribes of Israel. (Matthew 19:28)[17]

These short statements have two salient characteristics: they cannot have been invented as a pious wish by the later church, for they talk about an apocalyptic end which never happened, and they rely on the imagery of the apocalyptic past. The expression "son of man" comes explicitly from Daniel. Jewish mystical concepts of the "glory" of God—connecting Genesis 1:28, Ezekiel 1 and 10, and Exodus 24:10 as human figures that somehow represent divine power—are crucial for the meaning of this passage.[18] But what Jesus meant by the term is impossible to decipher.

The "son of man" problem represents one of the most mysterious and vexing of all New Testament quandaries. Jesus was presumably referring not to himself but to the apocalyptic passage in Daniel when he spoke these words. On the basis of the resurrection, his followers identified him with the passage he had discussed. But there is no unambiguous evidence of a preexistent title "son of man." It may merely have been an allusion to a well-known vision of the end of time.[19]

In any event, there is little doubt that much of Jesus' message was apocalyptic. This probably explains why names reminiscent of the Zealot movement, which in 66 C.E. fomented the Jewish revolution against Rome, show up in reference to the Christian movement. Judas Iscariot and Simeon the Zealot have names suggesting the Sicarii and Zealots, two groups of radical revolutionaries in 66 C.E. Exactly what these people expected of Jesus or how closely they can be connected with a revolutionary movement that flourished thirty years after Jesus' death is a moot point. But for political revolutionaries to have been attracted by Jesus' message would not have been surprising. For one thing, like the Dead Sea Scroll community and the Hasidim before him, Jesus seems to have been aware of and extremely critical of the Temple: "I will destroy this temple that is made with hands, and in three days, I will build another, not made with hands" (Mark 14:58).[20]

Opposition to the Temple is not unprecedented in Judaism. Nor is it innocent of political ramifications, considering that the Temple was the center of native government for Judea. On the contrary, this kind of action demonstrates the apocalyptic character of the message that Jesus taught. Because the earthly Temple is impure, Jesus and the apocalypticists maintained, only the reign of God would put events right again. However, this view does not necessarily imply that Jesus intended a political revolution.

Jesus and Political Revolution

Early Christianity was a religious revolution, but its political aims were still inchoate. The active and nonviolent motives of a movement are not easily unscrambled, as the modern data has made clear. But from the point of view of the central authority, most threats have active political consequences. Some of Jesus' followers seem to have had revolutionary expectations, though passivity was the stronger tradition in Jewish apocalypticism. Both the Qumran community and the Hasidim had a negative view of actual military combat with the oppressive, demonic forces. Rather, God himself with his angelic host was the direct agent of vengeance against wrong-doers, who more often than not were viewed as satanic envoys. Although this attitude is not pacifistic, it is very passively hostile.[21]

Then there is the evidence of the New Testament itself. When Jesus was arrested, he did not resist. The church followed his example. The direction that the Christian movement took was governed by its desire not to antagonize further the Roman authorities. This course may not have been intended from the outset, but it was consistent with the evidence of Jesus' own actions.

Although Jesus recommended passive resistance, he was still an apocalypticist and had strong feelings of scorn for the putative rulers of his country. The pietistic figure of a "gentle Jesus meek and mild" was a creation of Victorian Bible scholarship and is belied by the Gospels themselves at every turn. Jesus was a passionate advocate of political and individual justice who predicted a terrible and imminent end for the evil regime ruling Judea.

The mystery about the social message of early Christianity is not so complete as that about the Book of Daniel. As difficult as the Gospels are to evaluate, they still give a remarkable amount of evidence about the life of Jesus and his effect on his contemporaries. Early Christianity was a movement primarily of the disadvantaged and, even more so, of people who had little hope of improving their position. This is not to say that no one else could have joined. Paul's writing shows that more privileged people were also attracted. Like the Sadducees' close association with the traditional priestly aristocracy and the Pharisees' association with urban tradespersons, the association of Christianity with the deprived or those of ambiguous status is only a generalization. But the Gospels themselves testify that the early Christians had less access to the means of salvation than other people. For one reason or another they felt alienated from the roles that society had defined for them.

Jesus' original support came from the country folk of Galilee, whose ways and interests were different from those of the Jerusalemites. He appealed to a number of people in the society whose rank was inferior but who economic situation was not hopeless, including prostitutes, tax collectors, and others considered disreputable or impure by Sadducees or Pharisees, as well as many ordinary Jews, Samaritans, and Galileans with no specific party affiliation. These people often had some economic standing in the community. But their status was relatively low as compared to their economic attainments.

In some cases, the low status was based on a moral judgment about the ways in which the money was made. However, the presence of prostitutes and tax collectors among Jesus' supporters is probably symbolic as well as actual, vividly expressing the apocalyptic ethic of overturning the established order. Quite a number of ordinary people, who had other disadvantages, must have been among Jesus' most enthusiastic audiences. The ethic of making the last to be first appears to be addressed not only to social outcasts, in hopes of converting them, but also to people more generally with ordinary feelings of low self-esteem (Mark 10:31; Matthew 19:30; Luke 13:30).

The message of Jesus that, with repentance, all are equal before God is typical of all sectarian apocalypticism of the time. Christian practices of public repentance, baptism, and chaste communal living are likewise typical of the other contemporary apocalyptic groups. Yet the similarity only emphasizes the striking difference between Christianity and Essenism, for example. Essenism was priestly and largely interested in the cultic purity rules allowing priests to approach God's holy places. Christianity, in spite of its many similarities with other apocalyptic groups, was almost hostile to purity rules. Its corresponding emphasis on converting the distressed or sinful began in the teaching of John the Baptist, became characteristically Christian, and probably reflected the strong charismatic influence of Jesus. Through John the Baptist, baptism became the Christian rite uniquely demonstrating repentance, though there is no good evidence that Jesus performed it.

Jesus' unique lack of interest in purity rules was accompanied by another unique message: he did not stress a return to the old strict interpretations of Torah, as did the other apocalyptic groups. Although Jesus accepted Jewish law, he occasionally indulged in symbolic actions designed to provoke questions about the purpose of the Torah, such as healing the chronically ill or picking grain on the Sabbath. But these actions could have been directed at the Pharisees or other sectarian interpreters of the Torah without implying that the Torah itself was invalid.

Like many of the other apocalyptic groups around them, Christians often lived together and shared possessions. But

Christian communalism stressed only chastity, not monasticism. Although asceticism and perhaps monasticism were associated with the movement of John the Baptist, the majority of Jesus' early followers lived within the fabric of society. As the Christian movement developed, some Christians showed signs of a primitive communism, implicit in their pooling of resources.[22] Early Christianity did not adhere to the social code of the Essenes, yet it did contain the seeds of a radical criticism of private property and believed strongly in sharing all economic resources. "No man can serve two masters . . . You cannot serve God and mammon [money]" (Luke 16:13). Like the Pharisees and the Essenes, the Christians were equally religious and political in orientation.

Jesus was suspicious of people of means: "It is easier for a camel to go through the eye of a needle than for a rich man to enter the kingdom of God" (Mark 10:24). This statement does not prevent a rich man from becoming part of the movement. But it establishes a higher price for the rich than the poor. Early Christianity thus exhibited a deep suspicion of property. Given the command to share all things with the poor, few confident and successful people would have entered the movement at first. Those whose wealth had not brought with it feelings of achievement or worth would have been better targets for evangelism. Entering the Christian community at the beginning was a total commitment: "Give to every one who begs from you; and of him who takes away your goods, do not ask them again" (Luke 6:30).

Jesus himself did not come from the lowest economic classes but rather came from the class that provided most members of the rabbinic movement.[23] He came from an environment that valued property and skilled professions. His teaching was designed to appeal to the poor and otherwise underprivileged people, like the Samaritans, Galileans, and ordinary Jews unskilled in the Torah, yet unlike John the Baptist, he was not an ascetic. There is no evidence of his favoring the sanctification of sexuality by means of marriage, as did the Pharisees, but he accepted the institution of marriage as a given and participated in fellowship meals with food and wine.

Each of Jesus' followers apprehended and interpreted the

message according to his or her own powers and experience. Conflicting interpretations of Jesus' teachings were present from the very beginning. These different social responses competed with each other for dominance within the community. Some of Jesus' closest disciples and many of the apostles chose to live in a communal way, but others in his movement chose, or merely continued, to live in less radical styles. There was not a single orthodox interpretation of Jesus' mission.

Christianity as a Messianic Movement

The messiah was traditionally the reigning king of Israel, but after the Romans began to govern directly, claiming to be the messiah was tantamount to fomenting revolution against Roman order. Furthermore, because of the apocalyptic expectation that God would repay the Romans for their cruelty, the Jewish community believed that a messiah would, with supernatural assistance, bring about a victory against Roman government. "Messiah" was not a title that a Jew would have applied to himself lightly.

"Messiah" is also the most problematic of all titles to be applied to Jesus, because Jesus suffered and died before the coming of the kingdom of God, which he prophesized, although the messiah was supposed to bring about God's kingdom, usually by succeeding to the throne of David and effecting great victories. Nowhere in pre-Christian Jewish tradition is there the slightest evidence of an expectation of a messiah whose suffering will be redemptive for the people. The Christian idea had to come from somewhere else.

The simplest explanation would be that Jesus really was of royal lineage; therefore his messianic role was a normal expectation. Yet the stories of Jesus' Davidic lineage are suspect. They could have been provided by the church later, as part of a cycle of infancy stories. The shortest gospel, Mark, contains no record of the youth of Jesus. It may be that Matthew and Luke provided a messianic infancy to match Jesus' known messianic purpose. In short, the stories of Jesus' Davidic lineage do not satisfy the criterion of dissimilarity, because they may have been remembered by a church which automatically supposed Jesus to be a scion of David.

The best explanation for the enigma of Jesus' messiahship is that the Christian community did exactly what the other Jewish sects of the first century had done: they read Scripture in the light of events. Philo read Scripture in the light of allegory, finding in it a philosophical tract. The Essenes read Scripture in the light of *pesher*, finding in it a prophecy for the coming judgment. The Pharisees read Scripture in the light of *midrash*, finding in it a platform for their interpretation of the purity laws and resurrection. Christianity became messianic instead of merely apocalyptic—the messiah not being a necessary character for the coming of the apocalyptic millennium in Judaism—because the title was provided by a historic event experienced by the earliest Christian community. This event became the basis for a reinterpretation of Scripture.

N. A. Dahl has pointed out that the title "King of the Jews" on the cross has a high probability of historicity, because it was not one that the church wished to have remembered about Jesus.[24] The church preferred other titles of less nationalistic and universal scope. Ironically, Jesus is called a messiah by the church because he was executed by the Romans on the charge of being a candidate for the throne of Judea. This was not a charge that even traitorous Jews cooperating with Roman authorities would have invented. Whatever else his followers expected or desired from Jesus, they began after Easter Sunday, on account of the resurrection that they believed had then occurred, to preach of Jesus as the dying and rising messiah.

Jesus was sometimes recognized as a possible messiah even before his crucifixion, although there is little evidence that he sought the title for himself. In the Gospel of Mark, Jesus denies the title whenever it is applied to him except at his trial. However, some people besides the Romans must have understood Jesus as a messianic candidate, for neither the Romans nor their administrative advisers among the aristocrats in Judea would have fabricated a messianic role for Jesus, were he not already perceived to be a messianic threat. They would hardly have invented a title that so completely justified Jesus' opposition to them.

Jesus' movement presented a problem for the Romans and for members of the upper levels of Jewish administration, some of whom were cooperating with the Romans. Inasmuch as many of the other revolutionary movements destroyed by the Romans were not messianic, a revolutionary political movement did not have to be messianic in nature. Yet no matter how supernatural his actions, the messiah was also a political figure. Thus, the Bar Kokhba Revolt of 132 C.E., barely a century after Jesus, contained strong messianic overtones. When the revolt was quelled, the death of its messianic leader, as in Christianity, brought about the rise of a tradition that the messiah must suffer and die for the end to come.[25] But these examples only point up the anomaly of a messianic movement when the strong, charismatic figure at its founding has pacifist goals in mind.

The paradoxical use of this title in Christianity is borne out in the situations when the term *messiah* is used of Jesus. Jesus is usually called messiah at his trial and death. But in prophecies of his return, Jesus is usually called the "son of man," which identifies him with the angelic figure mentioned in Daniel. So Jesus is not called messiah on the basis of his return; rather, he is called messiah on the basis of his trial and death, which is in keeping with the hypothesis that he was arrested on this charge but is certainly not in keeping with the Jewish expectation of a messiah. The best explanation for the title of messiah, then, is that the historical events surrounding the trial accounted for the association, although it did not fit prior expectations. It was the charge leveled against Jesus by his detractors, with some justification from their point of view, once they were sure that he was in their power. But it was not a title that Jesus himself stressed in his ministry. Afterward, when Jesus was experienced as still alive by some of his disciples, the term *messiah* was reunderstood by the community to make sense of Jesus' suffering and death.

It appears, then, that Jesus was a man of powerful charisma whose teachings were innovative and popular; that he desired a quick apocalyptic end to this evil world, and that some people, including some of his followers, took this to be a messianic claim and a political statement. The movement must have been strong enough to come to the attention of Roman and Jewish authorities in Jerusalem. Moreover, the explicit purposes of a millennial movement are never clear to the social actors until historical events remove the ambiguity. Some movements turn into apolitical, symbolic rebellions; others are largely political in orientation. Presumably the borderline between violent revolution and passive resistance was never reached before Jesus' arrest. Jesus' lessons probably emphasized patience with contemporary political events. But the Romans did not understand the teaching, as shown by Jesus' arrest and the Roman policy toward Christians for centuries after his death.

Resurrection was one of the controveries of sectarian life in the time of Jesus. But expectations of both resurrection from the dead and ascension to heaven were strongest wherever the context was religious persecution or martyrdom. One event that passes the criterion of dissimilarity is Jesus' death as a martyr, for he was unjustly accused and illegitimately executed. And he died trying to protect and fulfill his preaching of the meaning of Jewish law rather than to subvert it.

It is understandable that several of Jesus' followers came to feel that Jesus was resurrected and had ascended to a new order of being. Since ascension and enthronement were common motifs of resurrection stories at the time, especially of stories dealing with martyrdom, it was entirely appropriate to identify Jesus with the enthroned figure about whom he had preached. This idea caused some readjustment in later New Testament writings. For instance, the Letter to the Hebrews, which strongly affirms Jesus' divinity, must argue that he was raised higher than the angels and was, in fact, God. It is characteristic of the later church that the Letter to the Hebrews does not mention the phrase "son of man." Since the later church was not particularly interested in this title for Jesus and it never acquired the same theological importance as "messiah," "son of man" is probably to be attributed to the earliest Christian tradition. Since Jesus distinguishes himself from the son of man in the New Testament, he is not likely to have preached that he was the figure of the prophecy.

The evolution from Jesus' preaching of the coming end of the world to the church's preaching of Jesus' return as the son of man, the sign that the coming apocalypse has already begun in a spiritual way, is one of the most striking factors in the success of the early Christian movement. It allowed the movement to succeed in an area where almost every other apocalyptic movement is doomed to fail, namely in institutionalizing the original impulse for reform into a stable religious system. Although it is practically impossible to discover how the evolution of thought took place, one can see how the church reunderstood the Hebrew Bible to make sense of the events of Jesus' life, and this is one major clue.

Christian Exegesis of the Hebrew Bible

The expectation of Jesus' ascension to heaven was given vivid actuality in the way that Christians brought the Scripture of the Old Testament to bear on their experiences after the resurrection. The most commonly used Hebrew scripture in the New Testament was not a traditional messianic prophecy. Indeed, no traditional prophecy would have solved the problem that history had given the Christians, to find a prophecy of messianic suffering. Psalm 110, however, contained the perplexing line:

> The LORD says to my lord: "Sit at my right hand,
> till I make your enemies your footstool."

This psalm was clearly intended to express something of the relationship between the Davidic, reigning king and God. Christians often interpreted this verse to imply that Jesus had been raised to the Father's right hand, giving it a new prophetic meaning which explained what God had intended for Jesus. When combined with the prophecy of Daniel that a manlike angelic figure, the son of man, will be enthroned in heaven and take part in the final judgment, this passage became the basis for Christian eschatology.

Although the Christian interpretation was new, this kind of reinterpretation of Scripture was a standard procedure during the period and was absolutely justifiable from the perspective of any contemporary. Even though the verse might have meant something quite different in its original historical context, there was nothing impious or unusual in interpreting Scripture as a prophecy fulfilled by the immediate historical occurrences. On the contrary, all the sects of Judaism would have automatically searched for a scriptural grounding for any important event in the life of their community, similar to the way in which American society searches for legal precedents when a new or puzzling situation arises. Since biblical traditions were so widely known throughout the society, a large part of the earliest Christian community would have been able to search the Scriptures. In short, the reinterpretation of Scripture was normal for any group of the first century.

The most important idea implied in the reinterpretation of Psalm 110 is the divinity of the two figures, "God" and "my lord." *Lord* is a term by which the Jews designated God. In Hebrew the word *Lord* for God is different from but extremely close to the ordinary word *Lord.* When translated into Greek or Aramaic, the two terms become one. In Christianity, the Greek word *Kyrios,* meaning "Lord," became a term describing not God himself, as in Judaism, but Christ. Thus, the earliest Christian exegesis already asserted the divinity of the figure of Jesus on the basis of his heavenly ascent and exaltation in Psalm 110. Hellenistic and mystical Judaism held similar views on the human form of God's glory (*kavod*), *logos,* the resemblance of Adam to God before sin, and the divine participation of some principal angels in God's divinity. The Qumran community asserted the "divinity" of Melchizedek, the angelic mediator, through a similar interpretation of the Hebrew word *El,* meaning "God" or "angel." Philo even describes Moses as divine when he ascends to Mount Sinai and allegorically, to heaven itself.[26] Against this background, Christian innovations are both natural and fitted to the events of the crucifixion. The events unique to Jesus' biography account for a postresurrection identification of the mediator or angelic figure with him and hence create a messianic candidate who succeeded at his messianic mission in a totally new and unexpected way. Since the interpretation is so novel, not all followers of Jesus may have approved of it. Nevertheless, if the New Testament is an indication of the variety of Christian writing in the first century, there was little diversity in the community on this point.

Psalm 118:15–25 is also used by the Christian community to express its surprise about the way in which Jesus fulfilled the prophecies of the Hebrew Bible:

> Hark, glad songs of victory in the tents of the righteous;
> "The right hand of the LORD does valiantly, the right hand of the
>   LORD is exalted, the right hand of the LORD does valiantly!"
> I shall not die, but I shall live, and recount the deeds of the LORD.
> The LORD has chastened me sorely but he has not given me over to
>   death.
>
> Open to me the gates of righteousness, that I may enter through
>   them and give thanks to the LORD.
>
> This is the gate of the LORD; the righteous shall enter through it.
>
> I thank thee that thou hast answered me and hast become my sal-
>   vation.
> The stone which the builders rejected has become the head of the
>   corner.
> This is the LORD's doing; it is marvelous in our eyes.
> This is the day which the LORD has made; let us rejoice and be glad
>   in it.
> Save us, we beseech thee, O LORD! O LORD, we beseech thee, give
>   us success!

This is not a messianic psalm but a psalm of thanksgiving after a military victory. After it is applied to Jesus, however, it receives a variety of new meanings. In 1 Corinthians 3:10–17, for instance, Paul interprets Jesus straightforwardly as the foundation stone of the church. Acts 4:11 stresses another aspect of the verse, that Jesus was the cornerstone whom the Jews have rejected. By then it was necessary for the church to maintain that the Jewish rejection of their own messiah was also grounded in scriptural prophecies.

Christians eventually saw that Isaiah 53, the Psalm of the Suffering Servant, was a prophecy applying to Jesus:

Who has believed what we have heard?
And to whom has the arm of the LORD been revealed?
For he grew up before him like a young plant, and like a root out of dry ground;
he had no form or comeliness that we should look at him, and no beauty that we should desire him.
He was despised and rejected by men; a man of sorrows, and acquainted with grief;
And as one from whom men hide their faces he was despised, and we esteemed him not.

Surely he has borne our griefs and carried our sorrows;
yet we esteemed him stricken, smitten by God, and afflicted.
But he was wounded for our transgressions, he was bruised for our iniquities;
upon him was the chastisement that made us whole, and with his stripes we are healed.
All we like sheep have gone astray; we have turned every one to his own way;
and the LORD has laid upon him the iniquity of us all.

He was oppressed, and he was afflicted, yet he opened not his mouth;
like a lamb that is led to the slaughter, and like a sheep that before its shearers is dumb, so he opened not his mouth.

By oppression and judgment he was taken away; and as for his generation, who considered
that he was cut off out of the land of the living, stricken for the transgression of my people?
And they made his grave with the wicked and with the rich man in his death,
although he had done no violence, and there was no deceit in his mouth.

Yet it was the will of the LORD to bruise him, he has put him to grief;
when he makes himself an offering for sin, he shall see his offspring, he shall prolong his days;

the will of the LORD shall prosper in his hand; he shall see the fruit
of the travail of his soul and be satisfied;
by his knowledge shall the righteous one, my servant, make many
to be accounted righteous; and he shall bear their iniquities.
Therefore I will divide him a portion with the great, and he shall
divide the spoil with the strong;
because he poured out his soul to death, and was numbered with
the transgressors;
yet he bore the sin of many, and made intercession for the transgressors.

The easy applicability of this passage to Jesus' life obscures
the curious fact that it was not often used explicitly by the earliest church, and the New Testament never uses it to prove the
vicarious atonement of the messiah. Yet the theory that the
passage silently informs all of the New Testament is difficult to
substantiate. Paul, the earliest New Testament author, who is
extremely interested in the concept of vicarious atonement,
does not quote Isaiah 53 at all. Only relatively late writers of
the New Testament explicitly quote the passage. Luke, for instance, quotes Isaiah 53 in Acts 8:26–40 when he relates the
story of the Ethiopian eunuch:

But an angel of the LORD said to Philip, "Rise and go toward
the south to the road that goes down from Jerusalem to Gaza.
This is a desert road." And he rose and went. And behold, an
Ethiopian, a eunuch, a minister of Candace the queen of the
Ethiopians, in charge of all her treasure had come to Jerusalem to
worship and was returning; seated in his chariot, he was reading
the prophet Isaiah. And the Spirit said to Philip, "Go up and
join this chariot." So Philip ran to him, and heard him reading
Isaiah the prophet, and asked, "Do you understand what you are
reading?" And he said, "How can I, unless someone guides me?"
And he invited Philip to come up and sit with him. Now the
passage of the scripture which he was reading was this:

As a sheep led to the slaughter or a lamb before its shearer is dumb,
so he opens not his mouth.
In his humiliation justice was denied him.
Who can describe his generation?
For his life is taken up from the earth.

And the eunuch said to Philip, "About whom, pray, does the prophet say this, about himself or about someone else?" Then Philip opened his mouth, and beginning with this scripture he told him the good news of Jesus. And as they went along the road they came to some water, and the eunuch said, "See, here is water! What is to prevent my being baptized?" And he commanded the chariot to stop, and they both went down into the water, Philip and the eunuch, and he baptized him. And when they came up out of the water, the Spirit of the LORD caught Philip; and the eunuch saw him no more, and went on his way rejoicing. But Philip was found at Azotus, and passing on he preached the gospel to all the towns till he came to Caesarea.

This passage reveals that before Christianity the meaning of Isaiah 53 was not clearly messianic. The eunuch asks whether the passage refers to the prophet himself or to someone else, never assuming it to apply to the messiah.[27] Only then does Philip tell the eunuch that it refers to Jesus. Furthermore, Philip uses the passage to prove that Jesus, the messiah, must die, not to prove that the suffering of Jesus was redemptive. It was the suffering of the messiah, not the concept of vicarious atonement (redemptive suffering), which needed demonstration. Vicarious atonement was hardly in need of proof in first century Judaism, for the Temple, with its system of vicarious animal sacrifice, was still operating. Paul, who stresses vicarious atonement in regard to Jesus, never feels the need to prove it by means of Scripture.

The novelty of the Christian exegesis of Isaiah 53 was to apply it exclusively to the messiah. Judaism identifies many different people as servants of Yahweh. Rabbinic tradition tried to understand the identity of the figure by applying Isaiah 53 to anyone who was called a servant of Yahweh in the Hebrew Bible—Moses, Abraham, Phineas, Elijah, and the messiah. But the messiah is only called "servant" in an oblique way. Psalm 89 identifies David as servant. Zechariah 3:8 calls the "branch," which was a messianic term, a "servant." But the future messiah is not explicitly called a servant. The identification of the servant in Isaiah 53 with the messiah is first attested by the Christians.[28]

In 1 Peter, Isaiah 53 is used to explain the death of the martyrs as an emulation of the Christ, but even here vicarious atonement is not proven by the scriptural passage. The Christian meaning of the Scripture arose in the same way as did the exegesis of the other sects, through the interplay between historical experience and the words of the Bible. This explains why Christianity had so much trouble persuading Jews that the messiah had come. Nothing that the Christians maintained seemed self-evident to the majority of the Jewish community, and the Jews were the only ones who expected a messiah. This situation illuminates the statement of Paul: "We preach Christ crucified, a stumbling block to Jews and folly to gentiles" (1 Corinthians 1:23). He means that for a Christian to persuade a Jew to convert, the Christian has to overcome the Jewish expectation that no messiah (Christ) can be crucified, and the Christian similarly has to persuade a pagan that a crucified man is worthy of veneration as a God. The passage testifies to the indomitable faith of Paul's generation of Christians. Later generations of Christianity, secure in the meaning of their faith, miss the poignancy of Paul's claim.

One of the most obvious differences between Christianity and other millenarian movements is Christianity's longevity. The normal lifespan of an apocalyptic group is brief.[29] Apocalyptic predictions are usually disproven in some radical way or quashed by the powerful establishment. Christianity differs from this pattern in its long-lived success.

One reason for Christianity's success is its effectiveness in revaluing Scripture. The Christians who revised the expectations about Scripture must have been Jewish Christians of one sort or another. In formulating the new Christian truth, they proved it so effectively that later generations missed the radical surprise everywhere expressed by Jesus' earliest followers. Yet the process was typical of the time.

Another reason for Christianity's success was its originally passive, nonviolent stance, which allowed for a much wider interpretation of the coming of the kingdom than did any political messianic group in Judaism. Christianity resembles rabbinic Judaism in this respect, since both were able to reinterpret the phrase "the kingdom of God" to refer to the individual's personal commitment of faith rather than to the cataclysmic end of earthly regimes, as the apocalypticists had specified. As it turned out, all overtly political rebellions against Rome were hopelessly doomed to failure. The Christian distaste for Roman rule, like the rabbinic opposition, evolved into a determinedly unenthusiastic compliance with Rome.

Christianity was not notably successful in converting Jews to its message. Its greatest achievement lay in its missionary work among the Gentiles. Moreover, the Christianity that spread throughout the Roman Empire had transformed its apocalyptic sectarianism into a religion of personal piety. It had not, however, given up its communal cohesion. Christianity did not so much abandon apocalyptic fervor as channel it into nonapocalyptic areas. The church maintained that Jesus' resurrection was the beginning of the apocalyptic end of time. Instead of quickening apocalyptic belief itself, the church transformed that belief into a means to form stable communities. This transformation was effected by Paul, the apostle, who was still very much an apocalypticist but who also laid the groundwork for the theology and fervor that brought Christianity into the wider world.

❧ IV ❧

Paul, the Convert and Apostle

Paul was not the first convert in the history of either Christianity or Judaism, though he was the most important one. Paul was not even the second founder of Christianity, for he converted into a vibrant, dynamic church.[1] It was a church that already contained a significant Jewish and Gentile population spread among the major cities of Asia Minor, Greece, and Rome.

Four factors helped the spread of Christianity: the respect already felt for Judaism in the Hellenistic world, in which Christianity joined as a similar cult based on piety and moral values; Christianity's apocalyptic sectarian organization and committed membership; the general mobility of peoples in the Hellenistic world, brought about by the expansion of trade; and a large population of economically self-sufficient but low-status people who were potential converts. Yet the overwhelming success of early Christianity cannot be explained merely by conditions accidental to its founding or in the general Hellenistic environment. The crucial factor in its success was the ability, which was virtually unique among Jewish sects, to convert Gentiles from a variety of milieus outside Judea and to transform itself into a single group unifying Jew and Gentile. Although Paul was a Jew, his experience of conversion became the model that would ensure the success of Christianity.

Christianity's Rise

In a work opposing Christianity, Celsus charges that Christianity excluded educated people and attracted only "wool-workers, cobblers, laundry workers and the most illiterate and bucolic yokels who enticed children and stupid women to come along to the woodworker's shop . . . that they may learn perfection."[2] This comment was no doubt meant to condemn Christianity as the religion of an uneducated crowd. Yet from his aristocratic distance Celsus actually gives evidence of a rise in status of Christians, who came from the respectable, skilled laboring classes.

Nothing in Judaism corresponds to the determination and effectiveness with which Christianity missionized. The dynamic that fueled Christianity's missionizing came partly from its apocalyptic Jewish roots and partly from the antinomian interpretation of Torah in some Christian communities, which allowed Christianity to transcend its apocalyptic and sectarian background within Judaism. By the time of Paul, a scant decade or two after Jesus, the church had already begun to attract a larger cross-section of the Roman world than one would expect from a Jewish apocalyptic movement of the purely disadvantaged. Just as in the Palestinian context of Jesus' movement, so in the Hellenistic setting of Christianity, disadvantage had a much broader meaning. The skilled trades were above average in economic security, though their ascribed status was sometimes low, leading to status ambiguity. The workshop provided an apt place for evangelization: conversation could take place between customers and tradesmen, and a master normally communicated to his apprentices not only his skill but a wide variety of opinions. Another group whose attainments were out of step with its official status were the "God-fearing" Gentiles, who were interested in Judaism and attended synagogue services but were unwilling to become fully Jewish and were perhaps afraid to undergo circumcision. Finally, as the New Testament shows, women who were of low status but high achievement found a comfortable home in early Christianity and other Hellenistic cults.[3]

In the end the audience that was most inclined to proselytism was found in the synagogues of the Diaspora. In these synagogues were found Diaspora Jews and semiproselytes to Judaism, who attended the synagogue but were unable or unwilling to take all the steps necessary to become Jews. They suffered from a double ambiguity in status, since they were no longer pagans but were not yet Jews. Luke reports that each time Paul arrived in a new town, he first turned to the synagogue for lodging and support but then used it as a pulpit from which to advance his mission. The reception he was accorded in synagogues changed when the Jews grasped the import of his message, and Paul was usually forced to withdraw. Thereafter Paul found lodging and continued preaching at a patron's house, which was insulated from the Jewish population. This practice of speaking in house churches under the sponsorship of a patron or patroness was common among religious and civic associations of the Hellenistic world. Synagogues themselves were often founded in the same way, though in their case the patrons were exclusively Jewish. For Paul, the arrangement led inevitably to a new and distinct Gentile church, separate from paganism and also separate from the established synagogues.

The population that Paul found in the synagogues was composed of native Jews, proselytes, God-fearers in the process of converting, and interested fellow travelers. The synagogues, which were themselves partly involved in actively converting Gentiles and partly concerned with protecting Jewish reputations, did not welcome competition or new interpretations from Paul. Many religions attracted the Gentiles' attention by virtue of their exotic beliefs and ceremonies or their ethics and morality. Jews were no exception. Evidence of the continuing attraction of Gentiles to the synagogue comes from Jewish literature of the period, which contains an occasional tractate, like *Joseph and Aseneth*, meant to fortify converts.

Even though Jews welcomed proselytes and sometimes went out of their way to explain Judaism to potential proselytes, the synagogue never indulged in the kind of proselytizing that characterized Christianity. The cellular social organization of the sect contributed to the effectiveness of the earliest Christians' mission. Living communally and doing only what was necessary to support their families before the expected end of the world, Christian apocalypticists formed a highly motivated group of proselytizers. But as Christianity began to attract Gentiles, a number of new issues, unanticipated in the time of Jesus, surfaced. As evidenced by Paul's letters, the Gentiles needed instruction to understand apocalypticism. A desire for equality in social relationships between Gentiles and Jews in Christianity constantly conflicted with Jewish law. This growing religious sect, no longer entirely Jewish, was the one with which Paul came into creative contact. In turn, Paul's experience among both Jews and Gentiles made him the ideal person to analyze and solve the problem of Christianity's Gentile future by coming to terms at a decisive moment with its Jewish past. Because Paul's life and experience thoroughly inform his letters to the Christian communities of the Roman world, Christianity received not just Paul's intellectual solution to these problems but also the stamp of his personality. That Pauline influence is summed up in two features of Christianity: it left Pharisaic Judaism behind and became entirely a missionary community of converts.

Conversion as a Religious Decision

Paul came to terms with two different religious systems and made a decision between them. He thus became a convert. But conversion in the ancient world was a relatively specialized religious experience. It involved an emotional commitment and a radical change of life. Although rare in the ancient world, conversion was characteristic of Judaism and Christianity, as well as of some philosophical schools and mystery religions. The commitment of a convert differed from the usual religious "adherence" to certain formal rites and rituals which were unique to each city. Most of these rites and formal pieties were merely civic rites, not demanding the kind of commitment that Judaism or Christianity found to be central to their way of life.[4]

Conversion today is sometimes viewed as a kind of "brainwashing," the term coined for the torture that American soldiers received at the hands of the North Koreans in order to secure their cooperation for propaganda purposes.[5] Yet this model does not apply to all conversions. Authentic conversions, which may involve strong emotions, as do most powerful psychological processes, also involve conscious, rational decisions. The conversion experience can be viewed less critically as a kind of decision-making. This model does justice to the believer's experience and also leaves open the possibility that the conversion can be affected by external conditions which the convert does not comprehend.

Because Paul's conversion was a difficult decision, the theory of cognitive dissonance advanced by Leon Festinger illuminates Pauline thought.[6] The concept of cognitive dissonance refers to the state of mind of a person going through the decision-making process. It includes the unpleasant anxieties encountered by all who have trouble making a decision or notice inconsistency in their actions after the decision is made. During a hard decision between alternatives, either one appears very attractive. After the decision, people revalue both the taken and the untaken choices so that they no longer appear close. As a result, the option not taken recedes in importance in the mind of the person as a way of reducing the dissonance or anxiety involved in the decision.

The commonest ways of reducing dissonance have nothing to do with disconfirmation or proselytism; rather, they are the mental processes of rationalization, reinterpretation, and disparagement.[7] The processes of Bible interpretation of the major sects of Judaism, such as midrash, pesher, and allegory, are at once dissonance-reducing mechanisms and strategies for constructing a new social world out of an old one. To limit the means of reducing dissonance to proselytism, increasing the size of the group, is to miss many of the other possibilities for analyzing religious discourse.

In exploring the survival of some apocalyptic communities and the failure of others, Rosabeth Kanter found that the stronger and more difficult the conversion experience, the stronger and more unshakable the resulting beliefs.[8] Group cohesiveness is therefore related to the strength or number of conversions in a group. In other words, if a group is made up largely or entirely of converts, its cohesiveness tends to be much greater than a group whose membership is filled by casual affiliation with no decisive rejection of other choices. The highest degree of cohesiveness is demonstrated in groups that represent a new type of moral community, such as those whose members share property or other resources and form a single household. One characteristic of sects that are highly dependent on conversion for membership is that they tend to be extremely cohesive, stressing the differences between themselves and the outside world. Furthermore, the groups themselves try to reduce the cognitive dissonance that arises in the mind of each of their members by reinforcing their own special construction or interpretation of reality. This tactic can be traced in the literature of each sectarian group.

The relationship between group cohesion and conversion helps to explain the spread and success of early Christianity. High group definition and communal sharing of property were common features of both Jewish and Christian apocalypticism.[9] The cohesiveness of the group was correlated with the individual commitment of its members in the Hellenistic world as in the modern one. Conversion suited Christianity to gain in popularity and conquer opposition. A highly personal piety, highly correlated with the conversion experience, characterized the most successful and most cohesive forms of religion in the Roman Empire. Once Christianity adopted its proselytizing mission, it became a true religious revolution in the late Roman Empire. Though not a unique phenomenon, it was at least one of the small number of successful new conversion religions that were characterized by personal piety in the first few centuries. Christianity was popular and attractive in the Roman Empire even before Paul. Christian communities organized all their resources for the dissemination of the Gospel and quickly spread throughout the Roman world.

The Christian emphasis on conversion, though inherited from Judaism, was specially suited to the new community. Many ancient sources report both a high esteem for Jewish practice and a high number of proselytes to Judaism. Matthew

23 certifies that the Pharisees were outstanding proselytizers. Yet the social cohesion of Judaism was not based on an active mission. It was rather based on the distinctive Jewish rites. The distinctive rites of Judaism and its high ethical standards attracted converts, for Jews displayed their beliefs in a variety of ways that brought favorable attention. Yet because most Jews were simply raised in the religion of their forefathers, Judaism *in toto* cannot be called a religion of converts to the same extent that Christianity became one. After the revolts against Rome, it was illegal for a time even to circumcise or preach conversion to Judaism, and proselytizing became an extremely dangerous activity.

Sectarian Judaism, like Essenism and the new religion of Christianity, depended on regular converts and operated educational programs for the purpose of recruiting or, as they would have phrased it, preaching to the populace about the value of repentance. The Dead Sea Scroll community's membership came only by conversion. No member of this group could be called an adherent, because members adopted a radically different way of life.[10] The single most obvious characteristic of the Dead Sea Scroll sectarians was their dualism, which functioned to create a high boundary between themselves and the rest of the population and hence to reduce postdecision dissonance. Strongly apocalyptic, the community divided the world into a battle between the children of darkness and the children of light. This division was not the same as a philosophical dualism, for the Qumran community believed in a single deity. Dead Sea Scroll dualism functioned to keep the converts away from the demonic attitudes tempting them to counterconversion.[11] It depended upon either a prior division of the world into the sons of light and the sons of darkness or, from another perspective, a strong distinction between pre- and postdecision conversion states in the community.

This distinction pervaded the members' thinking; they virtually identified themselves with the community of the saved at the end of time. There was thus a perfect symmetry between their personal decision states in joining their community and their views on the ultimate purpose of history. In this respect they were close to many of today's new religions, which set up monastic, ascetic, or retreat communities based on the notion that they alone will survive. Even though ecstasy appeared to be part of their rites, the Qumran group did not describe conversion in ecstatic or emotional terms; rather, they stressed the slowness of progress through educational grades into full membership and the rigors of their life of purity. They prescribed ritual immersion for purity, as did the Pharisees. But the immersion had an unequivocally Essene mark, for it made the community pure enough to fight with the angels at the end of time. Hence, the ritually pure convert would be saved at the final battle. This Essene practice filled in the gaps between the Jewish ritual bath and Christian baptism.

No matter how common or important was conversion within the general Jewish community, it was significantly more so to the emerging sects in Judaism, and spectacularly so to Christianity. Even the Essenes, who depended on conversion for most of their membership, never succeeded in spreading their message outside Judea to the same extent that Christianity did. Indeed, long after Christianity's apocalypticism had softened to an expectation of Christ's return and long after its spread had stopped being fostered by the dissonance of any supposed disconfirmation, Christianity continued to missionize actively.

Paul did not leave Judaism entirely in becoming a follower of Jesus. Nor can Paul be thought of as a pathological personality or a morally incomplete person who was unable to live under rabbinic auspices. He had, as Krister Stendahl remarked, a "robust conscience."[12]

But Paul was indeed a convert in the modern sociological definition of the word. Although it is not necessary to leave one's previous religion entirely to become a convert, a convert characteristically reports important changes in attitude and way of life. Think of James, who at first gave up no affiliation with the Jewish community and continued to practice the law. He could be thought of as a Jew who felt Jesus' teaching added to or completed his Judaism. Many Christians, especially the Torah-true Jewish Christians, grew into Christianity from Judaism. Not Paul, however. He says that he originally perceived

Christianity as an enemy. It is an almost universal human psychological process to revalue the past on the basis of important decisions, and Paul was no exception.

Paul's work is powerful precisely because he expresses what others must have felt in becoming Christian but could not express. He is a successful convert who reports that his life suddenly turned around on him. No matter how completely Paul had embraced Pharisaism, he found an even more important intuition about Judaism in the Christian faith which he had persecuted at first. In his letters Paul claims to have been a Pharisee and now to value it for naught on account of having become a Christian: "If any man thinks he has reason for confidence, I have more: circumcised on the eighth day, of the people of Israel of the tribe of Benjamin, a Hebrew born of Hebrews; as to the law a Pharisee, as to zeal a persecutor of the church, as to righteousness under the law blameless. But whatever gain I had, I counted as loss for the sake of Christ. Indeed, I count everything as loss because of the surpassing worth of knowing Christ Jesus my Lord" (Philippians 3:4–6; see also 2 Corinthians 11:21–22; Galatians 1:13–14; Romans 9:1–3).

This is a patent conversion. Paul was not merely a completed Jew. Paul relates that he had left the Pharisaic movement in becoming a Christian. Since Paul had come from a Diaspora city to study in Judea and membership in the Pharisees involved a commitment to more specialized laws within the Jewish community, Paul may be considered a religious quester. Even his study of Pharisaism raised the problem of dissonance. A more radical move was Paul's ultimate choice of an opposing group within Judaism which was apocalyptic and communal. There is no doubt of the gravity of these changes and the amount of dissonance that such a radical decision raised.

Yet Paul seemed unaware of leaving Judaism. Paul's subsequent training in the Christian movement did not require that he learn an entirely new world-view. So he did not have the most radical kind of conversion. Rather, he decided against following his previous sect of Pharisaism in favor of a new sect of Judaism that he had previously regarded as heretical. The fact that Paul perceived himself as having remained within Judaism, albeit with an entirely new understanding of Judaism, parallels his refusal to let go of the Torah. Paul's values about the Torah did not disappear after his conversion. His fundamental system of values stayed intact, but as John Gager pointed out, that system was reversed or transvalued.[13]

Paul's Exegesis

He grew up in Tarsus, a Hellenized city, yet he became a Pharisee. His Jewish past included Pharisaic as well as Hellenistic components, but no one feature can explain his mode of thinking. And his conversion overturned his past by giving him an entirely new perspective on it.

The passage of Paul's that best illustrates his Jewish past in tension with his Christian present is Galatians 3, where Paul appeals to Scripture to prove his point:

> Thus Abraham "believed God and it was reckoned to him as righteousness." So you see that it is men of faith who are the sons of Abraham. And the scripture, foreseeing that God would justify the gentiles by faith, preached the gospel beforehand to Abraham, saying, "In you shall all the nations be blessed." So then, those who are men of faith are blessed with Abraham who had faith. For all who rely on works of the law are under a curse: for it is written, "Cursed be every one who does not abide all the things written in the book of the law, and do them." Now it is evident that no man is justified before God by the law; for "He who through faith is righteous shall live," but the law does not rest on faith, for "He who does them shall live by them." Christ redeemed us from the curse of the law, having become a curse for us—for it is written, "Cursed be every one who hangs on a tree"—that in Christ Jesus the blessing of Abraham might come upon the gentiles, that we might receive the promise of the Spirit through faith.

Paul's argument is subtle and complex. He maintains that those who rely on the works of the law are under a curse, as in Deuteronomy 27:26: "Cursed be those who do not do it." But this conflicts with Habakkuk 2:4: "He who through faith is righteous shall live," which is to be understood by means of Leviticus 18:5 "He who does them shall live by them." The two passages contradict each other: either those who live by the law are blessed or those who live by faith are blessed. This contradiction has arisen in the reading because it previously arose in Paul's experience.

Though Paul's problem is caused by a personal crisis, his solution to the problem is rabbinic. Resolving apparent contradictions is a classic rabbinic approach to exegesis which Paul learned in his Pharisaic past.[14] His solution to this particular problem, while reflecting his Pharisaic training, also reflects his Christian perspective. He solves the contradiction by bringing in a third scriptural passage which shows how to interpret the first two passages so as to yield a unity, Deuteronomy 21:23: "Cursed be he who hangs on a tree." Paul interprets this passage, without any explanation, as referring to Christ. Perhaps he had once heard the passage used against Christianity, either before or after his conversion, for it is uniquely suited for such use. Paul searches, however, for a different meaning. He does not say that a curse is an impossible attribution for the crucified Christ. Rather, he turns the passage around in a surprising way to make it a prophecy, showing that Christ had changed the curse so as to bring the blessing of Abraham to the Gentiles. Gentiles do not have to follow the entire law. On account of Christ's salvific death, Gentiles may be adopted into Judaism by the process of conversion, yet now they do not have to keep the law. Just as in his conversion itself, Paul turns around the meaning of the scriptural passage.

Although Paul's method of analyzing the problem is rabbinic, his conclusion, which depends on a new understanding of Scripture, could only be made by a converted Christian interested in a Gentile mission. Paul's own conversion experience has shown him how to interpret this law for the first time, as a prophecy for the saving acts of Jesus. So Paul's own experience turns Jewish Scripture on its head and makes it come true in an ironic, unexpected way. If the law is a medium of salvation, then there can be no crucified Christ—or no messiah, since Jews did not expect a crucified messiah. And since Paul knows that Christ was crucified, the law is no longer the medium of salvation, at least in the way Paul expected.

No matter how sanctified Jesus' martyrdom may have been in its own right, Paul, as a Pharisee, knew that the messiah expected by Scripture would be a successful leader who would free Judea from oppression. What changes for Paul is first of all his description of the messiah and, of necessity, his interpretation of Torah. Torah's primary new importance is as a prophecy forecasting the crucified messiah and the conversion of Gentiles.

E. P. Sanders observed that in Paul's thought the solution precedes the problem.[15] That is, for Paul, Christianity does not remedy some failing in Judaism. Paul's Christianity rather arrives first, and then, in retrospect, Paul sees Pharisaic Judaism, the way not taken, in new and less positive ways. This kind of revaluation is characteristic of a person who has just made an important decision. Yet Paul is not an impartial and analytic observor of Judaism. He is a revolutionary. Paul does not forget his Jewish past; he rather inverts the values of his past in a way that is consonant with his new commitments.

Although the veracity of Paul's ecstatic conversion experience as related by Luke in Acts is doubtful, there is clear evidence of his ecstatic experience in Paul's own letters, as in 2 Corinthians 12:1–9:

> I must boast; there is nothing to be gained by it, but I will go on to visions and revelations of the Lord. I know a man in Christ who fourteen years ago was caught up to the third heaven— whether in the body or out of the body, I do not know, God knows. And I know that this man was caught up into Paradise— whether in the body or out of the body, I do not know, God knows—and he heard things that cannot be told, which man may not utter. On behalf of this man, I will boast, but on my own behalf I will not boast, except of my weaknesses. Though if I wish to boast, I shall not be a fool, for I shall be speaking the truth. But I refrain from it, so that no one may think more of me than he sees in me or hears in me. And to keep me from being too elated by the abundance of revelations, a thorn was given me in the flesh, a messenger of Satan, to harass me, to keep me from being too elated. Three times I besought the Lord about this, that it should leave me; but he said to me, "My grace is sufficient for you, for my power is made perfect in weakness."

Paul suggests here in an elliptical way that he himself has experienced ecstatic ascension. At the end of the passage, he admits having spoken with the Lord about an infirmity, but Christ has decided the infirmity perfects his power. Although the passage can be understood in other ways, the simplest sense is that Paul has had several ecstatic meetings with the Lord, the first of which was fourteen years previous to this letter. The meeting probably took place in a heavenly ascent to the enthroned Christ, since such ecstatic ascents to the divine throne appear in other apocalyptic and merkabah mystical traditions in Jewish Hellenism. Although there is no explicit proof that this was Paul's conversion experience, it certainly justified or confirmed a conversion.[16]

Conversion and Baptism

Being a Jew and then a follower of John the Baptist and Jesus, Paul defined one of the basic rites of conversion in Judaism, ritual immersion or baptism, as the prototypical rite of entrance to the new community as well. As an apocalyptic Jew, Paul also saw this rite as defining the boundary between outsiders and insiders. However, the purpose of the immersion is not to achieve ritual purity or even to allow the angels to descend and fight for the sons of light, as at Qumran. By means of baptism, a Pauline Christian is united with the death and resurrection of Christ, reborn as a new converted personality and eligible for the resurrection that has already begun. For Paul, as for the sect of John the Baptist and Qumran, these beliefs were still related to the apocalyptic beliefs of the coming end of time. In Christianity after Paul, baptism came to signify the purification of Christians for the heavenly journey at the end of life.

In Paul, baptism retains a strong apocalyptic sense. But it also has a present, social meaning: being in Christ, there is "neither Jew nor Greek, there is neither slave nor free, there is neither male nor female" (Galatians 3:28). All are part of a community of the last days. So to be "in Christ" is the same as to be a believer or a convert and a member of the new community. The effect of this unity on Christians, who remain brothers and sisters as long as they remain in the Christian community, is to define a new social reality, different from the reality of both Jews and Jewish Christians. By means of baptism the believers take off their old physical body and put on a new one. Upon rising from the baptismal water, they rise from the dead with Christ (Colossians 3:9–10). All are one in the new community, having risen with the body of Christ in baptism and being dead to previous lives in Torah or paganism. This understanding of baptism parallels that of the unique new cells of Gentile Christian house churches, which Paul shared in founding and at which he preached.[17]

Mary Douglas showed that the human body is often used as a symbol for society.[18] Paul's use of the metaphor of a new body for baptized believers in Christ defines the new social body of the new believers: all those who enter the new community by doing rites derived from Judaism but now developed uniquely for Christianity are to be resurrected. This new social body reflects the social reality of a predominantly Gentile house church. The new concept of Torah arises because nothing that Jews or Gentiles do within the community should destroy the unity of the saved. Exhortations of ethical behavior in Paul do not reflect Pharisaic exegesis so much as Hellenistic advice on proper familial virtue.

Paul's Reflection on Law

Paul revalued his life on the basis of his conversion. The traditional dichotomies in Paul's thought are due to his conversion experience. The dualism of flesh and spirit, of life apart from the law and under it, suggests a person who is trying to look at his previous values after having adopted new ones.[19]

Having been a Jew, Paul granted saving power to the law. But after his conversion he saw another vehicle to attain salvation. Since Paul valued his Jewish past, he still respected Torah. But he did not give it the same kind of soteriological status that the Pharisees did, because he had a new faith, depending upon an ecstatic experience of salvation confirmed by baptism. A Jew who entered Christianity and found it to complete his Judaism would not seek to limit the scope of Torah. In Romans 3:21–31, Paul still respects Torah but subtly changes the place of Torah in his life, so that it has ultimate authority as prophecy but not as a communal norm for salvation:

> But now the righteousness of God has been manifested apart from law, although the law and the prophets bear witness to it, the righteousness of God through faith in Jesus Christ for all who believe. For there is no distinction; since all have sinned and fall short of the glory of God, they are justified by his grace as a gift, through redemption which is in Christ Jesus, whom God put forward as an expiation by his blood, to be received by faith. This was to show God's righteousness, because in his divine forbearance he had passed over former sins; it was to prove at the present time that he himself is righteous and that he justifies him who has faith in Jesus. Then what becomes of our boasting? It is excluded. On what principle? On the principle of works? No but on the principle of faith. For we hold that a man is justified by faith apart from works of law. Or is God the God of Jews only? Is he not the God of gentiles also? Yes, of gentiles also, since God is one; and he will justify the circumcised on the ground of their faith and the uncircumcised through their faith. Do we then overthrow the law by this faith? By no means! On the contrary, we should uphold the law.

Paul says that the Torah is the proper guide for righteousness for the Jews. This view is in line with the understanding that the Torah is the national constitution of the Jews. Most Jews, even Hellenistic ones from Tarsus, like Paul, would begin from this point. As the national constitution, the Torah is admirable, even sublime. Paul also says that Jewish Christians may continue to practice the Torah if they choose to do so. But this practice is not the principle of salvation for Christians, whether they be Jews or Gentiles. The genius of Paul is to reflect on his conversion experience in such a way as to make it a new model for the whole community. In doing so, he develops a new principle of salvation in Christianity, for both the Jews and the Gentiles. The principle of salvation is the same as the principle of community: conversion through baptism in Christ.

Paul does not retreat to the position that the Torah is an ethnic characteristic of Jews. Paul understands that the Torah provides a universal standard of righteousness in ethical matters for Jew and Gentile alike. This understanding of the value of Torah is in keeping with later Jewish views that the Torah's general moral precepts, the Noahide Commandments, are incumbent on Gentiles as well as Jews. Only the special laws are incumbent upon Jews.

It is thus possible that what changes for Paul is merely his view of that medium of salvation for the Gentiles. In other words, Paul may rest all on faith but still maintain the validity of the Jewish faith including the Torah. This would be in keeping with the mature rabbinic view of the second century that salvation for Jew and Gentile alike is based upon righteousness and repentance, and that the ethics by which the Gentiles are judged excludes the special laws that apply to the Jews alone. Paul may thus be offering the convert the choice between becoming Jewish, with all of the rules operant, or becoming Christian. Either way, one achieves salvation. But it is simpler and more practical for a Gentile to become a Christian.[20]

This was the practical choice that many God-fearers or proselytes to Judaism faced in their own lives, but to see it also as the theology that Paul advocates is not easy. The church does not understand Paul to be advocating Christianity and Judaism as two equal choices. Although Paul seems to consider that the Gentiles can be righteous according to nature, a concept of universality that would evolve in Judaism (Romans 2:12–24), elsewhere he does not give Judaism much of a continuing positive place in God's plan (Romans 11:17–22). The reason is apparently not a lack of generosity or fellow-feeling; rather Paul is overcome with the conviction that faith is now the principle of salvation and that its measure is conversion through baptism in Christ. Yet Paul has to be read primarily as a preacher to the Gentiles. Moreover, Paul may never have actually solved this problem for himself in a systematic way.

Despite this liberal attitude, Paul thinks that special laws are no longer important for pagan or Jew within Christianity. In Galatians 2:11–12 he chides Peter, called Cephas, for his hy-

pocrisy on this issue: "But when Cephas came to Antioch I opposed him to his face, because he stood condemned. For before
certain men came from James, he ate with the gentiles; but
when they came he drew back and separated himself, fearing
the circumcision party."

Although eating only with one's brethren is not a law
explicitly enjoined upon Jews, Paul, having been a Pharisee,
would probably not have eaten with Gentiles or impure Jews,
because they carried ritual impurities to the table. From his
Pharisaic past, Paul learned how important table fellowship is
for unifying a community. Yet the Mishnah (Avodah Zarah
2:3) specifically mentions that Gentile wine and meat offered
to idols should not be eaten at all. After leaving Pharisaism,
Paul may have seen a way for Jewish Christians to eat with
Gentile Christians. Speaking to Jews and Gentiles together
about food prohibitions generally (Romans 14:1–6, 15–20; 1
Corinthians 8, 10:25–30), he suggests that all Christians should
eat together without fear. Addressing two different groups,
"the weak" who will eat only vegetables and "the strong" who
will eat meat and drink wine, he suggests that all Christians
should eat with each other, even if this means diplomatically
avoiding foods which other Christians despise. But Paul's personal feelings are with the "strong" (Romans 15:1), since he
states that no food is unclean of itself, only to him who thinks it
so (Romans 14:14).

Paul appears to be in complete opposition to James, who
feels that Jews and Gentile Christians should not eat together,
and Paul is in serious disagreement with Cephas (Peter) as
presented in Galatians. Paul feels that the church's unity is
more important than the food prohibitions: "Do not for the
sake of food, destroy the work of God" (Romans 14:20).
Though the referent of Paul's arguments is in question, his
general principle seems clear. The ambiguity in the situation
comes from the fact that no one knows exactly what ordinary
Jews or Gentiles would have practiced in the first century and
the New Testament assumes a context which is no longer self-
evident.[21] Paul's correspondence implies that his views were
still a minority opinion in his own lifetime. But when Pauline

Christians began to dominate Christianity, the effect of Paul's writing changed.

Paul puts the unity of the Christian community through faith above any law of the flesh, though he respects the Torah and knows the value of the rites of Judaism in ways that Gentiles would not. Although this decision shows Paul's commitment to eliminating the Gentile-Jewish boundary in the church, he was not victorious on the issue in his own day. The total abandonment of the special laws was not achieved in the church until later, for Peter, in spite of wavering, and James were against Paul, and they were far more powerful leaders. Only when Gentile Christians began to predominate in Christianity did Paul's position take hold.

Circumcision was an even more important issue for early Christians, and again the outcome in Paul's own day remains in doubt. For Jews, circumcision would have been the *sine qua non* for conversion of a male Gentile. Those Gentiles who became Christians by first becoming Jews also presumably had strong feelings about those who were not so willing. Paul's vituperation in Galatians 6 indicates the seriousness of the issue. For the circumcising party of the church, that rite continued to define entrance into the community, making Christianity, in effect, a new Jewish sect.

When Paul joined Christianity, he was baptized, but he did not need to be circumcised. Again, Paul's experience forms the basis for his opinions, since his idea of community is based upon baptism alone. Paul's Gentile converts to Christianity could not be understood as Jewish by either Jews or Jewish Christians, and this presented a grave threat to Jewish Christianity. As a result, Pauline converts were entirely different from both their Jewish and their pagan forebears. They existed by themselves, in some tension with the Jewish Christian church and probably in some tension with the Jewish community as well. But they were not actively involved in Jewish life.

That Paul, a Jew, provided the model for the Christian conversion experience for both Jew and Gentile is extremely important. On account of his Jewish background and his conversion, he was an especially effective spokesperson for his new Gentile concept rather than the old apocalyptic Jewish concept of community within Christianity. The proof of belongingness in the new community lay in the radical reorientation of everyone, not just of Gentiles, upon their entrance into Christianity. Paul was not a completed Jew. He was a Jew who did not have to convert to become a Christian. Theoretically, he could have just become a messianic adherent to the new sect. In that case, he would merely have insisted that the rules of Jewish life be imposed upon all Christians, as did the Jewish Christians. But Paul, even though he was Jewish and perhaps precisely because he had been a believing Pharisee, had to go through a radical reorientation of his life upon entering Christianity. Drawing on his own experience, Paul says that everyone needs radically to reorient his or her way of thinking in order to become a Christian. As a result, the conversion model operates for both Jews and Gentiles in a new social entity which reflects the house church of Pauline Christianity. Furthermore, this reorientation of life after so radical a decision fits the principles of social psychology.

For Paul, a Jew already socialized to the value of Torah, the subservience of Torah to faith meant the demotion in rank of an important concept, Torah. For a Gentile who had no understanding of or experience with the Torah, the subservience of Torah meant its complete irrelevance. For Paul, the secondary status of Torah was part of his dissonance upon leaving Pharisaism and entering an apocalyptic community based on faith. For the Gentile, the Torah was part of a sinful world to be left behind, on a par with paganism. For Paul, the value of Torah carried over into Christianity. For the Gentile convert to Christianity, Christianity was understandable without Torah. Paul's analysis of community was far more sweeping when read by an overwhelmingly Gentile church than when experienced by him or when used for self-justification by an embattled Gentile minority within the church.

Although Paul developed no systematic theology of conversion, his personal experience, expressed as death and rebirth in Christ, was an important factor in the future of Christianity. No other Jewish sect developed the same kind of cohesion that

Christianity did, with both Jew and Gentile wedded to a single concept of community. No other Jewish sect succeeded in turning that community so thoroughly into an engine for the further conversion of the world. Paul was not the first convert to Christianity, but his life became a model for Gentile Christians to follow. And his work fueled the Christian community even after that community's Jewish apocalyptic vision of the world had dimmed. In short, the Pauline idea of conversion into the community of repentant sinners was a potent factor in the success of Christianity, no matter how it may have offended the dominant Jewish-Christian sector of the church in Paul's own day.

In some ways, Paul's thinking was radical for the later church. He left open the possibility of a gnostic interpretation. In fact, his letters were the basis for the gospel of gnostic Christianity. Yet on Jewish-Gentile relations, the basic issue of the earliest church, his writings were invaluable. His conversion experience helped Christianity define its own unity. The dissonance that a Gentile felt on entering this new religion was as great as Paul's, if not greater, since it probably entailed a complete resocialization. Yet on the issue of Torah, the ordinary convert could feel little of the anguish and ambiguity that Paul evinces in Romans. Probably the Gentile convert ignored much of Paul's meditation on Torah since it was totally foreign to him. Furthermore, Christian communities formulated on Pauline conversion experiences had a much higher degree of commitment than Jewish Christian communities that continued to observe Jewish law. Based on the Pauline model, Christian communities valued conversion experiences as a proof of faith in the second and third generations of the movement, but for different reasons. Christians, even those socialized from birth, became imbued with the value of being in Christ through baptism and communion and looked upon all ecstatic experiences as proof of the faith. Gifts of the spirit, associated with the conversion experience, were looked upon as a sign of the imminent approach of God's kingdom. Hence, they artificially kept alive the concept of conversion, even when no actual conversion decision was made and so no dissonance was experienced. Yet when ecstatic gifts of the spirit later threatened the apostolic authority of the bishops, they had to be kept in line.

Paul's thinking was an extremely important development in the history of Christianity. But Paul's writing is not a dispassionate and fully accurate analysis of Torah. Paul attempted to describe his experience, not write a phenomenological description of the Torah. His writings are the result of a man who has experienced cognitive dissonance in a sharper way than many other Christians, especially other Jewish Christians. Paul's personal commitment helped Christianity explore the way to include the Gentile Christians within the original Jewish apocalyptic sect. Though some of the rites of passage of conversion, such as baptism, were kept, largely through the influence of John the Baptist's movement, Paul transformed them, giving them a new meaning for a new community. In the process he built what turned out to be the dominant model of Christian social life.

Paul, like most other Christians in his day, was profoundly apocalyptic in his thinking. But Paul's formula of conversion allowed Christianity to stimulate a high level of sectarian commitment even after the apocalyptic beginnings of Christianity had been left behind. In short, the use of Paul's Jewish conversion to Christianity as a role model for future conversion was another reason for the success of Christianity in attracting Gentiles. Paul's writing, by stressing his experience of conversion, helped bridge the gap between the apocalyptic Jewish sect and the dominant Hellenistic Christian community of piety and mystery.

❧ V ❧

Origins of the Rabbinic Movement

According to rabbinic tradition, the major leaders of the Pharisaic movement stand in a direct line of transmission between Moses and the Mishnah, the earliest datable rabbinic document, around 200 C.E. Such a straight line of descent cannot be proven, because sectarian movements are not biological creatures whose ontogeny can be precisely determined. But the rabbis' intent in the tradition is clear: they felt a close affinity to the Pharisaic teachers, even though the rabbinic movement developed considerably beyond its Pharisaic roots. The basic difference between the two phases of Judaism was the sectarian nature of the Pharisaic movement. When the Pharisees became the leading sect, consciously trying to be "catholic" for Israel, Pharisaism became rabbinic. The process occurred gradually throughout the second and succeeding centuries. Yet even in Judea and Galilee the rabbis were not the sole masters of the Jewish community, and in Babylonia the rabbis had to share power with the exilarch, involving themselves in a continuous conflict. In all places there were many Jews whose interest in the rabbinic movement was sporadic. Only in this sense did the rabbinic movement grow out of Pharisaism, as a response to the need for a new ruling party to govern Israel under Roman occupation after the disastrous failures of the two wars for independence in 66 and 132 C.E. The rabbinic justification for rule centered on the doctrine of the "oral law."

The Pharisees

Little is known directly about the Pharisees before the time of the New Testament. Josephus in *Antiquities of the Jews*, written at the beginning of the second century C.E., describes the place of the Pharisees' doctrines in the spectrum of Jewish belief in Palestine:

> Now at this time there were three schools of thought (*haireseis*) among the Jews, which held different opinions concerning human affairs; the first being that of the Pharisees, the second that of the Sadducees, and the third that of the Essenes. As to the Pharisees, they say that certain events are the work of fate but not all; as to the other events, it depends upon ourselves whether they shall take place or not. The Essenes, however, declare that Fate is mistress of all things, and that nothing befalls men unless it be in accordance with her degree. But the Sadducees do away with Fate, holding that there is no such thing and that human actions are not achieved in accordance with her decree, but that all things lie within our power, so that we ourselves are responsible for our well-being, while we suffer misfortune through our own thoughtlessness.   (13.171–173)

This is a peculiar description of the sects of Judea. The Essenes were only secondarily a fatalistic group by virtue of their overwhelming apocalypticism. But Josephus is writing for the benefit of philosophically educated Roman readers, not for the Jews, and his attention to Hellenistic philosophical values distorts the picture of the group he describes. Josephus's report on the Pharisees has the same problem. The rabbis of the third century C.E. and thereafter, when the rabbinic record is clear, believed that humanity was subject to fate in some in some things but that it had free will in moral decisions, so there is a rough correspondence between rabbinic doctrines and Josephus's description of the Pharisees. But it is unlikely that they expressed themselves in this way. Josephus does not attempt to capture the real qualities of the Pharisaic movement, even when describing his contemporaries, because he almost entirely ignores the legal and cultic aspects of the movement, as well as its sectarian rules.

Josephus's description of the Pharisees' history is even more perplexing. For instance, according to his story of the enmity between the Pharisees and John Hyrcanus, one of the principal Maccabean kings, the majority of the Pharisees had no objection to Hyrcanus, but at least one member, Eleazar, objected to Hyrcanus's assumption of the high priestly office. Hyrcanus became incensed at the Pharisees when they refused to put Eleazar to death for this insult: "Though many disapproved of Eleazar's actions, the Pharisees were lenient in the enforcement of punishments." Josephus maintains that the Pharisees' leniency was one of many laws handed down (*paredosan*) to which the Sadducees would not assent because they were not expressly written in Scripture.[1] By use of the term "tradition" (*paradosis*) Josephus signals his awareness that the Pharisees were already known for their special oral traditions—the Greek word itself implies oral traditions—and Josephus certainly means to contrast "tradition" with the "written law." But the technical term *Torah shebe'al peh*, "oral law," of the rabbinic period would not necessarily have been appropriate to the time of Hyrcanus. Josephus makes clear that the essential difference between Pharisees and Sadducees is not merely their position regarding providence but also tradition. The Pharisees usually shared power with the Sadducees until Josephus's day, when the Pharisees' party represented the people, while the Saducees represented only the aristocratic few.

The New Testament takes a perspective on the Pharisees that is hard to reconcile with Josephus. In the New Testament the Pharisees are often paired with the "scribes," an occupational group with whom they probably overlapped, and Pharisaic political maneuverings are scarcely discussed. Paul and the Gospels both attest to the existence of traditions beyond Scripture among the Pharisees. The Pharisees are to be found around the synagogues (Mark 1:21); they proclaim the traditions of the elders (Mark 7; Matthew 15); and they insist that God alone, not Jesus, can forgive sins (Mark 3:22; Matthew 9:2-4; Luke 5:20–21). Therefore, they do not condone the picking of grain (Mark 2:23) or healing of chronic diseases on the Sabbath (Mark 3:1–2); they do not eat with unwashed hands (Mark

7:1–8); they determine which oaths are binding (Mark 7:9); they assert that Elijah must come before the son of man (Mark 9:9–10); they allow divorce (Mark 10:2–4); and they disapprove of Jesus' anti-Temple stance (Mark 11:15–16).[2]

Matthew, writing at the height of the first century Jewish-Christian controversy, goes further in describing the Pharisees. They are said to be zealous in making proselytes, tithing, pursuing matters of ritual cleanliness and uncleanliness, and upholding righteousness. They ostracised members of the synagogues who challenged their authority. They took pride in the observance of law and gained seats of honor in public celebrations by means of their charity, fasting, and public prayer. Matthew scorns these ideas, maintaining that they are marks of hypocrisy.

Josephus does not give the same kind of detail about Pharisaic life as the New Testament because his Roman audience did not understand or care about Jewish ritual. But as Jacob Neusner pointed out, removal from the New Testament of the obvious Christian bias against the Pharisees leaves a picture that matches the Mishnaic literature on the Pharisees' concern with Sabbath rest, ritual cleanliness, eating, and tithing.[3] Thus there are two basic descriptions of the Pharisees, a religious description and a political description.

It would be wrong to conclude that the Pharisees were at one time largely a political movement and that they gave up political interests as they took on more and more sacral characteristics. This would be a misreading of Josephus who, even though he changes his opinion of the Pharisees, is interested primarily in their political maneuverings and not in the religious side of their character. Furthermore, the New Testament, some of whose traditions go back as far as 30 C.E., is a closer observer of the Pharisees' religious life than is Josephus, who wrote at the end of the first and beginning of the second century. Josephus uses historical sources and traditions to his own benefit in his recounting of early Pharisaic history in the first century B.C.E. The parties and sects in that society were both political and religious, there being no essential separation between the two. Even though Josephus himself subtly changes his opinion about the Pharisees, there is no reason to assume that the Pharisees underwent a sudden change.[4] Rather, the aims of the Pharisees, politically and religiously, were always in consonance. Different writers are chiefly concerned with one side of the Pharisees' character at the expense of the other. What changes is therefore the purpose of the writers who are describing Pharisees. Josephus is interested primarily in their political and philosophical values, while the writers of the New Testament are more interested in their religious ideas.

The reports about the Pharisees in Josephus and the New Testament are important in studying the Pharisees, because all rabbinic traditions are almost impossible to date. Few rabbinic reports are singled out as coming from the first century. Rather they come from almost every period in the first five hundred years of the Common Era and, as Jacob Neusner showed, reflect the editorial assumptions of the latest traditions far more than the earlier ones.[5] This is the same problem that plagues the evaluation of early Christian texts and underlines the irony of using the primary texts of each religion for the historical reconstruction of traditions of the other. Since the New Testament is datable to the first century, written within a much narrower period than the rabbinic ones, and is redacted a century earlier than the earliest rabbinic text, the Mishnah in 220 C.E., it is better evidence for the state of affairs within the Jewish community—if allowances are made for Christian disapproval—than the Jewish material is for early Christianity.

One characteristic upon which all sources agree is the Pharisaic reliance on *"paradosis"* or tradition, which by the time of the codification of the Mishnah had crystalized into an explicit doctrine of the oral law. The Pharisees claimed not only that they were entrusted to transmit the Torah constitution but that they had the exclusive right to comment and decide upon its authoritative meaning. In order to substantiate this claim, they expressed the idea that oral law went back to the Mosaic revelation itself and had been transmitted orally from Moses to them, not to the priests or apocalyptic Jews. Though they claimed that prophecy had ceased and thus there could be no legitimate contemporary prophets, they also claimed that all Israelites were the sons of prophets, heirs to the legal-prophetic writings. As is clear from their self-defined lineage, they felt that their biblical exegesis was the true descendant of prophetic insight. The priests, who had transmitted much ancient law and were responsible partners in the second Temple government, were in Pharisaic eyes merely cultic functionaries. This was a daring perspective for the early Pharisees, giving them a pretext for taking over the reins of government, which lay largely in the hands of the more Hellenized priestly class.

It is impossible to be sure whether the oral law was so-called because originally it was forbidden to be written down or merely because it had started its existence in oral form. Everything from rabbinic hands is now written. Therefore, the promulgation around 200 C.E. of the first rabbinic document, the Mishnah of Rabbi Judah the Prince, was an epochal event. In the first and second centuries, the Pharisaic practice of deriving rulings about contemporary customs from the written text of the Bible by means of imaginative principles of exegesis and then claiming that the interpretation was the original intention was analogous to the practices of other sects. Nevertheless, the oral law was uniquely suited for Pharisaic-rabbinic purposes. Highly legal and highly technical by comparison to apocalyptic or early Christian writing, the oral law gained adherents as the Pharisees gained respect. Though difficult to understand, its principles were derived from experience, reason, and precedent. They were divinely inspired but not deliberately puzzling or ecstatically received in the same way as apocalypticism. Nor were these principles secret. They were therefore more available to ordinary Jews. They represented life as most rural Jews knew it. Yet into the third and fourth centuries priests, landowners, and even lay Israelites turned to the rabbi only for a limited range of issues.

Equally important was the claim of Pharisees and rabbis that they were vested with authority to decide the meaning of legislation. Again and again the Pharisaic movement challenged the simple word of Scripture in an attempt to make the laws of Scripture more applicable to the society of their own day. By this means, as Ellis Rivkin showed, the Pharisees were able to keep the text of the Bible from becoming authoritative in itself.[6] They essentially tailored a primitive code of the tenth through the fifth centuries B.C.E. to the Hellenistic world by operating as if the Torah's ostensible meaning was but a pathway to the more relevant contemporary meaning, while claiming that they were actually unlocking its true meaning. Unlike the Sadducees, who limited the Torah to civil law and accepted Hellenistic custom in wide areas, the Pharisees extended the Torah into every area, allowing Hellenistic customs into Jewish practice only when they could be supported by their ingenious exegesis of Scripture. Sadducean principles probably coincided more closely with the popular Hellenism of Israel and hence were an earlier accommodation to Hellenistic life. But the Pharisaic scriptural interpretation rather than the Sadducean practice turned out to be the more effective accommodation and achieved wider acceptance because it did not appear to differ from or contravene the Torah, the root metaphor of the society.

Israelite Purity Rules

One of the key aspects of the Pharisaic interpretation of Scripture is its attention to ritual purity. Purity laws were long viewed as a kind of primitive hygiene, because societies tended to taboo substances that were harmful or noxious. An example is the taboo about touching corpses or human excreta. However, cultures often taboo completely harmless substances, while harmful ones are sometimes central to ritual events. Hebrew rules do not always have obvious medical value.

Ritual actions are now thought to function like metaphoric language, which sends dramatized rather than literal messages through the community. When the Pharisees turned their attention to the most arcane laws of the Torah constitution—the laws of ritual purity, tithes, and priestly offerings—they too were codifying a symbolic language system to send a complex social message.

The Hebrew purity laws outlined in Scripture postulated

that several substances were able to transmit states of impurity. The concept is widespread in ancient and modern cultures.[7] Impurity was an undesirable metaphysical state imparted by the material itself. Contact with a corpse might transmit this impurity, but so did childbirth or menstrual blood. Contact with these materials did not make a person a sinner, unless the contact itself was forbidden. For instance, a woman was unclean, not immoral, because of her menstrual period. A man who had sexual relations with her during her menstrual period might be immoral and unclean, since the action both was forbidden and conveyed uncleanness to the man. A woman who consented to sexual relations without being clean by rabbinic standards was also considered a sinner by the rabbis, though the status of a woman according to nonrabbinic custom might have been otherwise. But the status of an impure man was ambiguous. He could have accidentally received uncleanliness in a nonsexual way, or he could have deliberately violated the taboo in having sexual relations with an impure woman; hence, the language of uncleanness expresses immorality as well as impurity.

The impure state was remedied by means of a *mikveh* or ritual bath. The usual Greek translation for the process of ritual bathing was *baptisma;* hence the Christian practice of baptism has Jewish roots. When a sin was committed in the acquisition of impurity, community judgment might be severe. In many apocalyptic writings Jews are criticized for purposely seeking impurity by contact with impure Gentiles. In the *Testament of Levi* 9:10 the priests are enjoined to take wives only from Israel, and the story of the disobedient angels in Enoch 6–16 is partly a heavenly projection of the continually vexing problem of priestly intermarriage.[8] Thus, purity rules functioned to keep Hellenized priests from unstructured relationships with laity or Gentiles and also to keep laity from sexual relations with Gentiles. Many Hellenistic Jews ignored these rulings, occasioning the hostility of the more conservative members of Jewish society.

The Pharisees, along with most apocalypticists, wanted to extend compliance with purity rules. The apocalypticists controlled their own ritual baths, and so did the Pharisees. Insistence on purity was a practical device to enforce endogamy and a symbolic device to oppose contact with Gentiles. Although impurity need not necessarily express immorality, the ambiguity inherent in the concept was often exploited. In some sectors of Israelite society the language of impurity was used to clarify a position that could not be made plain in other ways. Apocalyptic writings stressed that immorality began with impurity. A positive function of purity rules was to enjoin Israel to a special responsibility as priests. A negative function was to keep Israel from close contact with Gentiles and especially from intermarriage.

The Hebrew tithe offerings were special duties or taxes on produce that were owed to the priests. The Pharisees refused to eat food from which the tithes had not been properly taken and insisted that all who joined their group be equally responsible. Neusner pointed out that the meaning of these actions in Hellenistic times is seen in the function and purpose to which they were put.[9] The Pharisees had to live near each other, forming small clubs called *havuroth* (singular: *havurah*), whose members ate together in order to ensure that none of them ate food which was unsuitable because the tithes had not been properly paid before consumption. The function of these rules was therefore to set off the Pharisees from the rest of Israelite society. The Essenes were set off by purity rules as well. They justified their beliefs by saying that the angels would help them fight against the sons of darkness only if they maintained heavenly standards of purity. Unlike the Essenes, the Pharisees did not live in isolation in monastic communities; they lived in the society, separated from it only by their rules of commensality—that is, eating together—and purity. Purity rules therefore kept them from impure tables and bedsides, without removing them from society. The Pharisaic model was eventually adopted as the ideal model for Jewish life in Diaspora, but not until the success of rabbinic Judaism itself.

The message of purity rules was based on the biblical injunction to Jews to separate from the other nations and become priests. In other words, each ordinary Jew was himself to behave as if he had to keep the rules of priestly purity. He had to be as ritually fit as possible to perform the sacrificial acts in the Temple. The purpose of these rules was to take the biblical injunction literally. Thus, the Pharisees believed in the sanctity of all Israel and passionately affirmed the obligation of all Jews, even those who were not from a priestly family, to keep themselves pure, as befit a priest of the Lord.

Hebrew society, like many non-Western societies, also contained a series of food prohibitions, including among other rules not eating blood, a kid seethed in its mother's milk, nor any of the birds and mammals that themselves violate these rules by predation. The Pharisaic-rabbinic party greatly expanded these ordinances, directing that the slaughter of all *kosher* ("ritually acceptable") animals be done in a humane way, and that meat and milk be kept strictly separate, as a safeguard against violating the biblical rules. The Bible says not to eat a young goat boiled in its mother's milk; it says nothing about keeping separate utensils for meat and milk or about not eating a fowl, which provides no milk for its young, at the same meal as cheese. Yet as the rules were interpreted, poultry was treated like meat and cheese was treated like milk, so that combining them became illegal as well. The Pharisaic-rabbinic expression of these rules illustrates what the rabbis called "making a fence around the Torah," setting up rules that prevented the inadvertent violation of Torah statutes.

These food rules were extensions of the same considerations that held the *havuroth* together. The biblical rules about acceptable slaughtering were extended beyond their original biblical symbolism of sacrifice to encompass the table of every Jew. The prohibition against eating blood, reflecting that only God has control over life, also emphasized the separation and sanctity of every Jewish home. The elaboration of the rules separating meat and milk had the same function, as did the rules requiring that only properly tithed produce be eaten, especially in countries other than Judea, where tithing obligations did not apply. Purity laws had a functional meaning for Pharisees. They separated Pharisees from the less pious and therefore provided cultural boundary markers for the areas of

Jewish life that were to be held sacrosanct from acculturation. As Pharisaism became rabbinism, the rules proliferated.

It is extremely difficult for a modern society with few rituals of this type to understand the complex messages implied by Pharisaic concepts of purity. In fact, Christian writing has traditionally portrayed the Pharisees as practicing a hypocritical religion, interested only in the forms, not in the substance of religion. This prejudice has kept many in the West from appreciating the value of ritual forms in any religion, not just Pharisaism. But these ritual actions are typical of much of the world's religious practice.

In the context of the first century C.E., the Pharisaic practice of Hebrew purity had the function of separating the Pharisees from their Hellenistic social context and imposing on them a high degree of group coherence. It also acknowledged the traditional role of the priests by having the duties payable to the priests properly set aside. Therefore, it supported the established social order, though it subverted that order to Pharisaic purposes. After the Temple had ceased to exist, the Pharisaic practice of purity in fact idealized the Temple and the social order that had maintained it. More important, it raised the ritual status of those Pharisees who practiced purity. Just as upward mobility can be achieved in modern society by means of higher income or more tasteful spending of newly gotten financial resources, so too upward mobility could be achieved in Israel by seeking greater ritual purity. The Pharisees represented many in the trades classes, as did the early Christians. Just as the Christians with an ambiguous status could remove that ambiguity by entering the Christian community, so the Pharisaic Jews could raise their status and eliminate ambiguity by taking on a higher ritual obligation. But the mechanism for the two groups differed.

Western societies contain no anologues to Hebrew purity laws, but Eastern cultures have them. Although Hindu purity rules are quite different from Hebrew ones, they were similarly manipulated by upwardly mobile groups in the twentieth century. Many untouchables, who had no stake at all in the caste system, became rich in the leather and shoe business from the burgeoning British trade, simply because, unlike high-caste Hindus, they had nothing to lose by touching these substances. It was not long before their new-found economic status brought about their desire for a higher ritual status. The Jatavs, for instance, soon found evidence that they were actually from the warrior Kshatriya caste and had fallen to untouchable status through an accident of history. The myth of fallen origins therefore functioned as a bid for higher sacral power. In the end, however, the Jatavs gained more from joining the labor movement, since most higher-caste Indians were not impressed by their exegesis. The Jatavs' attempt at Sanskritization to improve their ritual status paralleled the Pharisaic attempt at sanctification. Since traditional Jews all over the world still follow the rules that the Pharisees began, their effort was more successful than the Jatavs'.[10]

The Destruction of the Temple

The destruction of the second Temple in 70 C.E. was a major turning point in the history of Judaism, ending the institution of animal sacrifice and the primary cultic service to God for the past one thousand years and more. Because the Temple had been part of the complex of government destroyed along with Jerusalem, the entire machinery of the state had to be reconstituted. It fell to the Pharisees to accomplish this task. During the refurbishing of Pharisaic institutions for a new national purpose, the institutions of rabbinic Judaism were born. Other varieties of Judaism fared less well than the rabbinic, sometimes because they could not survive or had no interest in representing all Jews, and this left the rabbis more and more in charge of the people.

Since the Temple had been destroyed once before, there was a precedent for coping with the crisis, but the precedent was not particularly comforting. According to the most common view at the time, the first Temple had been destroyed for the sins of idolatry. Disobedience to God, though not often idolatry, was again used as the prime justification for the destruction of the second Temple. Josephus argues that the destruction was a punishment for the sins of the Zealot party, which had set off the first revolt. Furthermore, many of the sects of Judaism in the first century, in opposing the Temple, had pointedly raised the issue of the Temple's sanctity. The destruction of the Temple merely confirmed their opinions. In other words, the crisis brought on by the destruction of the Temple was both a religious and a political one.

The political crisis was soon resolved. A *modus vivendi* was worked out with the Romans, and though Jerusalem remained in ruins with many Jews killed or enslaved as a result of the revolt, government was re-established within the Palestinian Jewish community. The religious question needed a more innovative answer. For Judaism, the Pharisees were the ones who bridged the gap between a fractured national and a continuing religious existence; and in the process, they transformed Judaism into a universal religion. The Christians as well transformed their sectarian status into another kind of universal religion.

Various Judean groups responded differently to the challenge of the fall of the Temple. Apocalypticists, Sadducees, Essenes, Christians, and Pharisees all had to deal with the issue of the destruction of the nation-state. The destruction of Jerusalem was exactly what the apocalypticists had predicted. Like the literary prophets of the Bible, the apocalypticists would have been canonized on the basis of their perspicacity if the expected apocalypse had followed. As it was, the final consummation, of which the destruction of the Temple was just the first stage, did not arrive. Nor did the destruction bring about a new world order in which the righteous were saved. The result was a partial disconfirmation of apocalyptic beliefs: "So the Lord confirmed his word, which he spoke against us and against our judges who judged Israel, and against our kings and against our princes and against the whole of Israel and Judah . . . Righteousness belongs to the Lord our God but confusion of face to us and our fathers, as at this day. All those calamities with which the Lord threatened us have come upon us" (Baruch 2:1, 6–7). The apocalypticists' explanation for this failure, however, was the traditional one: "Why is it, O Israel

... that you are in the land of your enemies? ... You have forsaken the foundation of wisdom. If you had walked in the way of the Lord, you would be dwelling in peace forever" (Baruch 3:10–12).

Apocalypticism did not disappear. Much apocalyptic writing simply took a new, more comforting tone. Like literary prophecy, with which it had affinities, the message of apocalypticism turned to foreseeing the eventual reward of the righteous: "But I, how can I help you. For he who brought these calamities upon you will deliver you from the hand of your enemies . . . for I send you out with sorrow and weeping, but God will give you back to me with joy and gladness forever" (Baruch 4:17, 18:23).

The Qumranic responses differed, because in a sense the Qumran community had already replaced the Temple with the community, since it called itself the "holy of holies" and "the holy place." The Dead Sea Scroll community did not survive the revolt. Even though it was a casualty of that first war against Rome, its explanation for the irrelevance of the Jerusalem Temple exemplified the successful pattern that both Christianity and rabbinic Judaism followed in explaining the destruction of the Temple. Both Christians and rabbis changed the locus of purity from the Temple itself to the community of believers.

Each different Christian community designed a response to the destruction of the Temple to fit its own interpretation of history. Within Christianity the Temple characteristically became either the body of Christ, the church, or the Christian community itself. Later, Christianity used the passion of Jesus as justification for an end to the entire sacrificial cult. Jesus' sacrifice on the cross became the perfect sacrifice of the perfect priest on the perfect altar. This view is advanced in the Letter to the Hebrews, a late entry into the Christian canon and in fact neither a letter not an authentic piece of Paul's writing. Yet it meditates on the scriptural passages concerning the tabernacle, the institution that preceded the Temple, in order to demonstrate why Christ brought about the end of the cult of animal sacrifice. In the Revelation of John, the New Testament's prime example of apocalyptic writing, the new world envisioned at the end of time contains a new Jerusalem but not a new Temple.

The Christian community at this time was also involved in a fierce fight with the growing rabbinic community, which predisposed Christians to see the destruction of the Temple as a final punishment of the Jews for the sin of having rejected the fulfillment of Scriptures. The Christian community saw the destruction of the Temple as both a sign of the approaching end and an actual punishment of the Jews, but they spoke no words of comfort. In the liturgy, Jews said, "On account of our sins we were exiled from our land." The Christians agreed, as if saying, ironically "On account of *your* sins *you* were exiled from your land."

The response of the Pharisees to the destruction of the Temple can only be inferred from later rabbinic materials. But the story of Yohanan ben Zakkai and his disciple, Joshua ben Hananiah, gives the main outlines of the rabbinic view of the loss:

> Once as Rabbi Yohanan ben Zakkai was coming from Jerusalem, Rabbi Joshua followed after him and saw the temple in ruins.
>
> "Woe unto us," Rabbi Joshua cried, "For the place where the iniquities of Israel were atoned is destroyed!"
>
> "My son," Rabban Yohanan ben Zakkai said to him, "Do not grieve. We have another atonement as effective as this. And what is it? It is acts of lovingkindness, as it said: 'I desire mercy and not sacrifice.' " (The Fathers according to Rabbi Nathan 6)

For the rabbis, preserving the Temple was not an end in itself. They taught that there was another means of reconciliation between God and Israel, doing good deeds or "acts of lovingkindness," so the Temple and its cult, though tragically lost, were not necessary. In place of the Temple's sacred space, the table of every Jew was made sacred through the elaboration of rules for purity. Other aspects of the Temple service were transferred to the *mikveh* and the synagogue, a move for which there were already ample precedents.

Pharisaism as a Native Response to Hellenization

The Pharisees did not become rabbis on the day after the Temple was destroyed. Pharisaic Judaism made a bid to take over the responsibilities of earlier institutions. According to Neusner, the development of rabbinic traditions after the Pharisees was designed to unite Israel under a code of law that in its earliest layers was concerned with sectarian issues. There is even evidence for the arrival of rabbinic Judaism in Egypt, but only after the more varied Hellenistic Egyptian community had been almost totally destroyed by war, pogroms, and attrition.

The development of rabbinic traditions was hardly a straightforward process. The earliest stages may well have involved the codification of laws on the issues of most interest to the Pharisees—Sabbath law, purity, and tithing. Marriage and divorce law were also issues of primary interest to the early rabbis, for along with matters of ritual purity these rules of personal status defined membership in the Jewish community.

Together with this legal activity in the spheres of personal status went an enormous effort to discuss and record matters of the defunct sacrificial system in the Temple and purity issues depending upon the Temple. The motivations for this effort included a desire to be closely associated with the running of the Temple, should the Temple be soon rebuilt; an antiquarian interest in preserving laws; and even an interest in reconstructing the legal system with the rabbis more firmly in control. As it turned out, this whole enterprise was theoretical, for the Bar Kokhba Revolt made it painfully clear that the Temple would not soon be rebuilt. Yet the rabbinic commentary on Temple law continued, serving as a model for an idealized Temple populated by idealized assemblies of priests and rabbis, when God should choose to rebuild it in the messianic age.

For instance, in the Mishnah tractate devoted to Passover, only the last chapter is concerned with the liturgy of Passover. The first chapters deal mostly with the rules surrounding the Passover Temple sacrifice. Neusner suggested that the Temple itself, once it ceased to exist, formed a kind of imaginative locus for rabbinic method. These debates about Temple law were not an antiquarian interest but an imaginative enterprise for preserving the Temple mentally, transmuted by legal dispute as a new ideal for posterity. The Mishnah gives almost no narrative of the Temple. Instead, the Temple is reimagined, summoned to life through the application of legal method to the laws, precepts, and traditions surrounding the Temple cult. The Temple did not become a symbolic instruction to mystery, as the Bible became for Philo; it became an imagined place in which scholars could construct the Temple's glory through legal discussion.

The period of rabbinic activity surrounding Rabbi Judah the Prince around 200 C.E. is the foundation of rabbinism. It took a century and a half to go from Pharisaic sectarianism at the destruction of the Temple to the Mishnah of Rabbi Judah the Prince as the first canonical, analytically organized codification of law outside the Bible for the Jewish community. That codification, which served as the basis of both the Palestinian and the Babylonian Talmuds, was a much more ramified code than the sectarian Pharisees needed, and with it the rabbis became the principal legal spokesmen for the entire Jewish community.

The rabbinic writings that have survived were edited in the second century C. E. and later. They were redacted in an atmosphere of confident, albeit incomplete control by the Pharisees of the Jewish community. That sense of control was naturally projected backward onto traditions that had been laid down in totally different circumstances, some when Pharisaism was merely a sectarian movement in Judaism. By the second century it was taken for granted that the rabbinic movement was the majority movement in Judaism. The power and function of the competing sects in a complete and whole nation-state were forgotten. Indeed, the original social function for such sects, to ensure that conflicting perspectives in the Hellenistic world were expressed in a healthy and functional way, was taken over by the rabbinic movement itself. Schools and factions within the rabbinic movement fought each other with clearly defined rules for scriptural exegesis.

From another perspective the Pharisees were representative of the second stage of Hellenization. The Maccabean Revolt had ended the primary stage of Hellenization when the Maccabees, with popular support, said no to the proposal to make Jerusalem a *polis* in the Greek fashion. The Torah would continue as the constitution of the state, guaranteeing that the laws of the city would depend upon the divine word of God as set down in His books. The Judeans did not wish to be governed by a tribunal of educated men, like the *boulé* of Athens. However, the rabbinic movement, in putting the interpretation of the law in the hands of an educated class open to anyone, set the stage for rule by another kind of council, without threatening the cancellation of the Torah constitution. This was not the same as a democracy, but the oligarchical class had an open membership. Technically, the rulings of the Pharisees and the rabbis came from God. But in practice, the rulings were made by the majority:

> R. Eliezer used every argument to substantiate his opinion, but they [the other rabbis] would not accept them. He said, "If the law is as I have argued, may this carob tree argue for me." The carob tree uprooted itself and moved a hundred cubits from its place. Some say it moved four hundred cubits. They said, "From a tree no proof can be brought." Then he said, "May the canal prove it." The water of the canal flowed backwards. They said, "From a canal no proof may be brought." Then he said, "May the walls of this House of Study prove it." Then the walls of the house bent inwards, as if they were about to fall. R. Joshua rebuked the walls, and said to him, "If the learned dispute about the law, what has that to do with you?" So, to honor R. Joshua, the walls did not fall down, but to honor R. Eliezer, they did not become straight again. Then R. Eliezer said, "If I am right, may the heavens prove it." Then a heavenly voice said, "What have you against R. Eliezer? The law is always with him." Then R. Joshua got up and said, "It is not in heaven (Deut. 30:12)." What did he mean by this? R. Jeremiah said, "The Torah was given to us at Sinai. We do not attend to this heavenly voice. For it was already written in the Torah at Mt. Sinai that, 'By the majority you are to decide (Ex. 23:2).'" R. Nathan met Elijah and asked him what God did in that hour. Elijah replied, "He

laughed and said, 'My children have defeated me.'" (b. Baba Metzia 59b)

Although the story contains clear folkloric motifs, it still gives evidence of strongly held rabbinic values. The playful, even humorous narration of Rabbi Eliezer's miracles is emphasized by the meeting of Rabbi Nathan with the prophet Elijah which exposes even God's amusement. But the moral of the story is serious, too. It demonstrates the rabbinic suspicion of all sources of authority dependent on charismatic or miraculous claims, whether they be outside the rabbinic movement or even, as here, within it. The story of Rabbi Eliezer is meant to illustrate how to handle conflict with people claiming miraculous support for their religious opinions. The claims of such men, including holy men or even Christians as well as rabbis, are to be evaluated by the rules of legal discourse and decided by vote.

The story also illustrates a change in the way conflict was handled within the Jewish community, as a response to the destruction of the Judean state. In place of the old national system with its wide spectrum of political-religious positions—including Pharisees, Sadducees, Essenes, Christians, and a variety of other sects—the rabbis offered a limited democratization, oligarchical rule by an educated professional class of legal experts. The democratization of the interpretation of Torah did not eliminate all conflict. The rabbis still had to deal with conflict with other factions within the Jewish community. Although lack of conflict would have been impossible, stability involved making sure that the conflict was handled by rabbinic courts through rabbinic methods of exegesis. The rule of the majority, not miraculous actions, was to be the basic system for power brokerage.

This system was at once more differentiated and more controllable than the old sectarian system. Enforcing greater religious uniformity within, it also provided the necessary social and political control over a group under continuous suspicion by the Romans after the two unsuccessful revolts. Conflicts over the right to decree a new month, based on sightings of a new moon, or other issues were far less severe or dangerous to the Roman peace than the earlier sectarian conflicts between Sadducee, Essene, and Pharisee. The definition of allowable conflict had narrowed considerably in postwar Judah, because the disastrous wars against Rome and the spread of Christianity had made the rabbinic community chary of messianic or other movements of national independence. History had proved to them undeniably that the people of Israel were not destined soon to be the masters of their own land. Given the Roman forces, messianism and apocalyticism were dangerous to the community in the late second century and thereafter. The rabbis cautioned never to give up faith that the messiah would come, but they warned that, if one were ploughing a field and heard the report that the messiah had arrived, one should "finish ploughing and then go to see if the messiah has come." The point of the advice was clear: though one must not give up hope that the messiah will come, it would be foolhardy to give easy credence to anyone fomenting rebellion or heresy.

In like manner, the Mishnah of Rabbi Judah the Prince around 200 C.E. contains no reference to angels. It stays close to the categories of legal dispute. Though it makes no attempt to record all disputes, it makes critical distinctions and argues critical cases. As a code of community procedures, it presents principles and exemplars for cases rather than particular cases. The Mishnah attempts to be the guide, not for the Pharisaic community but for the nation as a whole. All who would accept its principles are included. Yet apocalyptic groups and groups with differing basic hypotheses about the meaning of Torah, such as Christians, could not easily accept the rabbinic rules for conflict resolution and were ostracized.

A more unified, less dissenting Jewish community was advantageous both to the Jewish community and to the Roman rulers. Rather than desiring the absence of unity in Judaism, the Romans desired stronger authority to prevent further rebellion and to guarantee the collection of imposts and taxes. A less conflicted Jewish community, one based on Mishnaic standards of law and theology and settling all conflicts by the exegetical priniciples laid out in Mishnaic and talmudic debate, replaced the earlier sectarian community as the common Jewish experience.

Judaism as a Religion of Personal Piety

The transformation of Judaism by the rabbis from a national ideology into a Hellenistic spiritual community was a characteristic development of the Hellenistic world, where some national religions, at first devoted to agriculture and the maintenance of the state, were successfully distanced from their national roots and transformed into religions of personal salvation. The cult of Isis, for instance, was a native Egyptian cult that originally celebrated the fertility of the Nile flood. In Hellenistic times it became a widespread, secret society, initiating its members all over the Roman Empire into quasi-secret rites with meals that guaranteed not the crops but the salvation and well-being of the initiate. These cultic meals were apparently based on the Greek tradition of formal dining exemplified in the *Symposium* of Plato, but they were augmented by special rituals suited to each mystery cult. The mystery religions also staged public parades and displays to attract new converts.

The mystery religions were quite successful. Among the educated classes in the burgeoning Roman Hellenistic world, personal piety replaced the old corporate concept of the good of the state. Besides the religion of Isis, the rites of Cybele, and the astral cult of Mithras, a myriad of other mysteries flourished in the Hellenistic world, all loosely remodeled on the Eleusinian mysteries outside Athens. The philosophical schools of this time also functioned as much like religions as like academic disciplines.

This pattern of spirituality suited Christianity as it traveled throughout the Hellenistic world. The transformation itself was a question more of emphasis than of a complete change in orientation. The eucharist memorial to Jesus was eventually transformed into a sacred meal resembling the mysteries. The dying and reviving messiah began to function in the same way as the dying and reviving vegetation gods in the transformed pagan agricultural religions. In the case of Christianity, the symbolism of rebirth into immortality was expressed through the ideas of personal resurrection, immortality, and ascension.

Before Christianity, Hellenistic Judaism had already accomplished part of this transformation. In a more limited way, the transformation can be seen in the kind of spirituality developed by the rabbis. Most varieties of Judaism were influenced by Hellenistic spirituality, since it was characteristic of the highest forms of Hellenistic thought. Philo, for instance, viewed the Exodus events as symbolic of the salvation from materiality which all Jews could experience if they read the Bible correctly and enacted its ordinances. For Philo, Moses was the spiritual hero par excellence, who, in ascending Mount Sinai to get the commandments from God, transcended material existence and gained a measure of divinity:

> What is the meaning of the words, "They appeared to God in the place and they ate and drank." (Ex. 24:11b) Having attained to the face of the father, they do not remain in any mortal place at all, for all such (places) are profane and polluted, but they send and make a migration to a holy and divine place which is called by another name, *logos*. Being in this place through the steward they see the master in a lofty and clear manner, envisioning God with the keen-sighted eyes of the mind . . . What is the meaning of the words, "Come up to Me to the mountain and be there?" This signifies that a holy soul is divinized by ascending, not to the air, to the ether, or to heaven (which is higher than all), but to a region above the heavens, and beyond the world where there is no place but God. And he determines the stability of the removal by saying: "Be there "(thus demonstrating the placelessness and the unchanging habitation of his divine place). (*Questions and Answers on Exodus* 39)

The purpose of the theophany is divine ascent, leading to immortalization. Philo's comments suggest the kinds of traditions that must have been current in the Hellenistic Jewish communities of the first century C.E. These traditions set up a paradigm for the believer to transcend materiality through mystical and philosophical contemplation of the text of the Bible. The communal meal of the Passover Seder served as an occasion to contemplate these divine truths for anyone with Philo's philosophical bent. There was no need to posit a new invention of secret Jewish mystery cult, for the Seder itself easily became an allegory emphasizing personal piety in Philo's thinking. The ritual derived naturally from the passage on eating and drinking in Exodus 24.

The rabbis naturally were influenced by the same religious sensibilities. They developed a Seder meal, however, that spiritualized the historical events of salvation from bondage. Using customs common in the Jewish community, they standardized a special liturgy called the Haggadah:

> Rabban Gamaliel used to say: Whosoever has not said (the verses concerning) these three things at Passover has not fulfilled his obligation. And these are they: Passover, unleavened bread, and bitter herbs: "Passover"—because God passed over the houses of our fathers in Egypt; "unleavened bread"—because our fathers were redeemed from Egypt; "bitter herbs"—because the Egyptians embittered the lives of our fathers in Egypt. In every generation a man must so regard himself as if he came forth himself out of Egypt, for it is written, *And thou shalt tell thy son in that day, saying: It is because of that which the Lord did for me when I came forth out of Egypt.* Therefore are we bound to give thanks, to praise, to glorify, to honour, to exalt, to extol, and to bless him who wrought all these wonders for our fathers and for us. He brought us from bondage to freedom, from sorrow to gladness, and from mourning to a Festival day, and from darkness to great light, and from servitude to redemption; so let us say before him *Hallelujah.* (*Mishnah Pesahim* 10:5)

The rabbinic Passover liturgy, the Haggadah, is a clear example of a formal Greek dinner party and philosophical evening of discussion, much like the one described in Plato's dialogue *The Symposium.* The rabbinic version of the Symposium described in the Passover Haggadah has been entirely adapted for Jewish purposes.

In the modern Passover liturgy there is no mention at all of Moses. This is because of the dangerously exalted role Moses played in Hellenistic Judaism. Philo says that Moses was virtually divine. The Samaritans also exalted the role of Moses. Consequently, the rabbis felt the need to expunge Moses from the Haggadah. In their eyes, Passover is the story of *God*'s deliverance of the people, not the story of the divinization of a single man, no matter how admirable he may be. By creating a liturgy which states that every Jew should look upon him or herself as having experienced the saving events of the Exodus personally through the dinner ritual dramatizing the event, the rabbis spiritualized the events of Israel's history to symbolize personal and communal salvation for each member of the Jewish people. Relying on the central events and meanings of the holiday, they de-emphasized the old national aspects of the holiday and transformed them into a mythological drama of salvation.

The rabbis transformed the other national festivals into celebrations of universal religious values as well. They changed the meaning of the Hanukkah holiday from an independence day of the Hasmonean dynasty into a celebration of God's deliverance by miracle. The eight day duration of one day's quantity of oil, the famous miracle dramatized by the Hanukkah menorah, was not nearly as dangerous a miracle as those confirming Rabbi Eliezer's legal opinion and the Hanukkah miracle had the additional function of giving religious sanction to a popular feast. Nevertheless, the rabbis were hardly enthusiastic proponents of the holiday, as evidenced by the lack of a tractate devoted to its celebration in the Mishnah. Perhaps they felt that its theme of national independence against Greco-Roman forces was too dangerous for the Jewish community. In other, less sensitive times, however, the same themes have ensured its continued celebration.

So, too, the rabbis changed the older, more important holidays. Besides Passover, the two other pilgrimage days—Sukkoth, which includes Rosh Hashanah ("New Year") and Yom Kippur ("The Day of Atonement"), and Shavuoth ("Weeks" or "Pentecost")—were transformed from agricultural festivals, into days of spiritual inwardness. The fall harvest holidays Rosh Hashanah, Yom Kippur, and Sukkoth were dedicated to atonement and self-searching even more than they had been in biblical days. The barley harvest, Shavuoth, was turned into a commemoration of the giving of the Torah to Moses.

The Christian community acted similarly in transforming the Jewish holidays into commemorations of the events in the life of Jesus. Most obviously, Pesach ("Passover") became Easter, the day on which the savior was resurrected. The Sabbath was eventually transferred from Saturday to Sunday on the basis of Easter. Shavuoth (" Pentecost") assumed a special significance for the Christian community on account of the outpouring of the spirit, the speaking in tongues, and the ecstatic behavior that occurred when the apostles gathered to celebrate this Jewish holiday (Acts 2). In modern English, Pentecostalism refers to those varieties of Christianity which put heavy emphasis on these ecstatic practices. Yet the relationship between the Christian and Jewish holidays was never completely lost, for the early church fathers often mention Christian temptations to attend daily, Sabbath and holiday synagogue services.

Both Christianity and rabbinic Judaism represented an evolutionary step forward in the Hellenistic time in that they both dictated a new way of life in a complex and changing world.[11] The ways in which Judaism and Christianity evolved, however, were very much affected by the conflicts between them.

❧ VI ❧

Communities
in Conflict

Conflict was characteristic of Jewish Christian relations from
the beginning. Yet the New Testament's many uncomplimentary references to Jews have been misinterpreted by both Jews
and Christians. The argument between Judaism and Christianity was at the beginning largely a family affair. After
Christianity separated from Judaism, the polemical passages in
the New Testament were read in an unhistorical way, as testimony of hatred between two separate religions, when they
should have been read as strife between two sects of the same
religion. Since many Christian communities insist on the literal
truth of the New Testament, the original context of the references has to be clarified to interpret them properly.

There was very little conceptual unity in the earliest Christianity. The doctrines of the Gospel of John, for instance, differ
significantly from those of the gnostic Gospel of Philip and
even from the Gospel of Mark. The communities that valued
the legends of Jesus' genealogy through his father Joseph,
which were probably Jewish, could not have been the same
communities that valued the story of his conception directly
from the Holy Spirit, which were probably Gentile. Since a
variety of Jews were attracted to the new sect, they brought
with them many exegetical styles. Accordingly, traces of Samaritan, Essene, Pharisaic, and even pagan styles of interpretation appear in the early writings of Christianity.

The Charge of Magic

Although some Jews became Christians, the general Jewish reaction to early Christianity was not favorable. Even the New Testament gives evidence that Jews found Christian doctrine to be controversial. On the whole, Jews were not convinced by the message of any of the different varieties of early Christianity. Most Jews opposed the idea of a dying and reviving messiah. In addition, most Jews objected to the doctrine that the Torah constitution, in either its ethical or its ceremonial dimensions, was no longer valid.

One of the earliest charges against Christianity by its Jewish detractors was simply that it was "magic." By this they undoubtedly meant that the stories of Jesus' healings could not be taken at face value. Since God had favored the Temple with His presence and Jesus had opposed the Temple, any power that Jesus possessed must have been satanic instead of divine. Charges of magic and witchcraft tend to multiply when there are highly antagonistic feelings and opposing claims of divine legitimation.[1] When the people in Jesus' time heard stories of miracles, they usually did not distrust them. Rather, if the stories contradicted their own feelings of correct religion, they necessarily ascribed the miraculous power to demonic rather than divine agency.

There was no universal definition of magical procedure in Hellenistic culture, because the charge of magic was an alternative political interpretation of the miracles of a wonder worker. Miracle stories were told about other personages than Jesus in the Mediterranean world, because wonder working was a conventional way to establish a charismatic leader's qualifications. In each case the wonder worker's enemies attributed his powers to magic instead of divinity. This was not pure name-calling. Legally, the use of magic in the Hellenistic world was a criminal offense if the intention was to do harm in some way. When a miracle worker took an antiestablishment line, as those involved in millennial cults invariably did, even such good deeds as healing could be interpreted by the authorities as harmful, because they gave credence to a movement that was against the social order. Therefore, it was a commonplace pattern in the ancient world for popular, charismatic figures to claim miracles and the political establishment to counter with charges of magic.[2] An accusation of magic could serve as the opening of a confrontation, the purpose of which was to clarify both the motivation of the accused and the values of the community. One result of a trial, or even an informal confrontation, was to try to produce clarity for all the various actors. But the truth or falsity of the claim usually depended on the perspective of the actor. Thus, the charge of magic helped distinguish among various groups of people from the perspective of the speaker but did not necessarily imply an observable difference in the actions of the participants. In a narrative about the event, the narrator often defined his own grounds for distinction.

The disputes about Jesus' healings and miracles occurred in this context. The different evangelists interpreted the Jewish charge of magic within their individual narrative frameworks and, in doing so, subtly changed the meaning of the accusation. Generally, they edited the exorcism stories to focus on the entire question of the source of Jesus' power, not merely the charge of magic. In Mark 3:19–27, Matthew 12:22–30, and Luke 11:14–23, three accounts of the incident known as the Beelzebul controversy are narrated, one from each of the three synoptic evangelists. In each account different opinions are ventured about the source of Jesus' power, the phenomenon of magic, and the issues of criticism both inside and outside the early Christian movement.

Jesus' followers raise the first criticism in Mark. Seeing the overwhelming crowds and anticipating the difficulty of feeding them, some of Jesus' own disciples begin to think that Jesus is either insane or in an ecstatic trance, "for they said that he was outside."[3] Only after the situation has been outlined do the scribes of Jerusalem introduce the charge of magic. The scribes are represented as believing that Jesus' power to heal is not from God but from Beelzebul (other versions list him as Beelzebub, meaning "Lord of the Flies"; in any case, the referent is Satan or one of his principal demons.) The logic from the scribes' perspective is that if Jesus were from God, he could not oppose the ideas of the legitimate authorities of Judea. Since he does oppose them, his power must have other sources. The New Testament portrayal, however, does not take the scribes' opinion seriously. Jesus points out that he is casting out demons, so he must be from God, since Satan would not consent to overthrow his own kingdom. This argument makes sense if one assumes a complete dualism, with a unified evil hegemony in opposing to God and the evil demons helping Satan—a presupposition central to the New Testament but not often shared by the Pharisees and certainly not by all Jews. More frequent is the Hellenistic idea that demons could provide both supernatural aid and harm.[4] A unified evil world involved in a cosmic battle with the good is, however, an apocalyptic motif. Mark's argument that Jesus must be divine because he is casting out evil demons is simple and forceful, but it is not the only possible analysis of the events.

According to Mark, those followers who criticize the marvelous deeds of the savior risk blasphemy in the name of the holy spirit, a sin much worse than the accusation of the scribes. For Mark, the charges of insanity and magic are already traditional ones, too authentic or relevant for him to leave out. But Mark has defused them by appending the warnings against internal dissent, which evidently was a more pressing problem for the developing church, as far as he was concerned.

In Luke and Matthew, the controversy is complicated by another argument: "If I cast out demons in the name of Beelzebul, in whose name do your sons exorcise?" This statement implies that there were other Jews who claimed to work similar acts to what Jesus had accomplished and who also claimed divine favor. It argues that Christianity was certainly a valid religion if other kinds of Jewish exorcism were. But the argument reflects a later time when the separation between Judaism and Christianity was more obvious, and its conclusion about magic is purchased at the price of the simpler logic of Mark's "house-divided" version, since there is no longer any assumption of a dualist world where all commerce with demons must be evil.

These later Gospels also fasten on the term *kingdom* which

occurs in the Markan version, converting the story into a prediction about the coming of the Kingdom, the end of time. Because it is a sensitive issue, Matthew even eliminates the original source of the charge in Mark—Jesus' followers—by attributing it to Jesus' enemies, who are for the first time called Pharisees. No doubt this reflects a later time than the period of Jesus when Pharisees were the principal spokesmen for Judaism and could have made such a charge about the Christian stories of Jesus' miracles and healings, based on their conviction that Jesus' power was not from God. The three gospel stories show the development of the issue of magic in the Christian community, as well as the difficulty and ambiguity in defining magic. Even more important, they illustrate the diversity of early Christian thinking in the first century.

Even with these three different discussions, there are some underlying uniformities. Unlike many other wonder-workers, Jesus did not, according to the evangelists, wish to claim the title of *magos*, or "magician." On the contrary, the Gospels represent Jesus' teachings, in addition to the titles of divine favor, as a defense against the accusation of magic.

Rejection of the Torah in the Gospels

The issue of the Torah caused a social breach between Jewish and many Christian communities. The Gospel of Matthew is the most clearly relevant gospel to the divorce between Judaism and Christianity, because it is concerned with the ordinary aspects of Jewish life. It is the most knowledgeable Gospel about Jewish law, especially divorce law, tithing, and purity. At the same time it is the most negative Gospel concerning the Pharisees and the Jewish population as a whole. For instance, Matthew 23 contains the longest denunciations of the Pharisees as hypocrites and includes what has proved to be the most unfortunate comment in the Bible because of its use to persecute Jews throughout the ages: "His blood be upon us and upon our children" (Matthew 27:25).

The Gospel of Matthew reflects one Christian community's opinions about its rupture with Judaism. Matthew feels more conflict with the Pharisees than with any other sect among the Jews. Some time during the first century C.E. the developing Pharisaic community must have run headlong into Matthew's Christian community. The sensitivity of Matthew to issues of Jewish law attests to his Jewish background and to the atmosphere of intense hostility and competition between the groups, for issues of marriage and divorce, the interpretation of the laws of personal status determine whether a person claiming to be Jewish is to be accepted within the Jewish community. Matthew is more aware of these issues and of their effect on communal definition than is Mark, with his apocalyptic sense of finality, or Luke, with his theory of history passing from Jerusalem to Rome through the person of Paul.

Rabbinic References to Christianity

In their writings, rabbinic Jews were no less restrained in their dislike of Christianity than were Christians in their writing about Jews, but they expressed less vituperation. More important, the rabbinic opposition developed at a much later time and was based on a reading of the Gospels rather than on eyewitness accounts of Jesus. There is little explicit polemic against Christianity within rabbinic literature, although many rabbis certainly opposed it. On the surface, therefore, rabbinic literature offers little help in reconstructing the earliest history of the church.

Because Jewish texts were redacted later and under different circumstances than the New Testament, it is hard to date the material and even harder to use it for reconstructing the early history of Jewish-Christian conflict. Censorship of rabbinic texts by Christians during the Middle Ages also eliminated many uncomplimentary references to the developing Christian sect. Even so, the original rabbinic texts, pieced together from versions surviving in Arab countries, contain less antagonism expressed specifically against Christians than does the New Testament against Jews. Probably this difference reflects the fact that for Christianity the continued existence of Judaism was a constant theological problem, whereas for rabbinic Judaism, Christianity represented only one more variety of sectarian heresy. The rabbis often treated heresy with stony silence, as if hoping that it would go away quickly, and certainly wishing not to serve as the unwitting agents for the spread of heretical ideas.

The geographical distributions of Christians and rabbinic Jews also differed. Just as Jesus left his small town in Galilee to be discovered by the world, so the rabbis retired to Galilee to escape the world. When the Mishnah was being written, rabbinic Judaism was centered in Galilee, while Christianity's membership was scattered in the Hellenistic cities of the Roman Empire. Christians certainly met the sizable Jewish communities in these cities as well, but these communities left no systematic literature. The rabbinic movement was just beginning to be felt in Hellenistic cities and was far from predominant. The rabbis did not at first distinguish Christianity from a variety of other Jewish sects.

A compendium of slander against Jesus, the *Toldoth Yeshu*, contains no historical material independent of the New Testament or the Talmud. In fact, it is an anthology of talmudic references assembled for easy use against Christianity. The talmudic references are in turn made up of reactions of Jews upon reading or hearing the stories of the New Testament and do not qualify as an independent historical report. *Toldoth Yeshu* is scurrilous on the subject of Jesus' life and death. It says, for instance, that Mary did not conceive as a virgin; she was merely an unwed mother. It maintains that Jesus' real father was a Roman legionnaire whose name was Panthera, a word meaning "tiger" but probably a pun or a corruption of the Greek word *parthenos*, meaning "virgin." The anthology, which covers the major events of Jesus' life, describes him as a magician.

In these circumstances, trying to identify the contemporary rabbinic and Jewish reaction to the rise of Christianity requires something like detective work. Any discussion of heresy in rabbinic literature, even where Christianity is not mentioned by name, may be obliquely describing Christian beliefs. Hidden in some later rabbinic discussion of heresy may be the clue to the first-century rabbinic views of Christians.

There are two aids to identifying oblique descriptions of Christianity. First, an identifiably Christian doctrine sometimes underlies the heresy that the rabbis discuss. Second, because of its unique composition, Christianity may appear as either a Jewish heresy or a Gentile group, or both, in the commentary: "R. Abahu said: If a man say to you, 'I am God,' he is a liar. If he says '(I am) the Son of Man,' in the end, people will laugh at him. If he says, 'I will go up to heaven,' he says so but he will not do it" (j. Taanith 65b). This may refer to Christian doctrine because the Christians, more than anyone else, were interested in describing a figure known as the son of man, who was alive and who ascended to heaven. Throughout rabbinic literature descriptions like this are the exception rather than the rule. Most of the time the literature outlaws a particular rite or custom: "*Minuth* (=Sectarianism:) He that saith 'I will not go before the ark in colored garments' shall not do so in white garments. (He that refuses to do so) in sandals, shall not do so even barefoot. And he that makes his phylacteries round, it is a danger and there is no fulfilling of the commandment in it. If he place it (the phylacteries) upon his forehead or upon the palm of his hand—lo, this is the way of *minuth*. If he cover it with gold and place it upon his robe—lo, this is the way of the outsiders" (m. Megilah 4:8, 9).

Knowing that the phylacteries are leather straps and boxes used by Jews in weekday morning prayers does not help in identifying these heretics. The practices may have been either individual idiosyncrasies or characteristics of organized sects, groups, or movements. It is impossible to ascertain not only the identity of these sects but the number of different sects implied in the passage. The rabbis find nothing harmful in the practices themselves. For instance, it is acceptable to go before the ark wearing white garments unless that is the only way one is willing to appear before the ark. The rabbis note that the implicit intention and symbolic value of the ritual actions are significant, but do not explain their significance for the heretics. So the context has been lost. Josephus claims that the Essenes wore linen and Philo claims that the Therapeutae wore white, but whether or not these are the groups meant by the rabbis is a moot point.

According to the Palestinian Talmud (j Ber. 9c), people leading services in the synagogue sometimes wanted to leave out prayers mentioning resurrection or the rebuilding of the Temple. Those who denied resurrection were probably not connected with Christianity, although some gnostic Christians denied resurrection in the literal sense. They were more likely Sadducees. But some of those who refused to pray that the earthly Temple be re-established included Christians.

Thus, even when Christianity is implicated, the rabbinic discussions reveal nothing specific about Christianity. They merely show that the rabbinic opposition to sects like Christianity was limited to short condemnations of its beliefs and practices. The rabbis' characteristic mode of controlling Christians was to prevent them from leading synagogue services or from influencing anyone else in the synagogue with their sectarian ways.

According to the rabbinic literature, Gamaliel instructed Samuel the Small to compose a prayer that would silence various kinds of Jewish sectarians. Samuel apparently added a few words to a curse against informers to the Romans which was already said in the synagogue. This prayer, after Samuel's revision, contained a reference to the *minim*, a category that included Christians, though again it did not refer to them exclusively. The prayer was recited in the central eighteen prayers of synagogue rite and was known as the *birkat ha-minim*.[5]

The church fathers mention that the Jews cursed the Christians, both generally and in synagogue services.[6] This report may correspond to Samuel the Small's addition to the prayer against blasphemers and informers. But if the church fathers have that particular prayer in mind, they present the action as if it were directed entirely against Christians. The reason may have been that the Christians were already the most notable of all Jewish heresies, or it may simply have been that church fathers' distaste for the practice prevented them from representing it as accurately as a modern historian would have liked.

Furthermore, John 9:22 reports that the Jews excluded the Christians from the synagogue. This is difficult to square with the rabbinic evidence. In synagogues following the rabbinic rule, sectarians may have been cursed but they were not bodily removed from the synagogue. They were only prevented from saying heretical benedictions when they were leading prayer. It is possible that the nonrabbinic synagogues, which still could have been in the majority at the time of John, exceeded the rabbinic directives. Such strong measures could have been illegal mob action. The writer of the fourth Gospel may also be exaggerating the actual action against Christians, on the basis of both panicky reports and his own fears. Yet the stories in Acts state that when Paul preached in synagogues, he was ejected for starting an uproar. The Jews also brought charges of "disturbing the peace" against him to the Roman authorities. These charges suggest that the rabbinic movement had not yet had a significant effect on the synagogue's behavior.

Two Powers in Heaven

When the rabbis mention a heretical group, they sometimes mention the scriptural passages upon which the heresy was built. For instance, the rabbis mention a strange group of heretics whom they call "those who say there are 'two powers in heaven.' " Sometimes the compare this group with other heretics who believed in "no power in heaven" or who believed in "many powers in heaven." The heresy is therefore designated by the title.[7]

At other times, the rabbinic reports about two powers contain a defense against the heresy which suggests it was Christianity. The defense is usually taken from the Bible itself; that is, Scripture is quoted to demonstrate the error of the heresy. Some of the favorite proofs that God is singular come from Deuteronomy 32: "I, even I am He and there is no God beside me; It is I that kill, and I that make alive. I wound and I heal." Deuteronomy 6:4 is another proof: "Hear O Israel, the LORD our GOD, the LORD is One." The most frequently used passages against those who said that there were two powers in heaven come from Isaiah 44–47, which is replete with lines like: "I am the first and the last ... I am the only God ... There is none beside Me ... I create weal and woe." That section of Isaiah was written in the fifth century B.C.E. by an author who was interested in showing that Yahweh was the author of both good and evil, because in the Persian Empire at that time a growing movement of Zoroastrians believed that there were two divinities, each seemingly equal and opposing.

Isaiah's arguments against paganism and Zoroastrianism, however, had taken place five hundred years earlier than the time of the rabbis. The rabbis, like every other Jewish group, used biblical passages to describe contemporary phenomena with which they were more familiar. The biblical text in Isaiah thus does not mean that the heresy to which the rabbinic texts refer is Zoroastrianism. Zoroastrianism was not a heresy of Judaism; it was a religion of itself. While the rabbis certainly knew something about Zoroastrianism, as shown by the Babylonian Talmud, most of the references to two powers seem not to have dualism in mind, as illustrated by the rabbinic exegesis:

I am the LORD thy GOD (Exodus 20:2): Why is this said? For this reason. At the sea He appeared to them as a mighty hero doing battle, as it is said: "The LORD is a man of war (Ex. 15:3)." At Sinai, he appeared to them as an old man full of mercy. It is said: "And they saw the God of Israel ... (Ex. 24:10)." And after they had been redeemed, what does it say: "And the like of the very heavens for clearness (Ibid)." Again, it says "I beheld 'til thrones were placed down (Dan. 7:9)." And it also says: "A fiery stream issued forth and came from before Him ... (Dan. 7:10)." Scripture therefore would not let the nations of the world have an excuse for saying that there are two powers, but declares: "I am the Lord thy God." I am He who was in the past and I am He who will be in the future. I am He who is in this world and I am He who will be in the world to come, as it is said: "See now that I, even I am He ... (Dt. 32:39)." And it says: "Even to old age, I am the same (Isa. 46:4)." And it says: "Thus says the Lord, the King of Israel and His redeemer, the Lord of Hosts; I am the first and I am the last ... (Isa. 44:6)." And it says: "Who hath wrought and done it? He that called the generations from the beginning. I, the Lord, who am the first ... (Isa. 41:4)."

Rabbi Nathan says: "From this one can cite a refutation

of the heretics who say: 'There are two powers.' For when the Holy One, Blessed be he, stood up and exclaimed: 'I am the LORD thy God,' was there any one who stood up to protest against Him? If you should say that it was done in secret—but has it not already been said: 'I said not unto the seed of Jacob . . .' (ibid)—that is, to these only will I give it. 'They sought me in the desert . . .' (ibid) Did I not give it in broad daylight? And thus it says: 'I, the Lord, speak righteousness. I declare things that are right.'" (Mekhilta Shirta 4 and Bahodesh 5)

These complicated arguments suggest that the tradition went through periods of glossing and interpolation. The heretics mentioned in the passage are described first as Gentiles and later as Jewish sectarians. This is a powerful hint that Christianity was involved. But more than one group could have been so designated, so one can never be sure that Christianity alone among all the sects was the group described.

Other subtle clues link this passage with Christianity. The passage relies on the meaning of the names of God in Hebrew. It says that just because in Hebrew God has two proper names, both *Lord* and *God*, there are not necessarily two gods. And then it gives countervailing scriptures.

First, in Christianity the two different names of God are used to designate two persons of the trinity, different in number though not different in essence. But such a subtle distinction is apparently irrelevant to the rabbis. Second, the scriptural citations characterizing the heresy are typical of Christianity. For instance, Daniel 7:13 appears to be a central part of the heresy. Since this is the passage in which the coming of the son of man is prophesied, it is also one of the key texts for early Christianity, which takes it to be a prophecy about the coming of the Christ upon the clouds of heaven at the end of time.

Christians were not the only sect because other scriptural passages refer to beliefs that were not necessarily part of orthodox Christianity. But the basic heresy appears to have been one of believing in two corresponding powers, not in two opposing divinities, as in Zoroastrianism. This appears to be one of the primary ways in which the rabbis polemicize against the

Christian message. They claim that the Christians, together with other groups of that time, compromised the unity of God.

It may seem odd that the rabbis would call Christians dualists, ditheists, or binitarians, since Christians are trinitarians. The rabbis may simply be ignoring the third member of the trinity, the Holy Spirit. Since the rabbis themselves could use the term *holy spirit* without any heretical connotations, they perhaps did not object to the Christian contention that it was an hypostasis of God. There is even some question as to whether at the beginning the Christians themselves understood the Holy Spirit as an entirely separate divine hypostasis. It was not until the Council of Constantinople in the fourth century that Christianity defined the concept of the trinity. Apparently, the rabbis have some justification for calling the Christians "those who believe in 'two powers in heaven,' " even if they also call other groups by the same name. The modern disposition to see Christians as trinitarians has obscured the relevance of these rabbinic reports.

Philo uses very similar biblical passages to the ones against which the rabbis warn, in order to describe the *logos,* a word he adopts for the biblical portrayal of God's powers and angels. He calls the *logos* a *deuteros theos,* a "second God":

> Yet there can be no cowering fear for the man who relies on the hope of the divine comradeship, to whom are addressed the words "I am the God who appeared to thee in place of God." (Gen. 31:31) Surely a right noble cause of vaunting it is, for a soul that God deigns to show himself to and to converse with it. And do not fail to mark the language used, but carefully inquire whether there are two Gods; for we read "I am the God that appeared to thee," not "in my place" but "in the place of God," as though it were another's. What then are we to say? He that is truly God is one, but those that are improperly so called are more than one.   (*On Dreams* 1.227-229)

Philo is exegeting the theophany of Jacob at "Beth El," which the Septuagint fortuitously translated as "Place of God." The resulting Greek sentence, unlike its Hebrew original, contains the word *God* twice and may therefore imply that two gods or two hypostases of God are present. Philo is careful to maintain that this concept of "place," which he has already defined as an allegorical synonym for the *logos*, does not imply a plurality in the divinity. Philo is even willing to use the expression *"second God"* to describe this intermediary form. The principal difference between Philo's understanding of the *logos* and the Christian understanding of the term is that Philo would have found it impossible for the *logos* to be made flesh, since for him divinity and mundane matter were impossible to combine.

The terms of Philo's argument illuminate the Christian controversy. Philo uses the same term that will later be used by Christianity in the Gospel of John to describe Jesus. For Philo, the issue is how to understand the biblical stories of angels, if Judaism is a monotheistic religion. He wants to preserve the truth of the Hebrew Bible by adopting Greek philosophical language to new purposes. He therefore claims that it was actually the *logos*, not angels, that appeared to the patriarchs in the stories of the Old Testament. Christianity follows the path of Philo, while the rabbis caution that this leads to heresy.

Philo was himself a practicing Jew, yet he was willing to use phrases like "second God," which appear to compromise strict biblical monotheism, rather than abandon the truth of the Bible. However, the rabbis were unwilling to argue in the same way. They were not interested in showing that the Bible understands the subtleties of Hellenistic philosophy. Rather they saw that speculation about the nature of angels and other divine figures in the Hebrew Bible had led to a diminution of monotheism. Some Christian views of the nature of Jesus' divinity grew out of the general intellectual discussion about the nature of angels. By the second century, the rabbis were warning that the depiction of various divine creatures violated monotheism. By that time, Christianity must have been a major, if not the only, offender.

Other Jews were involved in the heresy as well. Various obscure groups of mystical and apocalyptic Jews who wrote the Enoch literature or the hekhaloth texts cherished traditions about God's principal angelic mediator. They even said, as Philo sometimes did, that the angelic mediator was Yahweh or carried His name. Again, the issue was the repetition of the name of God in biblical passages or the fact that Hebrew uses two different words for the divinity, *Yahweh* and *Elohim* which are *Kyrios* and *Theos* in Greek.

These rabbinic stories reveal an aspect of Jewish opposition to Christianity that is evidenced but not emphasized in the New Testament. The Gospel of John gives the clear impression that the doctrine of the messiah per se was not the most important issue to the Jewish leaders. John claims continually that the Jews have misunderstood the title. The messiah is not the "King of the Jews." Rather, he has many of the qualities which apocalyptic and mystical varieties of Judaism gave to the principal angelic mediators. John 3:33, in fact, acknowledges that many other Jews accept traditions about heavenly ascensions and the descent of angelic mediators: "No one has ever gone up to heaven except He who is descended from heaven, the Son of Man." Furthermore, it is the claim of the messiah's divinity, not primarily the messianic claim itself, which accounts for the Jewish opposition to Johannine Christianity. In John the issue between Jesus and the Jews is precisely that Jesus seeks to make himself equal with God. Each time he does so, the penalty is stoning, the Jewish penalty for severe blasphemy, not crucifixion: "For this reason, the Jews sought all the more to kill Him—not only was He breaking the Sabbath; worse still, he was speaking of God as His own father, thus making himself God's equal" (John 5:18), and "We stone you for no good work but for blasphemy, because you, being a man, make yourself God" (John 10:33).

The degree of hostility described by John is anachronistic. Some in the Jewish community in the early first century may have rejected Jesus, but some obviously accepted him. The entire Jewish community was not united in this particular way during the life of Jesus. The Gospel writer is projecting the level of hostility that he felt in his own day back to the time of Jesus. The Gospel's report is also exaggerated for polemical effect, as is typical of groups in the process of defining internal differences and dividing.

This Gospel is evidence that a Jewish-Christian sect was in

the process of discovering that it was no longer part of Judaism. John uses the word *Jew* where the other Gospels would have used a word for one of the Jewish sects. Because the Gospel no longer discriminates between sects of Jews, it was presumably written by a group that may once have felt itself to be Jewish but did so no more. The result is unfortunately one of the strongest anti-Jewish polemics in the New Testament:

> They answered him, "Abraham is our father." Jesus said to them, "If you were Abraham's children you would do what Abraham did, but now you seek to kill me, a man who has told you the truth which I heard from God; this is not what Abraham did. You do what your father did." They said to him, "We were not born of fornication; we have one Father, even God," Jesus said to them, "If God were your father, you would love me, for I proceeded and came forth from God; I came not of my own accord, but he sent me. Why do you not understand what I say? It is because you cannot bear to hear my word. You are of your father the devil, and your will is to do your father's desires. He was a murderer from the beginning, and has nothing to do with the truth, because there is no truth in him. When he lies, he speaks according to his own nature, for he is a liar and the father of lies."   (John 8:39-47)

By the time that the Gospel of John was written, the lines between Christian and Jew were drawn in a way wholly inappropriate to the life of Jesus. In this passage the Gospel therefore sees the Jews as part of the Devil's conspiracy against the truth of Jesus' message. These words are unfortunate, not because dualism of this type was atypical of apocalyptic Judaism, but because the words were used subsequently, without any historical qualification, against the Jews by a church unaware of its own historical development. When the New Testament was canonized as the direct word of God and the original setting for the quarrel was lost, statements of hostility of this type were completely misunderstood and formed the basis of a virulent strain of anti-Judaism in Christianity. The quarrels show the intensity of conflict in an area where Jews and Christians were forced into close proximity. The function of this conflict was to force separation between the two communities and thereby protect each community from the other. The production of precise and opposing theologies of monotheism in Judaism and Christianity was the result of the conflict and helped contain the issue by defining the border between them exactly.

The Church Fathers on Christ

Even though the rabbis do not enter into detail about their Christian opponents, they seize upon a principal point of the kerygma of the primitive church, that Jesus ascended to the father and received the title of "Lord," one of the titles reserved for God in rabbinic tradition. Every document in the New Testament agrees that this ascension took place after or as part of Jesus' exaltation, though Paul in Philippians 2:9-11 states it most succinctly: "Therefore God has highly exalted him and bestowed upon him the name which is above every name, that at the name of Jesus every knee should bow in heaven and on earth and that every tongue confess that Jesus Christ is Lord to the glory of God the Father." This hymn, which is probably a quotation from Christian liturgy, proclaims that Jesus ascended to heaven to receive "the name which is above every name," a reference to Yahweh, the Lord. The rabbinic references are thus apt, for the Christians took a completely different tack than the rabbinic community on the definition of monotheism.

The New Testament portrayal of Christ was not forgotten by the church fathers. They in fact stressed it but refashioned its historical context. Justin Martyr in his *Dialogue with Trypho* uses most of the scriptural exegesis that the rabbis thought dangerous.[8] The setting for the *Dialogue* is Antioch, whither Justin had migrated in his Christian mission. The writing of the *Dialogue* must have corresponded closely with the Bar Kokhba Revolt, for Justin mentions it often, and Trypho is described as a Jewish fugitive who escaped from the turmoil.

Justin's use of midrashic traditions has sometimes been taken as evidence that the *Dialogue* is fictional, serving him as a purely literary framework for presenting his views. Yet it reflects one side of the debate between Judaism and Christianity in the early second century, whether the immediate incident be wholly fact, embellished incident, or pure fiction. The clearest parallel between Justin and the enemies of the rabbis occurs in Justin's argument, by means of Genesis 19:24, that a second divine figure, Christ, is responsible for carrying out divine commands on earth:

> "The previously quoted Scriptural passages will make this evident to you," I replied. "Here are the words: 'The sun was risen upon the earth, and Lot entered into Segor. And the Lord rained upon Sodom brimstone and fire from the Lord out of Heaven. And he destroyed these cities and all the country round about.' " (Genesis 19:24)
>
> Then the fourth of the companions who remained with Trypho spoke up: "It must therefore be admitted that one of the two angels who went down to Sodom, and whom Moses in the scriptures calls Lord, is different from Him who is also God, and appeared to Abraham."
>
> "Not only because of that quotation," I said, "must we certainly admit that, besides the creator of the universe, another was called Lord by the Holy Spirit. This was attested to not only by Moses, but also by David, when he said: 'The Lord said to my Lord: Sit Thou at My right hand, until I make Thy enemies Thy footstool,' and in other words: 'Thy throne, O God, is forever and ever; the sceptre of Thy kingdom is a sceptre of uprightness. Thou has loved justice, and hated iniquity; therefore God, Thy God hath anointed Thee with the oil of gladness above Thy fellows.' " (Ps. 45:7-8)   (*Dialogue* 56)

It is a Jew, not Justin, who admits that another divine being, "the Lord," was present at the destruction of Sodom and Gomorrah and that this divine being was different from God. Such heterodox Jews existed as early as Philo. Justin endeavors to prove only that this second divinity is Christ. The angelic figure is accepted by the Jew, who questions only his messianic status. This passage is another indication that Christianity was the first movement to connect the messiah and the principal angel but not the first to claim that the single God had multiple forms. Justin relies primarily on the various descriptions of vindication and enthronement found in the Psalm texts.

Like Philo, Justin calls the *logos* "another God" (*heteros theos*), distinct in number if not in essence (*Dialogue* 56). The sharply drawn personality of this manifestation, together with the doctrine of the incarnation, distinguish Justin's concept of *logos* from Philo's. But as E. R. Goodenough argued, both Justin and Philo are products of the same Hellenistic Jewish traditions.[9] Like Philo, Justin believes that the *logos* is an angel in that it is a power *(dynamis)* radiating from God. Like the angels, it has freedom of choice, but unlike the angels, Justin's *logos* has self-direction. Although Justin implies that the *logos* is the same as an angel, he emphasizes its distinctiveness in ways that never occurred to Philo.

The same biblical quotation from Genesis 19:24 is noted by the rabbis as having been used by heretics: "A min once said to R. Ishmael b. Yosi (ca. 170 C.E.?) It is written: *Then the Lord caused to rain upon Sodom and Gomorrah brimstone and fire from the Lord.* (Genesis 19:24) But 'from Him' should have been written. A certain fuller said: 'Leave him to me, I will answer him.' He then proceeded: 'It is written, *and Lamech said to his wives, Ada and Zillah, "Hear my voice, ye wives of Lamech."* ' But he should have said '*My wives.*' Such is the scriptural idiom. So here, too, it is the scriptural idiom " (b. Sanhedrin 38b). The reference to the fuller, a figure often portrayed in rabbinic literature as lacking the exegetical skills of the rabbis, suggests that the heretic's mistake is to misunderstand the ordinary sense of Scripture. Although this is a strange argument in the mouth of a rabbi, its intent is clearly to dismiss a "two powers" interpretation of Genesis 19:24, which Justin cites to prove that Christ was the angel who punished Sodom. Justin's christology grows out of pre-Christian, Jewish angelology; the rabbinic response, which takes issue with such exalted angelology, probably has Christians like Justin in mind.

The Dynamics of Separation

Comparing the charges, accusations, and vituperation in both communities yields a fuller idea of the nature and extent of the controversy than is available from the texts of one religion alone. The conflict encompasses aspects of sociology, law, politics, and theology. It comprehended many more serious issues than whether or not Jesus was to be acknowledged as a messiah. In fact, the number of issues separating Jews from Christians gradually escalated until all the serious questions facing the Jewish community in the Hellenistic world were involved in critical ways—the nature and meaning of Torah, its practice in a Gentile world, the definition of a Jew, and even the nature of Jewish claims to monotheism in a philosophically sophisticated and cosmopolitan world. As soon as the nature of the crisis became evident, the only solution was the separation of the two communities, for such different opinions on every definitive issue could not be contained by one community, especially when its independence in the Roman world had been so completely destroyed. The conflict with Christianity, together with the fall of the Judean state and the rise of rabbinic Judaism, forced a change in meaning of the word *Ioudaios* in Greek (or *Yehudi* in Hebrew) from its previous meaning of a resident of Judea to its modern meaning, incorporated in the word *Jew*, of a practitioner of the religion of Judaism, just as the word *Christian* began to designate those who adopted the religion of Christianity, whether they were Jews or not.

The breach between Judaism and Christianity resembles cases of friction and fission observable in modern societies as well, where charges of magic and witchcraft, together with a careful definition of the social and ideological components of the conflict on both sides, actually protect the society from the destruction brought on by internal strife. When the conflict cannot be handled within the society, division of the community into two parts becomes necessary. The positive function of the division is to contain the problem by excluding the opposition and protecting the members remaining inside the group by careful education about the crucial points of difference.

Once the communities of Judaism and Christianity had separated, the two religions forged individual understandings of their past, the conflict that had divided them, and their future goals. Christianity slowly became a church of Gentiles, for whom Luke expressed the theory of the future by writing the first truly universal history of Christianity and synthesizing the opinions of Paul with his fellow apostles. The rabbis in turn became the spokespersons for universalism in Judaism. The biggest casualty in this religious separation was the group that claimed to be both Jewish and Christian, since it was judged heretical by both religions. Once separated, the spiritual communities of Judaism and Christianity expressed theories of human destiny that were at once universal and opposing.

❧ VII ❧

The Ways Divide

The breakdown of ethnic boundaries in Christianity was a consequence of both its antinomianism and its emphasis on conversion. But neglect of ethnic boundaries was neither automatic nor immediate. After Paul's new definition of the Christian community, conversion to Christianity gradually became the true test of entrance into the movement. Although Paul himself did not live to see his evangelical efforts come to fruition in a predominantly Gentile church, by the time of Luke at the end of the first century and beginning of the second, the church needed a fuller and more coherent account of its Gentile mission.

The Christian Model of Universalism

Luke wrote two books that serve as a history of the early church. Because the books are separated by the Gospel of John in the New Testament, the scope of Luke's achievement has been obscured. The first volume of his history is the Gospel of Luke. The second volume is the Acts of the Apostles. In the second volume Luke attempts to synthesize the different interpretations of Jesus' message promulgated by the Jewish Christians and the Gentile Christians. In doing so, he reconciles the ideas of Paul and Peter. He idealizes their thoughts and lives, partly because he views them from a distance of fifty years and partly because he sees Christian destiny more clearly to lie with the Gentile church. Luke's ideals impose a particular evaluation on his narration of Christianity's past.

Luke's concept of the goal of Christian history emerges in the story of Peter's vision, which occurs in the context of the conversion of Cornelius, the centurian of the Italian cohort:

The next day, as they were on their journey and coming near the city, Peter went up on the housetop to pray, about the sixth hour. And he became hungry and desired something to eat; but while they were preparing it, he fell into a trance and saw the heaven opened, and something descending like a great sheet, let down by four corners upon the earth. In it were all kinds of animals and reptiles and birds of the air. And there came a voice to him, "Rise Peter; kill and eat." But Peter said, "No, Lord; for I have never eaten anything that is common or unclean." And the voice came to him again a second time: "What God has cleansed, you must not call common." This happened three times, and the thing was taken up at once to heaven . . .

And Cornelius said, "Four days ago about this hour, I was keeping the ninth hour of prayer in my house; and behold, a man stood before me in bright apparel, saying, 'Cornelius, your prayer has been heard and your alms have been remembered before God. Send therefore to Joppa and ask for Simon who is Peter; he is lodging in the house of Simon, a tanner by the seaside.' So I sent to you at once, and you have been kind enough to come. Now therefore we are all here present in the sight of God, to hear all that you have been commanded by the Lord." (Acts 10:1-33)

After the Gentile Cornelius has received baptism, the questions of Jewish Gentile relations raised by his admission to the community are eased by a vision given to Peter, which at first seems unrelated, since it is concerned with the dietary laws. Peter is so amazed by the command to stop observing the food laws that the vision needs to be repeated to him three times. The three-fold repetition may also have the literary function of persuading some Jewish-Christian readers of Acts of the desirability of giving up the food laws. The result of the vision is to settle both the question of the dietary laws and the issue of the Gentiles within the church. But the portrayal is a kind of idealization, since Paul's letters testify to the continuing and deeply divisive nature of the problem.

Although Peter's vision has some of the characteristics of apocalypticism in its symbolic use of kosher and nonkosher animals, angelic presence, and vivid revelations, it is purposefully different. Other Jewish apocalypticism stressed that salvation is available only within the confines of the sectarian group and defined that group through obedience to the purity laws and strict interpretation of Torah. Unlike apocalypticism, Luke's Christianity radically rejects the language of purity and insists on mixing Jews and Gentiles. But it maintains the sectarian concept of the salvation of believers alone.

The issue of the kosher laws is directly related to the issue of the admission of Gentiles. By placing the two issues together in this way, Luke is saying that the old symbolic distinctions separating Jew from Gentile cannot continue to disunite the Christian community. Luke is applying the Pauline principle of conversion to the Christian community in a way that Paul had probably not entirely anticipated, since Paul was not fully aware of any difference between Judaism and Christianity, living at a time when Gentile Christianity was a struggling new community. No use of the purity laws can be allowed to create distinctions within Christianity. The apocalyptic sectarian distinction between the saved and the damned has been extended by the call to proselytism.

This passage is a meditation on universalism, the philosophy of the destiny of Christianity within the history of all humanity. The Christian concept of universalism—salvation for those within, equal opportunity to join for those without—is a direct result of the historical issue of the Gentiles entering the Christian community and the attendant problems for Jewish purity laws. It is a logical and proper association, reflecting the social reality of the Gentile presence, though it is almost never discussed in that context by church historians.

The Jewish Model of Universalism

Within the Hellenistic Jewish world, those Jews who lived intimately with Gentiles were also forced by historical circumstances to articulate a theory for the role of Gentiles in world salvation. Philo accords to the morally highest members of pagan society the same promises of immortality that he gives to pious Jews. To a large extent he was defending a Jewish way of life in which Gentile values and culture played a significant part. Christianity, which began as a Jewish sect, was forced to come to terms with the same question but in different ways.

Rabbinic Judaism also had to face the issue of universalism, but since it encountered different historical circumstances, it developed a concept of universalism that differed from Christianity's. Even before the fall of the Temple, the Pharisees enunciated an expanded version of purity, prayer, and study within Judaism, which after the destruction of the Temple was able to preserve Jewish life by transforming it. As the rabbis gradually became the spokesmen for Judaism, they began to address the issue of Jewish universalism, the role of the Jewish people in world destiny. Because of the legal nature of rabbinic literature, the official doctrine of Jewish salvation is not outlined fully in any one place in rabbinic literature, but the basis is laid at the beginning of Mishnah Sanhedrin 10:

> All Israelites have a share in the world to come, for it is written: "Thy people also shall all be righteous, they shall inherit the land forever; the branch of my planting, the work of my hands, that I may be glorified." (Isaiah 60:21) And these are those who have no share in the world to come: he that says that there is no resurrection of the dead prescribed in the law, and that the law is not from heaven, and an Epicurean. Rabbi Akiba says: "Also he that reads from the heretical books or that utters charms over wounds, also he that pronounces the name with its proper letters."

The rabbis are here interested only in Israel. They claim that all Israel merits life in the world to come, except for some unpardonable villains singled out by the Bible as great sinners. The passage goes beyond merely Pharisaic Judaism to speak for all varieties of Judaism, though it excludes from immortality all those Jews who adopt atheism (Epicureanism), deny the prophecy of resurrection in the Torah, deny the divinity of the Torah, or practice magic. From the rabbinic perspective, those who are excluded from the world to come have warranted their ironic punishment, which fits their crime, for they have denied the doctrines that ensure their salvation. But they speak for all Israel, not for a particular sect. In rabbinic eyes all Israelites, even those who are sinners, will eventually share in the world to come. However, the rabbis are not of the same mind about the meaning of such an assertion. In many other places they maintain that future rewards depend strictly on the performance of good deeds and repentance. Rabbinic Judaism did not impose a single doctrine of the meaning of salvation on all its practitioners, and hence rabbinic writing, which anthologizes the opinions of the rabbis, does not evince one.

The early rabbis take some liberties in presuming to speak for all Israel. Yet by adopting the term *Israel* for the community of all believers, as the Christians will do, they are beginning to travel the distance toward universalism.

The next logical question for the rabbis to pursue becomes, "If Israel is to have eternal life, then what is the place given to Gentiles?" Rabbinic literature records no single answer but rather a variety of acceptable opinions. There is a difference of opinion on critical cases: "Rabbi Eliezer said: 'All the nations will have no share in the world to come, even as it is said, "The wicked shall go into Sheol, and all the nations that forget God." (Ps. 9:17) The wicked shall go into Sheol—these are the wicked among Israel.' Rabbi Joshua said to him: "If the verse had said, 'The wicked shall go into Sheol with all the nations,' and had stopped there, I should have agreed with you, but as it goes on to say 'who forget God,' it means there are righteous men among the nations who have a share in the world to come" (Tosefta Sanhedrin 13:2). Behind this statement lies an assumption that some nations may acknowledge God through their own rites and rituals so that the standard for judging their beliefs is their moral actions.

The positions attributed to Rabbis Eliezer and Joshua b. Hananiah are typical of other remarks that the midrash and Mishnah have attributed to them. Rabbi Eliezer is a severe critic of Gentiles. Rabbi Joshua b. Hananiah is more liberal. He removes all distinctions between Jew and Gentile in attaining salvation through the doing of good deeds. He says: "Everyone who walks in blamelessness before his Creator in this world will escape the judgment of hell in the world to come" (Tosefta Sanhedrin 13:2; Sanhedrin 105a).[1] He even disagrees with Rabbi Gamaliel by maintaining that the blameless children of wicked heathen will also have a share in the world to come. Though Rabbi Joshua does not allow conversion without circumcision, he at least looks at the positive side of the issue, saying: "Baptism without circumcision makes one a *ger* [a person in the process of converting]" (b. Yeb. 46a).

The consensus in rabbinic Judaism shortly became not merely that some righteous would have a place in paradise but that all righteous Gentiles would also enjoy the felicities of the world to come:

> Rabbi Jeremiah said: Whence can you know that the gentile that practices the law is equal to the high priest? Because it said, "which, if a man do, he shall live through them" (Lev. 18:5). And it says, "This is the Torah of man" (2 Sam. 7:19). It does not say, "the law of the priests, Levites, Israelites," but "This is the law of man, O Lord God." And it does not say, "Open the gates and let the priests and Levites and Israel enter," but it says: "Open the gates that the righteous gentile may enter" (Isaiah 26:2); And it says, "This is the gate of the Lord, the righteous shall enter it." It does not say, "The priests and the Levites and Israel shall enter it," but it says, "The righteous shall enter it" (Ps. 118:20). And it does not say, "Rejoice ye priests, Levites and Israelites," but it says, "Rejoice ye righteous" (Ps. 33:1). And it does not say, "Do good, O Lord, to the priests and the Levites and the Israelites." But it says, "Do good, O Lord, to the good" (Ps. 124:4). So even a gentile, if he practices the Torah, is equal to the high priest.   (Sifra 86b; b. Baba Kamma 38a)

Rabbinic discussions, which serve as the legal code of their community, are sometimes difficult to read when they rely on the interpretation of scriptural verses to derive their opinions. Here, however, there is little ambiguity about the critical issue of salvation which is open to all on the basis of righteousness and does not depend on anyone's prior conversion to Judaism. The Gentile need not become an Israelite. Rather, the issue is the future reward, not adherence to Torah.

Consequently, there is a critical and often misunderstood difference between rabbinic and Christian theology. In Christianity, the community defines the boundary of the elect and the saved. In rabbinic Judaism, if the Christian theological terms can be borrowed, election, which is being a member of Israel, is distinct from salvation or eternal life, which is earned by good deeds and repentance from evil. Thus, for the rabbis, Jewish nationality is a special privilege, just as priesthood is a privilege. But the privilege is not the same as salvation.

Apocalyptic Judaism claimed that most of Israel was condemned with the wholly sinful Gentiles. Rabbinic Judaism asserted that all Israel would be saved. In rabbinic Judaism, the distinction between Jew and Gentile was supposed to be one of purity, not of ethics or morality, though apocalyptic Jews constantly and rabbinic Jews occasionally were capable of extending the meaning of impurity and uncleanliness to immorality. Missionizing still remained an option for the rabbis, however theoretical it might have been under Christian Roman emperors, but the critical rabbinic doctrine was the openness of salvation to all mankind: the doing of good deeds and repentance defined salvation. Anyone, Jew or Gentile, who was able to do good deeds gained the rewards of them.

The Jewish so-called doctrine of works is often represented as a scoreboard religion. One simply totals up one's virtues against one's sins, and if the sum is negative, the result is damnation. But this is a misrepresentation, for repentance overrides any arithmetical calculations of reward and sin. Indeed, the rabbis were cautious in estimating the amount of good that the righteous could accomplish and were sometimes pessimistic about human nature in general. But they were complete optimists when discussing the value of sincere repentance. Most rabbis thought it impossible that whole sections of humanity could be condemned to perdition by a just and merciful God. Israel would surely see the world to come. The righteous Gentiles would be saved as well. That this doctrine of universalism might not command the assent of every rabbi or might contradict other, less broad-minded statements in Scripture was not crucial to them. Rabbinic literature, being made up of the opinions of different rabbis at different times, does not evince internal consistency on many doctrinal issues. In place of Pauline conversion, rabbinic Jews stressed the importance of repentance, of returning to the path and making full amends for any damage that a sin might have caused. Both conversion and repentance stress intention and motivation to change one's behavior as a fundamental component of moral development.

Since the Torah was given to Jews, the last logical question for the rabbis to answer was, "What are the standards of morality by which one can judge Gentile morality?" The rabbis linked the salvation of the Gentiles explicitly to the covenant made with Noah, and sealed with the rainbow, for in this covenant God promised mercy and deliverance to all mankind. The rabbis theorized that God gave all humanity "natural" laws at that moment, the so-called Noahide Commandments, so that the whole human race could comprehend the meaning of righteousness. The number of these commandments varies from six to ten, depending on the midrashic version, and include what the rabbis considered to be universally recognizable moral imperatives: prohibitions against blasphemy, idolatry, bloodshed, incest, theft, and eating flesh from live animals. Added to these is often the prohibition against idolatry and the recognition of the true God. The rabbinic formulation of all these specific ordinances, though somewhat puzzling to modern sensibilities, is determined by ingenious exegesis of the text of Genesis, where God gives specific commands to the survivors of the flood. Many of the Noahide Commandments are also consonant with the environment of antiquity, for even pious pagans in the late Roman Empire could justify ethical monotheism philosophically.[2]

In medieval Judaism these Noahide Commandments were related to Islam and Christianity. The rabbis acknowledged Islam as consonant with the intent of the Noahide Commandments, yet they often paused at Christianity with its trinitarian doctrines and rich Roman and Eastern traditions of devotion to *eikons* or "images." Some rabbis, especially those living in Christian countries, pointed out that while Christianity is not strict monotheism because it associates a mortal and his image with God, a *shittuf* (associationism) or "two powers" heresy forbidden to Jews, righteous Christians could still count on eternal life because the Noahide Commandments do not specifically prohibit *shittuf* for Gentiles. Rabbis living in Muslim lands sometimes judged Christianity as a violation of monotheism, as did the Muslims themselves, by means of the Muslim doctrine of associationism *(shirq)*.

Unlike some other rabbinic doctrines the Noahide Commandments can be dated from an independent source, the Book of Jubilees, found at Qumran and hence datable to the first century or probably earlier. Jubilees 7:20 attests to the content of the Noahide rules in Jewish thought, though it does not give them the explicit rabbinic name. It verifies that the Noahide Commandments were already being formulated in Jewish thought during the first century. The rabbis apparently expanded this outline of Gentile responsibilities from traditions that had antedated rabbinic control of the Jewish community. The doctrine that the Gentiles can effect their own salvation was not the only idea, and possibly not even the dominant idea, concerning the fate of the Gentiles in first century Judaism, since in most apocalyptic communities anyone outside the sect, especially Gentiles, was condemned as an oppressor of true Judaism. But the idea was already present.

Universalism and Monotheism in History

For Jews and Christians universalism, the concept of the community's place within the destiny of mankind, developed after the concept of election, God's special purpose for their community. But for each community election and universalism were related. Perhaps the most difficult problem for both Jews and Christians, even today, is to understand the difference between each other's respective conceptions of universalism and election. The concepts in both communities were laid down during the period of their initial separation and depended on their sectarian past. Each interpreted the concept of election to allow its own uniqueness and to legitimate its own community, yet also to cohere with their ideals of universality.

Christianity has traditionally regarded itself as the universal messianic fulfillment of all the promises of election in the Old Testament, proclaiming that the Israel of the spirit (Christianity) has completely replaced the old, particularistic Israel of the flesh (Judaism). Even Paul, who actually claimed that Israel remained God's elect, seems unwilling to allow the Jews any significant part in the salvation of mankind until the fulfillment of history, when they too will come to recognize the Christian savior. The doctrine that resulted from the New Testament polemic, together with the commentary of the church fathers, required that all salvation be mediated through conversion to the church.

For the Jews, this stance has been seen as ideological totalitarianism, the same kind of totalitarianism against which the Jews have fought since late antiquity. Yet their opposition was not merely a matter of refusing to exist within a politically and militarily superior regime. The rabbis were willing to adapt Judaism to deal with political domination. The two disastrous wars against Rome, with their terrible civilian and military losses, convinced even the strongest nationalists that fighting against Rome was hopeless. But Jews never resigned themselves to the destruction of their culture by complete assimilation to a dominant power. From the start of Greek domination, only the flag of religious freedom could be waved successfully to mobilize the country against foreign domination. Whatever the truth of the historical circumstances of the Maccabean Revolt, Jews of later times felt that their forebears had fought against the tyrannical totalitarianism of the Hellenistic world, whenever it was intolerant of ethnic and religious differences. The mythology of that fiercely independent loyalty to their own traditions still operates today.

The tyranny of Hellenism was itself a simplified recollection of the actual historical situation, composed centuries after the Maccabean Revolt and functioning as a myth to strengthen Jewish identity in situations of assimilation. Acculturation was not rejected by Hellenistic Jews. As long as their national and religious constitution remained intact, Jews felt comfortable in accepting a variety of Hellenistic institutions, provided they

could develop a native interpretation of them. When the traditional Jewish state was destroyed, each of the sects, including
the Christian one, fought for the continuance of its own interpretation of the Torah constitution. Each sect was reacting to a
universalism that appeared to mask imperialism and was intolerant of differences. For this reason, both Jews and Christians
stood out in different ways against the dominant Roman ideology as uncooperative minorities. After much conflict, both the
Jews and the Christians won grudging acknowledgments of
their differences from the Romans, but the Jews lost their en-
dorsement when the empire became Christian.

After the first and second Jewish wars against Rome, the
paths of Judaism and Christianity parted more rapidly. The
Christians, who blamed the Jews for the death of their savior,
saw God's destruction of Judea as God's vengeance. The Jews,
for their part, saw Christianity as an illegal interpretation of
the traditions in Judaism. Though Jews and Christians lived
together in the same land for centuries afterward, any shared
constitution was completely destroyed by these battles. Each
had started from such a different set of hypotheses that, although they claimed the same foundation document, the Bible
in Hebrew and Greek, they were no longer part of the same
community. The national fabric that had united them during
the early days of their battles was torn and could not be repaired.

Once the two communities separated, they erected new and
stronger boundaries, and these borders served to protect either
side from contamination by the other. Rejected from their
homeland and rejecting it, the Christians abandoned war-
ravaged Judea and spread throughout the cities of the Roman
Empire. Wherever they went, they met Jews caught up in the
same historical forces. But these Jews were not yet greatly informed on rabbinic ideology.

Most rabbinic activity was originally confined to the com-
paratively small towns of the Judean coast and the Galilee. In
the area around Judea Jews and Christians apparently met and
occasionally debated each other. The conflict between them
was bitter and not well informed, but it was functional in that

it sharpened each community's self-definition. Each found a way to become a universal community, but ironically, neither was prepared to acknowledge that same universality in the other.

The decisive theoretical issues dividing Christianity from Judaism were the interpretation of Torah and the concept of God's unity. These had been discussed theologically in the Jewish community before the rise of Christianity. But the social conflict unleashed by war and Christian messianism made it now impossible for anyone to discuss the issue theoretically. One had to choose between competing communities.

Rabbinic Judaism spiritualized the national institutions of the defunct state, creating a new communal power structure. This did not mean that after the Bar Kokhba Revolt, no rabbi ever sought political power within the Roman state. The exilarchate and the successors of Rabbi Judah the Prince viewed themselves as scions of David and, hence, as lawful heads of the Jewish community. They worked out an uneasy alliance with Roman authorities and accepted responsibility for good order within Jewish society, even if they did not completely control it. Yet Jewish attempts at independent rule in Judea proved futile. In its place, mystical concepts of the power of Israel's spirituality grew up, like the crucial effect of Israel's observance of the Sabbath on world redemption.

Within the Jewish community, the power of rabbinic scholarship and purity came to dominate secular and economic power when the rabbinic academy overtook the exilarchate as the chief Jewish institution in Babylonia. Rabbinic control was based upon positive sacramental power and the knowledge of proper interpretation of Scripture. The Temple, spiritualized and idealized in the Mishnah, continued to symbolize the center of the purity cult, but its actual function was taken over by table and eating rules.

Christian missionary activity made steady gains within the alienated client populations of the Roman Empire. Long before Constantine adopted the cross as his victory symbol, Christianity had become prominent in the religious life of the Roman Empire. Not long after Constantine, Christianity began a new career as the imperial religion of a factionated Roman Empire.[3]

The later historical roles of Judaism and Christianity were anticipated in the earlier ideals and theologies of each group. Confirming the thoroughgoing congruence between social role and theology in both religions, Mary Douglas has suggested that the chosen symbols of religious controversy are never arbitrary.[4] In Christianity, which attempted to break down the divisions between Gentile and Jew and hence create a new worldwide Israel, the orthodox doctrine of the incarnation insisted upon the perfect interpenetration of God and man. Christ was truly God, truly man. At the same time, the church was made of a mixing of Jew and Gentile. The divine body symbolized the same breakdown of categories as the social body, since the church was the body of Christ. Christian imagery broke through the strict categories of the age by accepting the baptismal formula recorded in Paul's writing, for in the idealized Christian world there should be neither Jew nor Greek, neither slave nor free, neither male nor female.

One of the reasons that gnosticism appeared so dangerous to Christianity is that it distinguished sharply between Christians. Gnosticism was not an organized movement; it was a term of derision, used by the orthodox against those Christians and non-Christians who felt that salvation was a matter of inner knowledge. Gnostics also expressed the view that the world was hopelessly corrupt, under the sway of a cruel or ignorant God, who was often portrayed with the standard attributes of the Hebrew God in the Old Testament. For the gnostic, this world could not be redeemed, as most of the early Christians had thought. It could only be transcended by ascension. If one lacked the saving knowledge *(gnosis)* that, despite the world's corruption, the oversoul *(pneuma)* was redeemable, one was doomed. Gnosticism therefore threatened to change the Pauline principle of conversion into an intellectual perception.

Gnosticism posed a social danger as well. It threatened the integrity of Christianity in two respects. First, it implied that non-Christians could have the same spiritual experience as

Christians, breaking the unity of the Christian community. Second, it distinguished the pneumatics, fully saved Christians who had received the saving *gnosis*, from the psychics, ordinary Christians who had merely come part way, just as completely as it distinguished both of them, the whole Christian community, from the sarkics, the unredeemed pagans and Jews. The result was a community with two distinct castes. Just as gnosticism divided the Christian community in two, it divided the divinity into two opposing deities—an evil demiurge, who made and ruled over an absurd world, and a redeemer, who was unknown to the demiurge and who made the secrets of salvation known only to his redeemed. This contrasted strongly with the Christian ideal of a single community of Gentiles and Jews grafted together, worshiping a single divinity composed of a father and son. Against the Jews and Jewish Christians, Christianity had to stress the unity of conversion through baptism into the rites of a dying and reviving divinity. But against the gnostics, it had to stress the value of the Jewish Scriptures and the unity of the Old Testament godhead. Thus, the concepts of community and theology were congruent.

The same congruence between theology and sociology characterized the radically different history of Judaism. In Jewish thought, God stayed strictly separate from man, just as the Jews stayed strictly separate from Gentiles. For the Jews, purity categories could remain strong without sacrificing universality because, when Jews distinguished between themselves and the Gentiles, they were not distinguishing between the saved and the damned. Nor were they suggesting that God communicated with or watched over only Jews. They were saying that the type of relationship between God and the Jews was unique because the Jews served as His priests. Just as in the Christian case, the social unity of all believers mirrored the doctrine, so in the Jewish case, the boundaries between sacred Jews and profane Gentiles were enforced by holiness laws. Dietary laws kept the purity of the people intact and kept the people intact as well. Instead of the old homeland with geographical borders, the rabbis relied on their sectarian past to define a people by means of purity boundaries alone. If Christianity created a new people, Judaism preserved an old one. If the object of Christian universalism was to create a universal role for a new people, the object of rabbinic universalism was to provide a viable environment and universal goal for an ancient people in danger of extinction. The universalism was real and sincere in both cases.

In Judaism, the urge to proselytize never abated until the Christian emperors made conversion to Judaism a crime. However, the equality of the righteous Israelite and Gentile under the Torah made missionizing unnecessary from a moral perspective. It was up to the individual alone whether or not to take on the burden of the extra commandments given to Israel. This was a quite different perspective from Christianity's, where the only way to be saved was to convert. The Christian doctrine was articulated in its strongest form after it achieved a firm hold on the Roman Empire, for it gave to the empire a sense of unity and religious purpose that had been lacking ever since the Republic had expanded its conquests beyond the Latium. Christianity gave Rome a universal religion and gave the empire a single philosophical justification.

The Jews had an entirely different historical experience awaiting them. Once Christianity took over the Roman Empire, it became more and more difficult to remain Jewish within it. The center of influence within the Jewish community quickly moved to Babylonia, where Jews were tolerated as a resident minority under Sassanian rule. Under succeeding Muslim empires there, Judaism occasionally flourished as it had in the Diaspora under Hellenistic rule, being one ethnic minority group among many. Judaism's model of universalism was based on its most favorable experience of toleration in an atmosphere of cultural pluralism.

Thus, the two religions represented different ways of arranging hierarchies: Christianity was committed to encountering the world in its universal mission to convert it; Judaism was committed to keeping the holiness of the people sacrosanct.[5] In the Christian case, religious hierarchy and political power were parallel and often identical. The head of the

Christian church would in later centuries claim to be a great prince. Alternate religious hierarchies, as in monasteries or in non-Christian kingdoms, were looked upon as threatening. Christianity committed itself to project religion into political institutions.

Traditional rabbinic Judaism, however, enclosed the people in a protective band of purity, enforced by rules of marriage and commensality. Just as the border between humanity and God was strictly maintained, so the border between sacred people and secular people was strictly maintained. As Mary Douglas has pointed out, marriage laws are related to symbolic categorizations in other areas.[6] When community law operates to prevent contact between the community and outsiders by forbidding contact with commonly eaten foods, it presumably operates as strongly to send the same symbolic message in the area of marriage, since the biological basis of kinship is sexuality, an urge as strong as hunger, and property is also entailed in the symbolic transaction. These symbolic messages were at work in Hellenistic Judaism, and historically they have played a role in Jewish national consciousness. Intermarriage is forbidden for the same reason that commensality is enforced. The rabbis preserved a people without a national homeland by enforcing ritual and purity separations between Jew and Gentile in as many areas as possible.

The issue of monotheism was parallel to the issue of community composition. The rabbis called various sectarians "two powers" heretics based upon the belief in any divine agents who shared power with the one God. They regarded Christians as perhaps the most important and dangerous manifestation of this heresy. In opposition to this heresy, the rabbis insisted that God and man be kept separate. Thus, they also assumed that a divine man was a violation of a fundamental principle within Judaism. This opposition in theology between Judaism and Christianity was directly parallel to the social history and destiny of the two communities. Philo's Judaism, which allowed for the possibility of divine mediators figured in human form like the Greek gods and the biblical descriptions of Yahweh, was a Judaism committed to acculturation within the

Hellenistic world. The dominant form of Christianity took the same course. But rabbinic Judaism took a different route.

Twin Sons with Different Missions

The prophecy about Jacob and Esau, Rebecca's twin children, in Genesis 25:23 was used by both Judaism and Christianity to further their competing claims to divine favor (e.g. Midrash Rabba *ad loc.*, Romans 9:6-13). Both Judaism and Christianity consider themselves to be the heirs to the promises given to Abraham and Isaac and they are indeed fraternal twins emerging from the nation-state of second commonwealth Israel. As brothers often do, they picked different, even opposing ways to preserve their family's heritage. Their differences became so important that for two millennia few people have been able to appreciate their underlying commonalities and, hence, the reasons for their differences. Though they are twins, it is difficult to judge which religion is the older and which the younger, for their birthright is one issue separating them. Both now claim to be Jacob, the younger child who received the birthright. Rabbinic Judaism maintains that it has preserved the traditions of Israel, Jacob's new name after he wrestled with God. Christianity maintains that it is the new Israel, preserving the intentions of Israel's prophets. Because of the two religions' overwhelming similarities and in spite of their great areas of difference, both statements are true. Furthermore, neither religion can be fully understood in isolation from the other. The witness of each is needed to show the truth of the other.

Both rabbinic Judaism and Christianity were successful in preserving and expanding their communities after the destruction of their Judean homeland. One of the reasons for their success was their ethical rigorousness. Both Judaism and Christianity set high standards of behavior for their adherents, binding them to treat both insider and outsider with fairness and dignity. However, neither Judaism nor Christianity were unique in upholding high ethical standards. The philosophical schools recommended ethical behavior to their adherents as well.

But unlike the philosophical schools, Judaism and Christianity practiced their ethical standards only in cohesive communities. Even though both Judaism and Christianity fashioned concepts of universalism, their basic patterns for achieving a highly cohesive community were different. The Christian community was composed of converted and repentant sinners whose unity was preserved by the equality of all believers and the equal opportunity of all humanity to join and be saved. The apocalyptic sectarian pattern of first century Judaism was extended in Christianity to include a larger and more unified community, but the sectarian model underlying it remained visible. Anyone could join, but only those who converted could be saved. Inside, all repentant members theoretically treated each other with complete equality in regard to their purity and status, no matter how different their material advantages.

Rabbinic Judaism evolved a completely different method of social cohesion. It expanded the ancient purity rules so that they functioned as a geographical boundary between a stateless Israel and the world. The rabbis related to the world as priests to its congregation, being centers of moral and ritual purity. And they claimed the priests' due, a special intuition about what was pleasing to God. But they did not claim an exclusive right to salvation, which was available to all humanity on the basis of moral action and repentance.

The danger inherent in Christianity was that it would expire quickly, as have so many apocalyptic movements of the ancient and modern world, fading out after a moment of feverish religious reform. The danger in Judaism was that it would expire from national catastrophe. Both Judaism and Christianity managed to survive by changing their national or sectarian ideals into universal ideals of personal piety.

Judaism and Christianity designed two different ways of understanding their universal missions. But Judaism and Christianity did not design theories of universalism that went substantially beyond their social experience. Rather, their ideals were based upon their history and expanded on it. Furthermore, through their universal principles each community sought to articulate and understand its changing position in the

Roman Empire. The two different theories reflected new Hellenized ideas, summarizing in theological form the different historical roles that Christianity and Judaism assumed. When Christianity promulgated its doctrine of the salvation of all believers, it understood itself to be the universal proselytizing religion for world salvation. By contrast, Judaism understood itself to be a kingdom of priests in a culturally plural world.

The social order for Judaism and Christianity had both a divine and a human context. In both Judaism and Christianity, the Torah, the national constitution of Judea, was the basis of historical being. Both attempted to preserve it after the collapse of national unity. The fact that they chose such different ways reflected their different social origins in the Judean state and presaged their later roles in history. Their different histories do not alter the fact of their birth as twins in the last years of Judean statehood. They are both truly Rebecca's children, but unlike Jacob and Esau, they have no need to dispute their birthright. It can belong to both of them together.

Notes

Introduction

1. The abbreviations B.C.E. (before the common era) and C.E. (common era) are used here to avoid the theological implications of B.C. (before Christ) and A.D. (Anno Domini, or year of Our Lord). The terms are otherwise similar in meaning.

2. Van Harvey, *The Historian and the Believer* (New York: Macmillan, 1966).

3. See e.g. Paul Tillich, "The Significance of the History of Religions for the Systematic Theologian," in Jerald C. Brauer, ed., *The Future of Religion* (New York: Harper and Row, 1966); Victor Turner, *Dramas, Fields, and Metaphors: Symbolic Action in Human Society* (Ithaca: Cornell University Press, 1974); Talcott Parsons, *The Social System* (New York: Free Press, 1951); Bernard Barber, *Science and the Social Order* (Glencoe, Ill.: Free Press, 1952); Stephen C. Pepper, *World Hypotheses: A Study in Evidence* (Berkeley: University of California Press, 1942); Mary Douglas, "Self Evidence," *Implicit Meanings: Essays in Anthropology* (London: Routledge and Kegan Paul, 1975), pp. 276–316; Ian G. Barbour, *Myths, Models, and Paradigms* (New York: Harper and Row, 1974).

4. The proper name of the Hebrew divinity is considered blasphemy to pronounce by many modern Jews and thus is usually translated by the four Hebrew letters YHWH. For convenience, however, it is rendered Yahweh in this book.

5. See Norman Gottwald, *The Tribes of Yahweh* (Maryknoll, N.Y.: Orbis Books, 1979); Guy Swanson, *The Birth of the Gods: The Origin of Primitive Beliefs* (Ann Arbor: University of Michigan Press, 1960); Swanson, "Monotheism, Materialism, and Collective Purpose: An Analysis of Underhill's Correlations," *American Journal of Sociology* 81 (1975): 841–861; Swanson, "Comment on

Underhill's reply," *American Journal of Sociology* 82 (1976): 421–423; Swanson, "Sovereign Groups, Subsistence Activities and the Presence of a High God in Primitive Societies," in *The Religious Dimension: New Directions in Quantitative Research* (New York: Academic Press, 1978), pp. 299–310; John Simpson, "Subsistence Systems and High Gods," prepared for the CSSR Annual Meeting, Vancouver, 1983.

6. Unless otherwise noted, all quotations from the Hebrew Bible, the New Testament, and the Apocrypha are from the Revised Standard Version, *The New Oxford Annotated Bible with the Apocrypha* (New York: Oxford University Press, 1973).

7. See Delbert Hillers, *Covenant: The History of a Biblical Idea* (Baltimore: Johns Hopkins, 1969).

8. See D. J. McCarthy, *Old Testament Covenant: A Survey of Current Opinions* (Richmond, Va.: John Knox Press, 1972); K. Baltzer, *Das Bundesformulaer*, WMANT 4 (Neukirchen, 1964); R. E. Clements, *Prophecy and Covenant*, Studies in Biblical Theology 43 (London: SPCK, 1965).

9. See Jacob Neusner, *The Way of Torah: An Introduction to Judaism* (Encino, Ca.: Dickenson, 1974); Yosef Yerushalmi, *Zakhor: Jewish History and Jewish Memory* (Seattle: University of Washington Press, 1982).

1. Israel between Empires

1. See Ezra 1:1; Isa. 41:2, 44:28, 45:1.

2. See Morton Smith, "II Isaiah and the Persians," *Journal of the American Oriental Society* 83 (1963): 415–421.

3. See F. M. Cross, "A Reconstruction of the Judean Restoration," *Journal of Biblical Literature* 94.1 (1975): 4–18.

4. Cross, p. 16. Cf. Morton Smith, *Palestinian Parties and Politics That Shaped the Old Testament* (New York: Columbia University Press, 1971).

5. See Isa. 56:3; Ezra 6:21; Neh. 9:2, 10:29, 13:3; Esther 9:27; Za. 2:15.

6. See Smith, *Palestinian Parties and Politics*, p. 73.

7. The marketing process normally tends to uphold the values of the particular regime promoting the religious reform, which can be effected in the service of either modernization or, just as often, conservative reaction to change imposed from the outside. This process was already evident in the government set up by Ezra and Nehemiah. In their case, the new order of imperial rule was legitimated by a conservative religious revolution to rebuild the old values. Whether

or not this process appears positive usually depends on the actors in the social drama. A contrast to the second commonwealth is contemporary revolutionary Iran where, in an attempt to impose a renovated form of traditional Shiism on the people, the religious system had a powerful, sometimes uncontrollable effect on the modernization process. See Peter Berger, *The Sacred Canopy: Elements of a Sociological Theory of Religion* (Garden City: Anchor Doubleday, 1969). Religion always reacts to events in the political, economic, and social realms. It also causes changes to those realms.

8. Menahem Stern, ed., *Greek Authors on Jews and Judaism* (Jerusalem: Israel Academy of Sciences and Humanities, 1974, 1980), I, 10, 26–35.

9. Elias Bickerman, *The God of the Maccabees*, trans. Horst R. Moehring (Leiden: Brill, 1978); Bickerman, *From Ezra to the Last of the Maccabees* (New York: Schocken, 1962, orig. ed. 1947).

10. See Milton Gordon, *Assimilation in American Life: The Role of Race, Religion, and National Origins* (New York: Oxford University Press, 1964).

11. See Victor Tcherikover, *Hellenistic Civilization and the Jews* (Philadelphia: Jewish Publication Society, 1961).

12. Epispasm, the operation in which the mark of circumcision was covered by drawing the flesh of the penis forward over the glans, was in those days a difficult and painful operation. That there were some who would submit to this needless and vain operation attests to the strength of their convictions about Hellenistic institutions.

13. See Victor Turner, *Dramas, Fields, and Metaphors: Symbolic Action in Human Society* (Ithaca: Cornell University Press, 1974), p. 26. The dynamic interaction of people within a certain society resembles drama when concerned with the understanding of these root metaphors. Since both sides of the conflict understood the implications of the covenant differently and yet accepted the basic metaphor, their interactions can be understood as a drama, exploring the limits of the covenantal metaphor.

2. Society in the Time of Jesus

1. The best examples of supposed first century C.E. synagogues are Masada, Herodium, and Gamle. The first two are clearly royal buildings of Herod the Great, which may have been fashioned into synagogues, perhaps by the zealots in the first war against Rome. The third, Gamle, is not in Judea but probably represents an authentic first century synagogue, though it may date from later than the destruction of the Temple in 70 C.E.

2. Josephus, *Against Apion* 2.178; Philo, *Concerning the Creation* 128; Jacob Neusner, "The Idea of Purity in Ancient Judaism," *Journal of the American Academy of Religion* 43 (1975): 15–27.

3. See Lee I. Levine, ed., *Ancient Synagogues Revealed* (Jerusalem: The Israel Exploration Society, 1981).

4. E. R. Goodenough, *Jewish Symbols of the Greco-Roman World* (New York: Pantheon Books, 1953–1968), 13 vols.

5. See Eric M. Meyers and James F. Strange, *Archeology, the Rabbis, and Early Christianity* (Nashville: Abingdon, 1981).

6. See Josephus, *Antiquities* 14.165–177, 20.200, 20.251.

7. S. B. Hoenig, *The Great Sanhedrin* (Philadelphia: Dropsie College, 1953); H. Mantel, *Studies in the History of the Sanhedrin* (Cambridge: Harvard University Press, 1961); Ellis Rivkin, "Beth Din, Boulé, Sanhedrin: A Tragedy of Errors," *Hebrew Union College Annual* 46 (1975): 181–199.

8. "Sects" is the usual translation of Josephus's word *haireseis.* Some of these groups would be considered sects in modern sociological parlance, but others would be closer to "denominations" or "parties."

9. All translations are from *Josephus in Nine Volumes,* Loeb Classical Library (Cambridge: Harvard University Press, 1927). This volume was translated by H. St. J. Thackeray.

10. See S. Isser, *The Dositheans* (SJLA XVII) (Leiden: Brill, 1976); J. Fossum, *The Name of God and the Angel of the Lord* (Ph.D. diss., University of Utrecht 1981).

11. See also Josephus, *The Jewish War* 2.119–161; Philo, *That Every Good Man Is Free* 75; Philo, *Hypothetica* 11.1; Philo, *On the Contemplative Life.*

12. See N. A. Dahl, "History and Eschatology in Light of the Dead Sea Scrolls," *The Crucified Messiah* (St. Paul, Minn.: Augsburg, 1974).

13. See Josephus, *Antiquities* 14.158–160, 20.102; Josephus, *Jewish War* 1.204–205, 2.433–488, 7.253; Acts 5:37.

14. See Morton Smith, "The Zealots and Sicarii," *Harvard Theological Review* 64 (1971): 1–19.

15. See e.g. Jacob Neusner, *The Rabbinic Traditions about the Pharisees before 70* C.E. (Leiden: Brill, 1971).

16. See E. R. Goodenough, *Introduction to Philo Judaeus* (Oxford: Blackwell, 1962); Samuel Sandmel, *Philo of Alexandria* (New York: Oxford University Press, 1979); H. A. Wolfson, *Philo* (Cambridge: Harvard University Press, 1947).

17. All translations are from *Philo,* Loeb Classical Library, 10 vols. (Cambridge: Harvard University Press, 1929), trans. F. H. Colson and G. H. Whitaker.

18. See W. A. Meeks, *The First Urban Christians: The Social World of the Apostle Paul* (New Haven: Yale University Press, 1983), pp. 51–73.

19. Lewis Coser, *The Functions of Social Conflict* (New York: Free Press, 1956), p. 80.

20. See Donald Gowan, *Bridge between the Testaments* (Pittsburgh: Pickwick Press, 1976); Job 3:17–19; Ps. 88:12; 2 Sam. 12:23.

21. See G. W. E. Nickelsburg, *Resurrection, Immortality, and Eternal Life in Intertestamental Judaism* (Missoula: Scholars Press, 1972); H. C. Cavallin, "Leben nach dem Tode im Spaetjudentum und im fruehen Christentum," *Aufstieg und Niedergang des roemischen Welt*, II vol. 19, 1 (Berlin: de Gruyter, 1979), pp. 240–345.

22. See Ben Sira 14:16–17.

23. See E. R. Goodenough, *The Politics of Philo Judaeus: Practice and Theory* (New Haven: Yale University Press, 1938), pp. 115–199, 279.

3. Jesus, the Jewish Revolutionary

1. Albert Schweitzer, *The Quest for the Historical Jesus*, 3rd ed. (London: A. and C. Black, 1954).

2. See e.g. Norman Perrin, *Rediscovering the Teaching of Jesus* (New York: Harper and Row, 1967).

3. See James Charlesworth, *The Pseudepigrapha in Modern Research* (Missoula, Mont.: Scholars Press, 1976); Michael Stone, *Scriptures, Sects, and Visions: A Profile of Judaism from Ezra to the Jewish Revolts* (Philadelphia: Fortress Press, 1980).

4. See Yonina Talmon, "Pursuit of the Millennium: The Relationship between Religions and Social Change," in W. Lessa and E. Vogt, ed., *Reader in Comparative Religion: An Anthropological Approach*, 2nd ed. (New York: Harper and Row, 1965), pp. 522–537; Bernard Barber, "Acculturation and Messianic Movements," in Lessa and Vogt, ed., *Reader in Comparative Religion: An Anthropological Approach*, 3rd ed. (New York: Harper and Row, 1972), pp. 512–516; Ralph Linton, Anthony F. C. Wallace, W. W. Hill, J. S. Slotkin, Cyril S. Belshaw, David Aberle, and Clifford Geertz, "Dynamics in Religion," in Lessa and Vogt, ed., *Reader*, 3rd ed., pp. 496–543.

5. Peter Worsley, *The Trumpet Shall Sound: A Study of "Cargo" Cults in Melanesia* (New York: Schocken Books, 1968, 1970); Kenelm Burridge, *New Heaven, New Earth: A Study of Millenarian Activities* (New York: Schocken Books, 1969); John Gager, *Kingdom and Community: The Social World of Early Christianity* (Englewood Cliffs: Prentice Hall, 1975); S. R. Isenberg, "Millen-

arism in Greco-Roman Palestine," *Religion* 4 (1974):26–46; I. C. Jarvie, *The Revolution in Anthropology* (Chicago: Henry Regnery, 1967), p. 52; *Max Weber: Essays in Sociology*, trans. and ed. H. H. Gerth and C. Wright Mills (New York: Oxford University Press, 1946); Weber, *Ancient Judaism*, trans. H. H. Gerth and Don Martindale (New York: Free Press, 1952); Weber, *Gesammelte Aufsaetze zur Religionssociologie*, 3 vols. (Tübingen: Moehr, 1920–1930); Robert C. Tescher, "A Theory of Charismatic Leadership," *Daedalus: Journal of the American Academy of Arts and Sciences*, Summer 1968, pp. 73–74.

6. Worsley, *The Trumpet Shall Sound;* Vittorio Lantenari, *The Religions of the Oppressed: A Study of Modern Messianic Cults*, English ed. (New York: Alfred A. Knopf, 1963); D. Aberle, "A Note on Relative Deprivation Theory As Applied to Millenarian and Other Cult Movements," in Sylvia Thrupp, ed., *Millennial Dreams in Action: Studies in Revolutionary Religious Movements* (New York: Schocken Books, 1970); Gager, *Kingdom and Community.*

7. See Victor Turner, *The Ritual Process: Structure and Anti-Structure* (Ithaca: Connell University Press, 1977); Barber, "Acculturation and Messianic Movements," in Lessa and Vogt, ed., *Reader*, pp. 512–516; Gerd Theissen, *The First Followers of Jesus: A Sociological Analysis of the Earliest Christianity*, trans. John Bowden (London: SCM Press, 1978), originally published in German and published again as *Sociology of Early Palestinian Christianity;* M. I. Finley, *The Ancient Economy* (Berkeley: University of California Press, 1973); Wayne Meeks, *The First Urban Christians* (New Haven: Yale University Press, 1983), pp. 53–54. The movement of Sabbatianism in Judaism is an example of this phenomenon. Pogroms alone do not account for the rise of the messianic movement around Sabbatai Zevi in the years around 1666 in the Turkish Empire, for that was not the place where pogroms actually took place. Instead, the threat of pogroms, together with the rise of Lurianic Kabbalah, a mystical movement given to messianic speculation, accounts for the rise of the mystical messiah. See Gershom Scholem, *Sabbatai Zevi* (Princeton: Princeton University Press, 1976). The same is true of conversion to marginal religious sects in contemporary American life. See John Lofland and Rodney Stark, "Becoming a World Saver: A Theory of Conversion to a Deviant Perspective," *American Sociological Review* 30 (1965): 862–875; Bernard Barber, "Function, Variability, and Change in Ideological Systems," in Bernard Barber and Alex Inkeles, ed., *Stability and Social Change* (Boston: Little Brown, 1971).

8. See e.g. V. Lantennari, *Religions of the Oppressed: A Study of Modern Messianic Cults* (New York: Knopf, 1963). Sabbatianism provided a clear example of the moment of political decision in Judaism. See Scholem, *Sabbatai Zevi.* The radically mystical and apolitical nature of Sabbatianism became clear only after Sabbatai Zevi was apprehended by the Sultan in Constantinople as a political threat and offered the choice of conversion to Islam or death. Zevi's choice of conversion began a reinterpretation of the mystical tradition to account for a Muslim messiah, and it also clarified a future nonpolitical role for Sabbatianism.

9. See also Sibylline Oracles 3:381–400.

10. D. S. Russell, *The Method and Message of Jewish Apocalyptic* (Philadelphia: Westminister, Press, 1964), pp. 286–287.

11. J. J. Collins, *The Apocalyptic Vision of the Book of Daniel* (Missoula, Mont.: Scholars Press, 1977), esp. pp. 167–170, 191–218.

12. Frank Cross, *The Essene Library at Qumran and Modern Biblical Studies* (Garden City, N.Y.: Doubleday, 1958), pp. 80–120.

13. See J. T. Milik, *The Books of Enoch* (Oxford: Oxford University Press, 1976); Gershom Scholem, *Major Trends in Jewish Mysticism* (New York: Schocken Press, 1967); Scholem, *Jewish Gnosticism, Merkabah Mysticism, and Talmudic Tradition* (New York: JTS, 1965).

14. See Hagigah 14b; Sanhedrin 38b.

15. Hymns 6:13; 3:20; 11:10; 2:10; Manual of Discipline 2:5–10.

16. See Gilles Quispel, "Gnosis," in Maarten J. Vermaseren, ed., *Die orientalischen Religionen im Roemmerreich* (Leiden: E. J. Brill, 1981).

17. See e.g. A. J. B. Higgins, *Jesus and the Son of Man* (Philadelphia: Fortress Press, 1964).

18. See Alan F. Segal, *Two Powers in Heaven* (Leiden: Brill, 1977).

19. The "son of man" was once mistakenly thought to be the Jewish name for a widespread Persian and Indian mythical figure who represented a less nationalistic and more universal messianic hope. Another theory has it that "son of man" means merely "I," as does "that man" in Aramaic, and that Jesus only meant to be referring to himself. See Geza Vermes, *Jesus the Jew* (London: SPCK, 1973).

20. The Matthew 26:61 version reads: "I am able to destroy the temple of God, and to build it in three days." John 2:19 reads: "Destroy this temple, and in three days, I will raise it up."

21. Martin Hengel, *Was Jesus a Revolutionist?* (Philadelphia: Fortress Press, 1971).

22. See Martin Hengel, *Property and Riches in the Early Church: Aspects of a Social History of Early Christianity,* trans. John Bowden (Philadelphia: Fortress Press, 1974).

23. Like his father, Jesus was an artisan, a *tekton,* a Greek word that means mason, carpenter, cartwright, and joiner all rolled into one (Mark 6:3). According to Justin Martyr, he had "made yokes and ploughs" (*Dial.* 88:8); Hengel, *Property and Riches,* p. 27.

24. N. A. Dahl, *The Crucified Messiah* (Minneapolis, Minn.: 1974).

25. Messiah ben Joseph: "What is the cause of this wailing? Rabbi Dosa and the rabbis disagree. One says: It is on account of the killing of the Messiah son of Joseph. Another says: This is on account of the killing of the evil inclination. But the former interpretation is to be adopted, for it is written, 'And they shall look on him whom they have transpierced, and they shall wail over him as over an only child.' Why should he who says that it is on account of the killing of the evil inclination be sorrowful? He should rejoice rather than weep." (b. suk. 52a.) See also Vermes, *Jesus the Jew,* p. 139.

26. See the Dead Sea Scrolls, 11 QMelch; Philo, *Life of Moses;* Philo, *Questions and Answers* on Exod. 24:10–12.

27. The servant in Isaiah 53 may have originally referred to a specific character, as opposed to other servant psalms, which are metaphorical descriptions of Israel. However, the death of this servant is not necessarily implied by the reference to his grave being dug, which may merely mean that he was expected to die.

28. In the Aramaic Targum to Isaiah 53 the rabbis maintain a surprising messianic interpretation where, against the literal meaning of Isaiah 53, the servant messiah makes all the enemies of God suffer. This is clearly polemic against Christianity inserted into rabbinic commentary.

29. Gager, *Kingdom and Community.*

4. Paul, the Convert and Apostle

1. See *The Writings of St. Paul,* ed. Wayne A. Meeks (New York: W. W. Norton, 1972), pp. 277–319.

2. Origen, *Contra Celsum* 3:44, ed. Henry Chadwick (Cambridge: Cambridge University Press, 1965), p. 158; Wayne Meeks, *The First Urban Christians: The Social World of the Apostle Paul* (New Haven: Yale University Press, 1982), p. 51. Although there is evidence for wealthy patrons of Christianity, such as the centurion in Acts 10, the earliest church was drawn largely from the lower echelons of the society.

3. See Meeks, *The First Urban Christians,* p. 52; Gerd Theis-

sen, "Soziale Integration und sakramentales Handeln: Eine Analyse von 1 Cor. XI 17-34," *Novum Testamentum* 24 (1979): 290–317; Abraham Malherbe, *Social Aspects of Early Christianity* (Baton Rouge: Louisiana State University Press, 1977), pp. 29–59; N. A. Dahl, "Paul and Possessions," *Studies in Paul* (Minneapolis: Augsburg Press, 1977); R. Hock, *The Social Context of Paul's Ministry: Tent Making and Apostleship* (Philadelphia: Fortress Press, 1980); Ross Kraemer, "Women in the Religions of the Greco-Roman World," *Religious Studies Review* 9.2 (April 1983): 127–139. By now, not all Christians were apocalypticists, but apocalypticism was still one of the dominant motifs of the earliest church.

   4. A. D. Nock, *Conversion: The Old and the New in Religion from Alexander the Great to Augustine of Hippo* (Oxford: Oxford University Press, 1933).

   5. See William Sargant, *The Battle for the Mind: A Physiology of Conversion and Brainwashing* (New York: Harper and Row, 1957); Robert J. Lifton, *Thought Reform and the Psychology of Totalism* (New York, 1961); Flo Conway and Jim Siegelman, *Snapping: America's Epidemic of Sudden Personality Change* (New York: J. D. Lippincott, 1978); Christopher Evans, *Cults of Unreason* (New York: Dell, 1973).

   6. See Leon Festinger, Henry W. Riecken, and Stanley Schacter, *When Prophecy Fails: A Social and Psychological Study of a Modern Group That Predicted the Destruction of the World* (New York, 1956); Jane Allyn Hardwyck and Marcia Braden, "Prophecy Fails Again: A Report of a Failure to Replicate," *Journal of Abnormal and Social Psychology* 65 (1962): 136–141; Leon Festinger, Stanley Schachter, and Kurt Bach, *Social Pressures in Informal Groups: A Study of Human Factors in Housing* (Palo Alto: Stanford University Press, 1950); Leon Festinger, *A Theory of Cognitive Dissonance* (Evanston: Row Peterson, 1957); Robert B. Zajonc, "The Concepts of Balance, Congruity, and Dissonance," *Public Opinion Quarterly* 24 (1960): 280–296; Robert A. Wicklund and Jack W. Brehm, *Perspectives on Cognitive Dissonance* (New York: Lawrence Erlbaum, 1976).

   7. Leon Festinger, with the collaboration of Vernon Allen, Marcia Braden, Lance Kirkpatrick Canon, Jon R. Davidson, Jon D. Jecker, Sara B. Kiesler, and Elaine Walster, *Conflict, Decision, and Dissonance* (Stanford: Stanford University Press, 1964); Robert P. Carroll, *When Prophecy Fails: Cognitive Dissonance in the Prophetic Traditions of the Old Testament* (New York: Seabury Press, 1979), p. 87.

   8. Rosabeth Kanter, *Commitment and Community* (Cambridge:

Harvard University Press, 1972), p. 64; Rosabeth Moss Kanter, "Commitment and the Internal Organization of Millennial Movements," *American Behavioral Scientist* 16.2 (Dec. 1972): 129–143; Leon Festinger, "The Psychological Effects of Insufficient Reward," *American Psychologist* 16 (1961): 1–11; Festinger, *Conflict, Decision, and Dissonance.*

9. There were also nonapocalyptic Christians. Early Christianity was far more varied than the New Testament suggests. Christianity soon appropriated very different interpretations of Jesus' word and purpose, depending on the disposition of the various communities. The dominant mode, however, continued to be apocalyptic, whatever other wisdom or protognostic communities it also subsumed. As time went on, Christianity became even more varied. Paul's genius was to unify the various parts of the Christian community with his new mythological metaphor of the body of believers, which was coupled with the new social reality of house churches.

10. See Lawrence Schiffman, *Sectarian Law in the Dead Sea Scrolls: Courts, Testimony, and the Penal Code* (Chico, Cal.: Scholars Press, 1983), pp. 155–174.

11. The Gospel of John's dualism has sociological implications and is a key for understanding Gnosticism.

12. Krister Stendahl, "The Apostle Paul and the Introspective Conscience of the West," *Harvard Theological Review* 56 (1963): 200.

13. See John Gager, "Some Notes on Paul's Conversion," *New Testament Studies* 27 (1982): 697–704.

14. See N. A. Dahl, "Widersprueche in der Bibel, ein altes hermeneutisches Problem," *Studia Theologica* 25 (1971): 1–19.

15. E. P. Sanders, *Paul and Palestinian Judaism: A Comparison of Patterns of Religion* (Philadelphia: Fortress Press, 1977), p. 442.

16. See Seyoon Kim, *The Origin of Paul's Gospel* (Tuebingen: J. C. B. Mohr, 1981).

17. See Meeks, *The First Urban Christians*, p. 87.

18. Mary Douglas, *Natural Symbols: Explorations in Cosmology*, 2nd ed. (London: Barrie and Jenkins, 1973).

19. See Gager, "Some Notes."

20. See John G. Gager, *The Origins of Anti-Semitism: Attitudes towards Judaism in Pagan and Christian Antiquity* (New York: Oxford University Press, 1983); Lloyd Gaston, "Paul and the Torah," in *Antisemitism and the Foundations of Christianity*, ed. Alan T. Davies (New York: Paulist Press, 1979), pp. 48–71; Krister Stendahl, "Judaism and Christianity: A Plea for a New Relationship," *Cross Currents* 17 (1967): 445–458.

21. The scholarly position that Paul is talking about only Gentile food laws and that he never himself ceased practicing Jewish dietary laws needs careful reconsideration and nuancing.

5. Origins of the Rabbinic Movement

1. Rabbinic legend narrates a similar incident during the time of Alexander Jannaeus (Yannai Hamelekh). Probably rabbinic tradition, with its longer stage of oral transmission and different values, has reinterpreted the story for its own purposes over the years.

2. See Ellis Rivkin, *A Hidden Revolution: The Pharisees' Search for the Kingdom Within* (Nashville: Abingdon, 1978), p. 270.

3. Jacob Neusner, *From Politics to Piety: The Emergence of Pharisaic Judaism* (Englewood Cliffs: Prentice Hall, 1973), pp. 67–80.

4. See Morton Smith, "Palestinian Judaism in the First Century," in Moshe Davis, ed., *Israel: Its Role in Civilization* (New York: Seminary Israel Institute, 1956).

5. Jacob Neusner, *The Rabbinic Traditions about the Pharisees before 70*, 3 parts (Leiden: Brill, 1971).

6. Rivkin, *A Hidden Revolution.*

7. See Leviticus 17:10–11; Numbers 18, 19:14.

8. See David Suter, "Fallen Angel, Fallen Priest: The Problem of Family Purity in I Enoch," *Hebrew Union College Annual* 50 (1979): 115–135.

9. Neusner, *From Politics to Piety.*

10. See Owen Lynch, *The Politics of Untouchability: Social Mobility and Social Change in a City of India* (New York: Columbia University Press, 1969); M. N. Srinivas, *Social Change in Modern India* (Berkeley: University of California Press, 1966); Louis Dumont, *Homo Hierarchicus: The Caste System and Its Implications*, complete rev. English ed., trans. Mark Sainsbury, Louis Dumont, and Basia Gulati (Chicago: University of Chicago Press, 1980).

11. See Talcott Parsons, *The Social System* (New York: Collier-Macmillan, Free Press, 1951); Parsons, *Societies: Evolutionary and Comparative Perspectives* (Englewood Cliffs, N.J.: Prentice Hall, 1966).

6. Communities in Conflict

1. Morton Smith, *Jesus the Magician* (San Francisco: Harper and Row, 1978); Alan F. Segal, "Hellenistic Magic: Some Questions of

Definition," in R. van den Broek and M. J. Vermaseren, ed., *Studies in Gnosticism and Hellenistic Religions: Presented to Gilles Quispel on the Occasion of His 65th Birthday* (Leiden: Brill, 1981), pp. 349–375.

2. Ramsey MacMullen, *Enemies of the Roman Order: Treason, Unrest, and Alienation in the Empire* (Cambridge: Harvard University Press, 1966), pp. 95-162.

3. See the rabbinic comment about Simeon b. Zoma, b. Hagigah 15a. He is also described as "outside," which may be either ecstasy or insanity.

4. E. R. Goodenough, *Jewish Symbols of the Greco-Roman World* (New York: Pantheon Books, 1953–1968).

5. Joseph Heinemann, *Ha-Tefilah bi-Tequfat Ha-Tannai'im ve-ha-'Amoraim* (Jerusalem, 1964).

6. Justin, *Dial.* 16, 47, 96, 137; Origen, *H. Jeremiah* 10.8.2; Epiphanius, *Panarion* 29.9.1; Jerome, *Epis. August.* 112.13. See also Klijn and Reinink, *Patristic Evidence for Jewish-Christianity, Supplements to Novum Testamentum* 36 (Leiden: Brill, 1973); Reuven Kimelman, "*Birkat Ha-minim* and the Lack of Evidence for an Anti-Christian Jewish Prayer in Late Antiquity," in E. P. Sanders with A. I. Baumgarten and Alan Mendelson, ed., *Jewish and Christian Self-Definition*, vol. 2. *Aspects of Judaism in the Greco-Roman Period* (Philadelphia: Fortress Press, 1981), pp. 226–244, 391–403.

7. See Alan F. Segal, *Two Powers in Heaven: Early Rabbinic Reports about Christianity and Gnosticism* (Leiden: Brill, 1977); Alan F. Segal, "Ruler of This World: Attitudes about Mediator Figures and the Importance of Sociology for Self-Definition," in Sanders et al., ed., *Jewish and Christian Self-Definition*, II, 245–268, 403–413.

8. See A. H. Goldfahn, *Justinus Martyr und die Agada* (Breslau: Glutsch, n.d.); Moritz Friedlaender, *Geschichte der juedischen Apologetik als Vorgeschichte des Christentums* (Amsterdam: 1903); Adolf Buechler, "The Minim of Sepphoris and Tiberias in the Second and Third Centuries," *Studies in Jewish History* (Oxford: Oxford University Press, 1956), pp. 245–274. Justin Martyr was born at the beginning of the second century in Shechem, then called Flavia Neapolis, in Samaria. He called himself a Samaritan, which meant only that he was descended from people living in that part of the country and not that he was a member of that religious sect, because he stated that he was uncircumcised. Justin's life shows the relationship between Samaritans and early Gentile Christianity.

9. E. R. Goodenough, *The Theology of Justin Martyr: An Inves-*

tigation into the Conceptions of the Earliest Christian Literature and Its Hellenistic and Judaistic Influences (Jena, 1923), pp. 147-148.

7. The Ways Divide

1. See Samuel Helfgott, *The Doctrine of Election in Rabbinic Literature* (New York, 1954), p. 69; Midrash Prov. 17:1. An attribution to a first century rabbi can also be scrutinized for authenticity, in the way that the criterion of dissimilarity can be used to scrutinize Jesus' words. There is a difference, however, in that much less hangs on an attribution in Jewish literature than in Jesus' case. Here, the story does not present a consistent theological position. Moreover, it is slightly embarrassing in that all the Gentiles are lumped together and weighed as a single group. That a rabbi can state that they should all be condemned by God is also startling, because the later mature rabbinic position favors the salvation of righteous Gentiles. Furthermore, in the first century both Josephus and Philo, as well as Christianity, touch on these issues in their own characteristic ways. Universalism is a feature of Hellenistic Jewish apologetic. The criterion of dissimilarity, adapted to midrashic use, tends to verify the historicity of the rabbinic debate, if not its exact wording. The frankness of the discussion, combined with the historical appropriateness of discussions of universalism, suggest that the dispute between Rabbis Joshua and Eliezer is authentic. Were it not an authentic tradition, there would have been little reason to preserve such a grudging admission. And there is no particular gain for the rabbis to give the story a false antiquity.

2. See W. D. Davies, *Paul and Rabbinic Judaism: Some Rabbinic Elements in Pauline Theology* (New York: Harper, 1948), p. 114.

3. See Peter Brown, *The Making of Late Antiquity* (Cambridge: Harvard University Press, 1978); Ramsey MacMullen, *Christianizing the Roman Empire A.D. 100–400* (New Haven: Yale University Press, 1984).

4. Mary Douglas, *Natural Symbols: Explorations in Cosmology,* 2nd ed. (London: Barrie and Jenkins, 1973), p. 196.

5. Louis Dumont, *Homo Hierarchichus: The Caste System and Its Implications* (Chicago: University of Chicago Press, 1980); Mary Douglas, *Implicit Meanings in Anthropology* (London: Routledge and Kegan Paul, 1975), pp. 190–191.

6. See Douglas, *Implicit Meanings.*

Scriptural Index

(for noncanonical works, see General Index)

Genesis 1:28, 79; ch. 15, 5–6; 19:24, 159, 160; 25:23, 179

Exodus 15:3, 16, 152; chs. 19–34, 78; 20:2–17, 8, 152; ch. 24, 139; 24:10, 14, 79; 24:10–12, 152, 190

Leviticus 17:10–11, 193; 18:5, 105, 168; 21:11, 60

Numbers 6:6, 60; ch. 18, 193; 19:14, 193: 23:19, 58; 24:15–17, 51; 24:17–19, 49–50

Deuteronomy 6:4, 151; 18:18, 51; 21:23, 106; 27:26, 105; ch. 32, 151; 32:39, 152; 33:8–11, 51

2 Samuel 7, 65; 7:19, 168; 12:23, 187

Ezra 1:1–2, 15, 184; 6:16–18, 36; 6:21, 184

Nehemiah 8:13–9:38 (10:1 in Hebrew), 18; 9:2, 184; 10:29, 184; 13:3, 184

Esther 9:27, 184

Job 3:17–19, 187; 14:14, 61; 14:20–22, 61; 19:25–27, 61

Psalms 29, 14; 33:1, 168; 45:7–8, 159; 88:12, 187; ch. 89, 93; ch. 110, 88, 89; 118:15–25, 90, 168; 124:4, 168; 137:1–6, 13

Ecclesiastes 3:19, 61

Isaiah 11, 65; 11:3–4, 66; 25:8, 62; ch. 26, 62; 26:2, 168; 26:15–16, 62; 26:19, 62, 63; 40:1–2, 16; 41:2, 184; 41:4, 152; 43:15–19, 16; chs. 44–47, 151–152; 44:6, 152; 44:28, 184; 45:1, 184; 46:4, 152; ch. 53, 91–92, 93, 94, 190; 56:3, 184; 60:1–3, 17; 60:21, 53, 166

Jeremiah 23, 65

Lamentations 5:19–22, 14

Ezekiel 1, 79; ch. 10, 79; 11:16, 41; ch. 34, 65; ch. 37, 62

Daniel 7–12, 73; 7:8, 73; 7:9, 66, 73, 152; 7:10, 152; 7:13, 73, 77, 78, 153; 7:27, 73; 8:9, 73; 11:2, 74; 11:31, 73; 11:34, 74; 11:40–45, 74; ch. 12, 66, 77; 12:2, 62–63, 74; 12:11, 73

Hosea 2:16–20, 10

Micah ch. 5, 65

Habakkuk 2:4, 105

Zechariah 2:15, 184; 3:8, 93

Matthew 9:24, 119; 10:23, 79; 12:22–30, 144; ch. 15, 119; 16:28, 79; 19:28, 79; 19:30, 82; ch. 23, 101–102, 146; 26:61, 189; 27:25, 146

Mark 1:21, 119; 2:23, 119; 3:1–2, 119; 3:19–27, 144; 3:22, 119; 6:3, 190; ch. 7, 119; 7:1–8, 119–120; 7:9, 120; 8:38, 78; 9:9–10, 120; 10:2–4, 120; 10:24, 83; 10:31, 82; 11:15–16, 120; 14:58, 80

Luke 5:20–21, 119; 6:30, 83; 11:14–23, 144; 12:8–9, 79; 13:30, 82; 16:13, 83

John 2:19, 189; 3:33, 156; 5:18, 156; 8:39–47, 157; 9:22, 150; 10:33, 156

Acts ch. 2, 141; 4:11, 90; 5:37, 186; 8:26–40, 92–93; 10:1–33, 164

Romans 2:12–24, 111; 3:21–31, 110; 9:1–3, 104; 9:6–13, 179; 11:17–22, 111; 14:1–6, 112; 14:14, 112; 14:20, 112; 14:15–20, 112; 15:1, 112

1 Corinthians 1:23, 94; 3:10–17, 90; ch. 8, 112; 10:25–30, 112
2 Corinthians 11:21–22, 104; 12:1–9, 107
Galatians 1:13–14, 104; 2:11–12, 111–112; ch. 3, 105; 3:38, 108; ch. 6, 113
Philippians 2:9–11, 158; 3:4–6, 104

Colossians 3:9–10, 109

4 Ezra 7:28–30, 66–67
Ben Sira 14:16–19, 46, 187
1 Maccabees 1:11–15, 32; ch. 2, 75; 14:41, 75
2 Maccabees ch. 7, 63

General Index

Aaron, 51
Ab Beth Din, 44
Aberle, David, 187–188
Abraham, 1, 5–8, 19, 106, 157, 159, 179
Acculturation, 25, 31, 33, 70, 172
Acts of the Apostles, 43, 107, 151, 163
Adam, 60, 78, 89
Adam and Eve, 21
Adoption, 20
Adultery, 10–11
Alabarch, 55
Alexander Jannaeus, 193
Alexander the Great, 22–24, 28
Alexandria, 24, 27, 33, 36, 48, 54–55, 57
Allegory, 53, 55, 100, 139, 154–155
Altar, 35, 74
Amos, 9
"Ancient of Days," 73
Angels, 14, 51, 56, 66, 73–74, 76–78, 80, 87, 89, 109, 155–156, 160
Animals, 6, 93, 126, 170
Anointing, 64–65
Anthropomorphism, 14, 56–57
Anti-Christian, 69
Anit-Judaism, 26–27, 157
Antinomianism, 97, 163
Antioch, 28, 112, 158
Antiochus III the Great, 28
Antiochus IV Epiphanes, 27–30, 34–35, 37, 73–74, 76–77
Anti-Semitism, 26–27, 157
Aphrodisias, 43
Apion, 26–27
Apocalypticism, 10, 53, 63, 66, 68–73, 74–75, 76, 77, 78–81, 82, 84, 85, 87, 88, 94, 95–97, 99, 100, 102–104, 108, 114, 118, 121–122, 124, 129–131, 136, 147, 155–157, 165, 171, 180, 192
Apocrypha, 184
Apollonius, 30
Apollonius Molon, 27
Apostasy, 31–32
Apostles, 84, 95
Apostolic authority, 116
Arab conquest, 23
Arab countries, 147
Aramaic, 27, 73, 76, 89, 190
Archangels, 73
Archisynagogos, 43
Archontes, 43
Ascension, 77, 87, 138, 175
Asceticism, 83
Asia Minor, 96
Assimilation, 31, 33
Assyria, 21, 47
Atonement, 92, 94, 108, 131, 137–138
Athens, 134, 137
Avodah Zarah, 112

Ba'al, 11, 62
Babylonia, 1, 4, 12–17, 19, 21, 41, 62, 74, 174, 177
Bach, Kurt, 191
Baltzer, K., 184
Baptism, 9, 11, 21, 24, 45, 47, 55–56, 82, 103–104, 108–111, 113, 116, 124, 164, 168
Baptismal formula, 175
Baram, 42
Barber, Bernard, 183, 187–188

Bar Kokhba, 50, 86, 132, 158, 174. *See also* Revolt: second
Barbour, Ian G., 183
Baruch: 2:1, 129; 3:10–12, 129–130; 4:17, 130; 18:23, 130
Baths, ritual, 103, 124–125
Beelzebul, 144–145
Belshaw, Cyril S., 187
Bema (podium), 42
Ben Sira, 28, 64; 14:16–19, 46, 187
Berger, Peter, 185
Beth Alpha, 42
Beth Din (rabbinic court), 44
Bible, 76, 94, 100, 126, 129, 133, 138, 146, 151, 166, 173, 184
Biblical narrators, 5, 8–9, 19
Bickerman, Elias, 185
Binitarians, 154
Birkat Haminim, 150
Bishops, 116
Blasphemy, 156, 170
Boulé, 44
Braden, Marcia, 191
Brehm, Jack W., 191
Brith, 4
Bronze Age, 7
Brown, Peter, 195
Buechler, Adolf, 194
Burridge, Kenelm, 187

"Camping-Out Festival of Kislev," 36
Canaan(ites), 7–8, 10–11, 19, 50, 62
Capernaum, 42
Carroll, Robert P., 191
Cavallin, H. C., 187
Cephas, 111–112. See also *Peter*
Charismatic, 143–144
Charlesworth, James, 187
Cherubim, 14
Children of darkness and light, 51, 77–78, 102
Christ, 88, 94, 104, 106, 108–111, 130, 153, 159–160, 175
Christianity, 1–3, 12, 22, 39, 43, 49, 51, 54, 57, 60, 64, 66–69, 73, 78, 79–83, 84–87, 88, 90, 91, 93–96, 98–99, 102, 109, 113, 116, 130, 135, 141–147, 150, 153–155, 158–159, 161–181, 194
Christos, 64–65
Church, 68, 78, 80, 84–85, 87–88, 90, 92, 95

Church fathers, 150, 172
Circumcision, 32–34, 97, 102, 104, 108, 110, 112–113
Class, 16, 26, 31, 81–83, 97
Clements, R. E., 184
"Cognitive dissonance," 100–101, 103–104, 114–116
Cohesion, 101–102
Commonwealth: first, 47; second, 17, 20–22, 25
Communion, 115
Communitarian idealism, 71, 83
Community, 48, 82–85, 89–90, 108–110, 113, 115, 127
Conceptual archetype, 3
Constantine, 174
"Constitutional assembly," 18
Conversion, 19–20, 56, 64, 65, 94–95, 99–110, 114–116, 137, 163, 168, 170, 175
Coser, Lewis, 59, 187
Cosmopolitanism, 2, 59–60
Cosmos, 3, 5
Council of Constantinople, 154
Counterconversion, 102
Covenant, 4–12, 17–18, 20, 31–33, 38, 57–60, 68
Creation, 17, 21
"Criterion of dissimilarity," 68–69, 78–79, 84–87, 194
Cross, Frank M., 75, 184, 189
Crucifixion, 64–65, 85, 94
Cybele, 137
Cyrus, 13–17, 22, 65, 73

Dahl, Nils A., 85, 186, 190–192
Daniel, 46, 62–64, 66, 69, 73–78, 86, 88
David, 5, 7, 17, 20–21, 38, 65, 93, 174
Davidic kings, 17–18, 20–21, 47, 65, 84–85, 88
Davies, Alan T., 192
Davies, W. D., 195
Dead Sea Scrolls, 48–51, 69, 75–77, 80; *Hymns* 2:10, 3:20, 6:13, and 11:10, 189; *Manual of Discipline* 1QS 9:10–11, 51; *War Scroll* 1QM, 70; 11:6–10, 50; 11 QMelch, 89–90. *See also* Qumran
Demiurge, 176
Demons, 145
Denominations, 186

Desert tabernacle, 38
Deuteronomy, 19
Diaspora, 12, 25, 39, 41, 43, 55, 97, 104, 125
Dietary laws, 112, 123, 126, 164–165, 176–177, 193
Divorce, 146–147
Douglas, Mary, 109, 175, 178, 183, 192, 195
Dumont, Louis, 193, 195
Dura Europos, 42

Easter, 85, 141
Ecclesiastes, Book of, 28
Ecstasy, 107–108, 194
Egypt, 12, 24, 28–29, 74, 76, 139
Eikons (images), 170
El, 89
Eleazar, 119
Eleazar (revolutionary), 52
Election, 17, 169, 171
Eleusinian mysteries, 137
Elijah, 93, 120
Elohim, 156
"End of time (days)," 46, 51, 69–70, 74, 79, 100, 102, 146, 153
Endogamy, 10, 18–20, 32, 124–125, 178
Enoch literature, 70, 155
I Enoch, 63, 76, 78, 193
Ephraim, 47
Epicurean, 166
Epiphanius, *Panarion*, 29.9.1, 194
Epispasm, 185
Esau, 1, 179, 181
Essenes, 38–39, 48–51, 58, 67, 69, 75–77, 82–83, 85, 102–103, 118, 129, 135, 142, 149
Ethiopian eunuch, 92–93
Evangelists, 97, 144, 146
Evans, Christopher, 191
Evil, 55–56, 74, 77
Exegesis, 38–39, 41, 44–46, 49–51, 53–55, 78–79, 85, 88–95, 105–106, 122–123, 128, 133, 142, 151–154, 158, 170
Exodus, 12, 16, 138
"Extreme allegorizers," 57
Ezekias, 52
Ezekiel, 14–15, 41, 78
Ezekiel the Tragedian, 78
Ezra, 1, 5, 15, 18, 20, 22, 36, 184
4 Ezra (*2 Esdras*) 66–67

Family, 20
"Father of the Court," 44
Fathers according to Rabbi Nathan, The, ch. 6, 131
Fertility cults, 10–11
Festinger, Leon, 100, 191–192
"Festival of Lights," 36
Finley, M. I., 188
Flavia Neapolis, 194
Fossum, J., 186

Gabriel, 73
Gager, John, 105, 187–188, 190, 192
Gaius Caligula, 55
Galilee, 28, 42, 44, 48, 52, 54, 81, 83, 117, 173
Gamaliel, 150
Gamle, 42, 185
Garden of Eden, 55
Gaston, Lloyd, 192
Geertz, Clifford, 187
Genesis, 21, 170
Gentiles, 39–40, 43, 48, 50, 56, 66, 95–99, 105–106, 110–113, 114, 115–116, 124–125, 153, 161–171, 175–177, 195
Gnosis, 175–176
Gnosticism, 47, 115, 142, 150, 175–176, 192
"God-fearers," 43, 98, 111
Golan heights, 42
Goldfahn, A. H., 194
Goodenough, E. R., 160, 186–187, 194
Gordon, Milton, 185
Gospels, 81, 84, 101, 119, 146–147, 157
Gottwald, Norman, 183
Gowan, Donald, 187
Greece, 22–24, 31, 96

Hades, 60
Haggadah, 139–140
Haireseis, 186
Hammurabi, 4
Hanukkah, 28–29, 34–37, 140
Hardwyck, Jane Allyn, 191
Harvey, Van, 183
Hasidim, 75–76, 80
Hasmoneans, 30, 35–40, 44, 75, 140
Havuroth, 125–126
"Healers," 48
Heavenly council (court), 61, 73
Heavenly journey, 63–64, 76–77

Hebrew, 24, 27–28, 89, 153–156, 173
Hebrew Bible, 4, 46, 56, 64–65, 69, 88, 90, 93, 155
Hebrews, 4–5, 18, 20, 30
Hecataeus, 26
Heinemann, Joseph, 194
Hekhaloth texts, 76, 155
Helfgott, Samuel, 195
Helios Mithras, 77
Hell, 63
Hellenism, 14, 18, 23–26, 28–34, 37–41, 43, 46, 55–56, 59–60, 63–65, 70, 76, 88, 97–98, 108, 109, 116, 123, 132, 134, 137, 143, 145, 148, 155, 160–161, 178, 181, 185
Hellenistic Jews (Judaism), 28, 31–33, 35, 38, 45–46, 50, 54–58, 74, 89, 110, 123–124, 134, 137–139, 141, 161, 165, 167–168, 172, 177–178, 195
Hellenistic world, 26, 27, 30–31, 33, 42, 46, 59, 96, 101, 179
Hellenization, 22, 24–28, 33, 37, 45, 105, 122, 134
Hengel, Martin, 189–190
Hercules, 63
Heresy, 47, 148–149, 151, 153, 160, 162, 171, 178
Herod, 39–40, 52, 185
Herodium, 185
Higgins, A. J. B., 189
High Priest, 19, 29, 37, 39–40, 44, 49, 75–76
Hill, W. W., 187
Hillers, Delbert, 184
Hindus, 127
History, 2–4, 11–12, 50, 94
Hock, R., 191
Hoenig, S. B., 186
Holy of Holies, 19, 40
Holy Spirit, 142, 145, 154, 159
Homer, 46, 55
Hosea, 10–11
House churches, 109, 114, 192

Ideal kingship, 65
Idolatry, 112, 170
Immortality, 55, 61, 63–64, 76–77, 138
Incarnation, 160, 175
Individualism, 2, 59–60
Indo-European languages, 23
Indus River, 23

Inkeles, Alex, 188
Iran, 23, 185
Isaac, 1, 5, 8
Isaiah, 16–17, 54, 152
Isenberg, S. R., 187
Isis, 137
Islam, 76, 171, 176, 189
Israel, 4, 7, 10–12, 13, 17, 19, 24–25, 28, 35, 39, 41–42, 46, 47, 55, 59, 66, 68, 84, 117, 131, 140, 167
Israelites, 3–4, 8, 10–15, 17–19, 20–21, 24, 29–30, 38–39, 41, 122, 166–168, 177, 179, 190
Isser, S., 186

Jacob, 1, 5, 7, 154, 179, 181
James, 103, 112–113
James (revolutionary), 52
Jarvie, I. C., 188
Jason, 29
Jeremiah, 68
Jerome, *Epis. August.* 112.13, 194
Jerusalem, 7, 13, 17, 25, 29–30, 32–36, 40, 42, 47–49, 52, 66, 74, 76, 81, 129, 134, 147
Jesus, 1, 2, 12, 44–45, 55, 64, 68–69, 78–93, 95, 97–98, 106–107, 119, 130, 137, 141, 144–145, 148, 155, 161, 190, 195
Jew, 18, 157, 161
Jewish community, 2, 12, 70, 87, 133, 139
Jewish-Christian, 94, 116, 120, 142
Jewish holidays, 141
Jewish home, 42, 126
Job, 61, 64
John, 48, 57, 156–157
John Hyrcanus, 48, 119
John of Gischala, 52
John the Baptist, 82–83, 108, 116
Jordan river, 28
Joseph, 142
Joseph and Aseneth, 98
Josephus: *Against Apion* 2.178, 185; 2.79–80, 26–27; *Antiquities of the Jews*, 36; 13:171–173, 118; 13.297–298, 52–53; 14.158–160 and 14:165–177, 186; 18.16–17, 45–46; 18.18–22, 48–49, 77; 20.102, 20.200, and 20.251, 186; *The Jewish Wars* 1.204–205, and 2:119–161, 186;

2.162–163, 52; 2.164–166, 45;
2.433–488, 186
Joshua, 51
Joshua ben Hananiah, 131
Josiah, 5
Jubilees 7:20, 171
Judah, 4, 7, 13–15, 17–19, 47, 74–75,
185
Judaism, 1–3, 12, 13, 22, 24, 26, 32–34,
43, 56, 57, 59, 62–63, 70, 77, 80, 85,
89, 93–94, 96–113, 128, 130, 137,
141–142, 146, 155–159, 161–162,
170–181
Judas Iscariot, 79
Judas Maccabees, 36–37, 76
Judas of Galilee, 52
Judea, 13, 17–20, 24–28, 30–31, 34–36,
38, 39, 40–41, 47–48, 54–55, 58–60,
72–73, 80–81, 85, 96, 104, 107,
117–118, 126, 145, 173, 179, 181
Judgment day, 73–74, 85, 88
Justin Martyr, 159–160, 190, 193; *Dialogue with Trypho*, 158; chs. 16 and
47, 194; ch. 56, 159–160; 88:8, 190;
chs. 96 and 137, 194

Kanter, Rosabeth, 100, 191–192
Kavod, 89
Khirbet Shema, 42
Kim, Seyoon, 192
Kimelman, Reuven, 194
Kingdom, coming of the, 84–85, 111,
145–146. *See also* "End of time"
"King of the Jews," 85, 156
Kraemer, Ross, 191
Kshatriya caste, 128

Lantenari, Vittorio, 188–189
Levine, Lee I., 186
Levites, 40
Lifton, Robert J., 191
Linton, Ralph, 187
Liturgy, 9, 12, 132, 158
Logos, 56–57, 154–155, 160
LORD, 17, 89, 153, 156, 158
Luke, 43, 84, 92, 107, 145, 162–165
Lurianic Kabbalah, 188
Lynch, Owen, 193

Maccabean Revolt, 30–39, 62, 73–75,
134, 172

Maccabees, 30–31, 33–35, 39, 51, 75–76,
120
I Maccabees, 30–33, 35, 75–76
II Maccabees, 36
McCarthy, D. J., 184
MacMullen, Ramsey, 194–195
Magic and witchcraft, 76, 143–146, 161,
166
Malherbe, Abraham, 191
Manasseh, 47
Mantel, H., 186
Marduk, 15
Mark, 84–85, 144–146
Marriage, 10, 18–21, 132, 146–147, 178.
See also Endogamy
Martyrdom, 35, 63–64, 75, 87, 94
Marxism, 71
Mary, 148
Masada, 52, 185
Maskilim (wise), 74
Mater, 43
Matthew, 84, 102, 120, 145–146
Meeks, Wayne A., 186, 188, 190, 192
Megilat Antiochus, 30
Meiron, 42
Mekhilta: Bahodesh and *Shirta*,
152–153
Melanesia, 70
Melchizedek, 77, 89
Melekh, 17
Menahem, 52
Meneleus, 29
Menstrual period, 124
Merkabah, 14–15, 108. *See also* Hekha-
loth texts; Mysticism
Messiah (*mashiah*), 15–16, 18, 51,
64–67, 84–87, 90, 92–94, 106–107,
156, 159, 188–189, 190
Messiah ben Joseph, 190
Messianism, 49–50, 64–65, 85–88, 90,
93, 135–136, 174
Meyers, Eric M., 186
Michael, 73–74
Middle Ages, 147
Midrash, 85, 100, 158; *Midrash Rabba*,
179; *Midrash Rabba Prov.* 17:1, 195
Mikveh (ritual bath), 124, 131
Milik, J. T., 189
Millenarianism, 70–71, 74, 87, 94
Minuth (sectarianism), 149
Miracles, 135, 140, 143–144

Mishnah, 54, 112, 117, 120–122, 132–133, 136–137, 140, 148, 174; *Avodah Zarah* 2:3, 112; *Megilah*, 149; *Pesahim* 10:5, 139; *Pirke Aboth* 1:1, 53; *Sanhedrin* 1:1, 44; *Sanhedrin*, ch. 10, 166
Mithras, 76–77, 137
Moab, 50
Modernization, 25, 31
Modiin, 35
Moehring, Horst, 185
Monasteries, 178
Monasticism, 26, 48, 51, 58, 83
Monotheism, 5, 26, 56, 155, 158
Moses, 1, 5, 9, 11, 19, 26, 31, 37, 41, 46, 48, 50–51, 54, 78, 89, 93, 117, 138–139
Mystery religions, 99, 137; Jewish, 76, 79, 89, 139
Mysticism, 63, 77–78. *See also* Hekhaloth texts; *Merkabah*
Myth, 3–4, 11–12, 22, 50, 61, 94

Naiskos, 42
Nasi, 17
Nature, 11
Near East, 4, 6, 9, 11, 15, 23, 61
Nebuchadnezzar, 13, 73
Nefesh, 60
Nehemiah, 18, 22, 36
Neusner, Jacob, 120–121, 132, 184, 186, 193
"New covenant," 68
New Testament, 18, 40, 43–45, 48, 52, 64–65, 68–69, 79–80, 87–88, 90, 92, 97, 112, 119–121, 131, 142–148, 157–158, 163, 172, 184, 192
Nickelsburg, G. W. E., 187
Nilvim, 20
Noah, 170
Noahide Commandments, 111, 170–171
Nock, A. D., 191
Numbers, 50

Oath, 4, 6, 120
Old Testament, 64, 69, 175–176
Onias, 29
"Oral law," 117–119, 121–122
Origen, 190; *H. Jeremiah* 10.8.2, 194

Panias, 28
Paradise, 6, 63, 70, 107
Paradosis (tradition), 119, 121

Paris Magical Papyrus, 76
Parsons, Talcott, 183, 193
Parthenos (virgin), 148
Passover, 12, 132, 138, 139, 140
Pater, 43
Patriarchs, 5, 7, 65, 69
Paul, 24, 44, 53, 55, 64, 81, 90, 92–97, 99, 100, 103, 113–114, 116, 119, 147, 151, 162–163, 172, 193
Pentacostalism, 141
Pentateuch, 21, 47
Pepper, Stephen C., 183
Perrin, Norman, 69, 187
Persecution, 73, 76, 84, 87
Persia, 15, 17–18, 21–24, 39, 47, 62, 65, 74, 152
Perseus, 63
Pesach, 141
Pesher, 49, 52, 85, 100
Peter, 111–113, 163–165. *See also* Cephas
Pharisees, 38–40, 44, 52–54, 58–60, 64, 81–83, 85, 99, 103, 104–106, 109, 114, 118–135, 136, 142, 145–147, 166
Philip, 93
Philip, Gospel of, 142
Philo, 24, 33, 41, 48, 51, 54–58, 67, 85, 89, 133, 138–139, 149, 154–155, 159–160, 166, 178, 185–186, 195; *Concerning the Creation*, § 128, 185; *Hypothetica* 11.1, 186; *Life of Moses*, 190; 2.17, 56; *On Dreams* 1.227–229, 154; *On Rewards*, § 115–119, 67; *On the Contemplative Life*, 186; *On the Migration of Abraham*, § 89, 57; *On the Sacrifice of Cain and Abel*, § 94–97, 57–58; *Questions and Answers on Exodus*, § 39–42, 138, 190; *Special Laws*, 33; *That Every Good Man Is Free*, § 75, 186
Philosophical schools, 99, 137
Phineas, 93
Phoboumenoi, 43
Phylacteries, 149
Piety, personal, 2, 95, 101, 180
Pilgrimage, 39–40, 48
Pneuma, 175
Pneumatics, 176
Pogroms, 188
Pompey, 35, 40
Pork, 34, 63
Posidonius, 27

Priestly messiah, 51, 67
Priests, 21, 34–35, 40, 51, 122, 124, 126–127, 176, 180
Property, 83, 101
Prophets, 9–11, 13–15, 62, 64, 93, 121–122, 179
Proselytes, 98, 99–100, 101, 111, 120, 177
Prostitution, ritual, 8
Proverbs, 28
Psalms, 90, 159
Psalms of Solomon, 17:36–37a, 17:39–40, 66
Pseudepigrapha, 63, 66, 69
Psychics, 176
Ptolemies, 24, 28, 39
Purity, 39–40, 49, 51, 85, 102, 123–127, 130–131, 146, 165–166, 169, 176–180

Quispel, Gilles, 189
Qumran, 48, 50, 58, 67, 75–78, 80, 89, 102–103, 108, 130, 171. *See also* Dead Sea Scrolls

R. Abahu, 149
R. Akiba, 166
R. Eliezer, 135, 140, 167, 195
R. Gamaliel, 139, 168
R. Ishmael b. Yosi, 160
R. Joshua, 167, 195
R. Judah the Prince, 122, 133, 136, 174
R. Nathan, 135, 152
Rabbinic evidence for Pharisees, 53–54
Rabbinic institutions, 41, 44, 58–59
Rabbinic literature, 147–150
Rabbinic movement, 1–2, 36, 40, 52, 64, 83, 94–95, 128, 131, 134, 158
Rabbinic traditions, 36, 40–41, 44, 93, 111, 117–118, 121
Rabbis, 39, 48, 50–51, 122, 128, 158
Rebecca, 1, 12, 179, 181
Redemption, 12, 50–51, 66, 174–175
Red Sea, 16
"Reformers," 30, 32–34
Repentance, 102, 111, 115, 167, 169–170, 180
Resurrection, 45–46, 60–64, 76–77, 79, 85, 87, 89, 95, 138
Revelation of John, 69, 131
Revolt: first, 12, 44, 55, 60, 67, 79–80, 95; second, 50, 86, 95, 132, 158, 174

Revolutionaries, 48, 51–52, 76, 79–80, 107
Riecken, Henry W., 191
Righteousness, 63, 110–111, 167, 169–170
Ritual, 4, 8, 9, 18, 64–65, 99, 102–103, 108, 113, 120, 123–127, 137–140, 149, 167
Rivkin, Ellis, 123, 186, 193
Roman rule, 2, 22, 35, 38–40, 44, 48, 50–52, 60, 66, 70, 72, 79, 81, 84–87, 95
Romans, 12, 23, 26–27, 97, 99, 117–118, 120, 129, 135–137, 150–151, 161, 169–170, 173–175, 177
Rome, 27, 68, 96, 147, 172, 177, 185
Root metaphor, 3–4, 7, 9, 22, 33, 38, 123
Rosh Hashanah, 140
Royal messiah, 51, 67
Russell, D. S., 189

Sabbath, 30, 35, 41, 82, 119–120, 132, 141, 156
Sabbatianism, 188–189
Sacrifice, 6, 7–8, 10–11, 19, 40, 93, 132
Sadducees, 38, 44–46, 53–56, 58–59, 64, 81, 118–119, 123, 135
Salvation, 12, 81, 106, 109–110, 137, 139, 166–168, 170–172, 181, 195
Samaria, 38, 47–48, 81, 83, 139, 194
II Samuel, 21
Samuel the Small, 150
Sanctification, 128
Sanders, E. P., 107, 192, 194
Sandmel, Samuel, 186
Sanhedrin, 38, 41, 43–45, 58
Sarkics, 176
Satan, 50, 80, 107, 144, 157
Saul, 65
Schacter, Stanley, 191
Schiffman, Lawrence, 192
Scholem, Gershom, 188–189
Schweitzer, Albert, 187
Scribes, 119, 145
Scripture, 105–107, 119, 122–123, 131, 151–152, 159–160, 168, 174, 176
Sebomenoi, 43
Sectarianism, 45, 54, 58–60, 68–69, 85, 94, 98–99, 102, 135, 142, 147–148, 153, 156–157, 165, 178, 180, 186, 188

Sects, 45–54, 74–76, 79–80, 98, 102, 115, 117, 129, 132, 153, 173, 187–188
Secularization, 25, 31
Seder, 139
Segal, Alan F., 189, 193–194
Seleucids, 28, 37, 39
Semitic language and literature, 23, 27–28
Septuagint, 24, 78, 154
Shamash, 4
Shechem, 194
Sheol, 60, 167
Sheshbezzar, 17
Shiism, 185
shirq (associationism), 171
Sibylline Oracles 3:381–400, 189
Sicarii, 79
Siegelman, Jim, 191
Sifra 86b, 168
Simeon b. Zoma, 199
Simeon the Zealot, 79
Simon (revolutionary), 52
Simon bar Giora, 52
Simon Maccabee, 75
Simpson, John, 184
Sinai, 8–9, 54, 78, 89, 138, 152
Slotkin, J. S., 187
Smith, Morton, 184, 186, 193
Sociodrama, 33, 38, 184–185
Socrates, 46
Sodom and Gomorrah, 159–160
Solomon, 5, 7, 13, 28, 35, 38, 47, 66
"Son of Man," 66, 73, 77–79, 86–88
"Son of the Star," 50
Sophia (Wisdom), 28, 68
Soul, 7, 55, 60
Srinivas, M. N., 193
Stark, Rodney, 188
Status ambiguity, 71–72, 97–98, 128, 132, 147
Stendahl, Krister, 103, 192
Stern, Menaham, 185
Stoicism, 28, 46
Strange, James F., 186
Stone, Michael, 187
Suffering, 63
Suffering Servant, 91–92
Sukkoth, 18, 35–36, 140
Swanson, Guy, 183
Symposium of Plato, 137, 139
Synagogue, 38, 41–43, 58, 150–151
Syria, 28, 42

"Tabernacles," 18
Talmon, Yonina, 187
Talmud, 16, 77, 133, 137, 148, 150, 152; *b. Baba Kamma* 38a, 168; *b. Baba Metzia* 59b, 134–135; *b. Hagigah* 14b, 189; *b. Sanhedrin* 38b, 160, 189; *b. Sanhedrin* 105a, 168; *b. Sukkoth* 52a, 90; *b. Taanith* 65b, 149; *b. Yebamoth* 46a, 168; *j. Berakhoth* 9c, 150
Tarsus, 105, 110
Tcherikover, Victor, 185
Teacher of Righteousness, 49
Tekton, 190
Temple, 19, 35–36, 40, 49, 54, 77–78, 120, 126–129, 131–133, 143, 150, 174, 189; first, 1, 12–13, 17–18, 35, 38–39, 65, 76; second, 12, 15, 17, 19, 27, 29–30, 34–35, 38–42, 45, 47, 54, 58, 73, 75, 80, 93, 128–130, 132, 166, 185
Ten Commandments, 8–9
Tescher, Robert C., 188
Testament of Levi 9:10, 124
Theissen, Gerd, 188, 190–191
Theocracy, 21
Theophany, 138
Theophrastus, 26
Theos, 156
Therapeutae (Healers), 48, 149
Thrupp, Sylvia, 188
Tillich, Paul, 183
Toldoth Yeshu, 148
Torah, 4–5, 20, 31, 38–39, 41, 45–46, 49, 51, 53–55, 63, 82–83, 103–105, 106–107, 109–111, 114, 116, 123, 126, 134–136, 140, 146, 165–166, 168, 170, 174
Torah constitution, 21, 29–30, 34, 37–38, 44–46, 54, 68, 121, 123, 134, 143, 173, 181
Tosefta Sanhedrin 13:2, 167–168
Trade routes, 15, 23
Trinitarians, 154
Trypho, 158
Turner, Victor, 183, 185, 188
Twins, 179, 181
Two powers in heaven, 151, 153–154, 171

Unity, 113, 142, 179
Universalism, 129, 162–165, 167, 169–180, 195
Universality, 11, 129, 176

Vermes, Geza, 189–190
Vicarious atonement, 92, 94, 137–138

Wallace, Anthony F. C., 187
Weber, Max, 188
Western societies, 2, 25, 70
Wicklund, Robert A., 191
Wisdom literature, 27–28
Wolfson, H. A., 186
"Word," 56
Worsley, Peter, 187–188

Yahud, 18
Yahweh, 4, 6–11, 13–17, 19, 23, 30, 32,
    38, 47, 62, 93, 152, 155–156, 158, 178,
    183

Yehoiachin, 17
Yehudi, 18, 161
Yerushalmi, Yosef, 184
Yohanan ben Zakkai, 131
Yom Kippur, 19, 40, 140

Xenophobia, 26
Xerxes, 73

Zajonc, Robert B., 191
Zealots, 52, 79, 129, 185
Zerubbabel, 17
Zeus, 30
Zevi, Sabbatai, 188
Zionism, 16
Zoroastrians, 152–153